This Wasn't on the Syllabus

Stories from the front lines of campus
activism against sexualized violence

Curated by Addy Strickland and Emma Kuzmyk

#ThisWasntontheSyllabus
#WritingActivism

Follow Rising Action on our socials!
Twitter: @RAPubCollective
Instagram: @risingactionpublishingc
Tiktok: @risingactionpublishingco

Contents

Content Warning

This book contains stories that talk about sexual assault, sexualized and physical violence, self-harm, body image, discrimination, mental illness, suicide, and other potentially triggering or difficult topics. Please note that *all* stories and poems mention or discuss sexualized violence to some degree.

You'll find more specific warnings throughout the book, at the beginning of certain stories.

Please take care engaging with this material, and make time for self-care if you need to.

This book will still be here when you're ready!

Land Acknowledgement

We respectfully acknowledge that this book was written on unceded Indigenous territory across the settler state of Canada, whose sovereignty relies on continued exploitation, violence, and the ongoing settlement of stolen lands.

Given the subject matter of this anthology, we would be remiss to begin without specifically acknowledging the high rates of physical and sexualized violence faced by Indigenous peoples—particularly by women, girls, and Two-spirit individuals—that are part of both an historical and ongoing genocide of Indigenous populations.

Many, if not all of the post-secondary institutions written about in this anthology are complicit in this violent, ongoing colonization.

As an editorial team made up of settlers, we take responsibility for learning and seeking long-term transformation in our relationships with Indigenous peoples and land, particularly as they pertain to organizing and taking action on issues of sexualized violence.

This anthology is dedicated to every campus activist fighting sexualized violence who has ever felt discouraged, let down, burned out, or defeated. We hear you. We see you. We believe you.
Change is possible.

Foreword

MANDI GRAY

Over the last decade, there has been a resurgence of anti-violence activism on post-secondary campuses across Canada. Much of this labour has been fuelled by *what we faced* when we reported sexual violence or supported a friend who had been harmed. In 2015, I was in the first year of my PhD when I was sexually assaulted by another student. Only a decade ago, there was no sexual assault policy nor were there any dedicated staff for supporting students like me. There have been many changes that have happened on campus that we can attribute to the dedicated labour of survivors and their allies. This work has filled massive policy gaps and challenged discriminatory rape myths in institutional responses (or lack thereof).

We couldn't have done this without the labour of the feminist activists who came before us. We are indebted to the feminists of the 70s and 80s. They provided us with the language of sexual violence to identify our experiences as such. They advocated for much-needed legal reform in criminal law. They identified sexual harassment as a critical problem on campuses across the country. The feminists of the 90s and 00s fought for sexual harassment offices, circulated *Chilly Climate* reports to document the sexism and racism in many university departments across the country, and created feminist-led safety audits to assess the physical safety of campuses for women and racialized community members.

For many of us, the institutional failures have been just as harmful as the initial act of violence—whether it is senior administrators minimizing the report of sexual violence as simply an interpersonal conflict, long waiting lists for counselling, or being forced to continue taking a class with the perpetrator. Experiencing sexual violence while attending a post-secondary institution has unique consequences. Survivors often continue to attend classes with the person who harmed them, or the perpetrator might even be their instructor who has incredible power over their future. The campus, which may have felt at one time like a safe community, now feels like an absolute betrayal after their disclosure wasn't taken seriously. Some may abandon their studies and future career plans altogether. Some survivors face backlash for reporting, as demonstrated by the growing number of defamation lawsuits that faculty members accused of sexual violence have initiated with the intention of intimidating survivors into silence.

Survivors who face numerous forms of intersecting structural marginalization also come up against unique barriers to justice. For example, international students risk losing their visas if they fail or drop out after they experience sexual violence. Students who engage in sex work might be fearful of reporting out of fear of blackmail by the perpetrator. Black, Indigenous, racialized, members of the 2SLGBTQ+ community, and disabled students are often subjected to intersecting discriminatory stereotypes that diminish their victimization and are often even far less likely to make formal reports despite experiencing disproportionate rates of gendered violence. While we should be proud of how far we have come, we still have a lot of work to do to ensure that all members of the campus community are safe from violence and oppression.

This Wasn't on the Syllabus is critical because it documents the many challenges that survivors and their allies face when advocating for much needed change in institutions that are often resistant and at times out right hostile. The pieces included in this collection provide stories of feminist victories, survival, and collective rage, which help us to see just how much work has been done and provide future generations with lessons learned to continue fighting for a future that ensures that all campus community members are safe.

The latter chapters of this book provide a glimpse into the possibilities for the future. It is important that we spend time dreaming and imagining a future that is safe for everyone and what that could look like. Safety is far more than simply the absence of violence. It is a space where everyone is heard, validated, cared for, and accountability is not just a hollow word. This is what we must continue to strive for.

Introduction

ADDY STRICKLAND AND EMMA KUZMYK

No one gets into activism on purpose. When it comes to combatting sexualized violence, you don't wake up one morning and decide "I'm going to fight my university's administration," or "I'm going to rewrite my school's sexualized violence policy;" rather, you listen as an upper-year student tells you which professors to worry about. You cringe while reading poorly worded emails from administration. You decide not to go out because you don't feel like being cat-called or groped and the walk across campus is dark and empty. By the end of your first year, you listen as every single one of your female friends tells you they've been harassed or assaulted.

For far too many, sexualized violence is an unfortunate and unexpected side-effect of the post-secondary experience. It's something you're forced to learn about, even though it might not appear on any of your course syllabi. Statistics Canada found that one in ten women were sexually assaulted while attending post-secondary institutions in 2019 alone, and that 71% of all students experienced some form of unwanted sexualized behaviour.[1] These statistics are shocking enough at face value,

---

1. "One in Ten Women Students Sexually Assaulted in a Postsecondary Setting." Statistics Canada, September 14, 2020. https://www150.statcan.gc.ca/n1/daily-quotidien/200914/dq200914a-eng.htm.

but those involved in prevention and response work will also concur that both are most likely under-representations due to ongoing barriers in reporting.

For decades, activists and allies have been fighting to change those statistics and to rewrite the culture of sexualized violence on post-secondary campuses. There have been protests, petitions, sit-ins, walkouts, and endless campaigns, alongside tireless work towards policy and systems change. Our own experiences encompass only four short years of activist work—much of which would not have been possible without the work of those who preceded us—and it often feels as if we crammed decades of learning into what is, in the grand scheme of things, not a whole lot of time.

Coming to the end of those four years, as most senior students are prone to do, we started to reminisce on everything that happened. What went on in the classroom was, perhaps unsurprisingly, only a small part of our conversation. Instead, we remembered writing an open letter to university administration part way through our first semester. We remembered marching onto the basketball court in the middle of an open house with megaphones and linked arms. We remembered planning protests from the basement of an old residence hall, and painting words of resistance onto the windows of another. We remembered how it felt to march across campus in a pack of badass women, and to scream our worth at the top of our lungs. We also remembered how it felt to be told "no" and "never" and "not here" over and over again. We remembered the dozens, if not hundreds of stories of trauma we heard from our peers, and we remembered sitting across the boardroom from administrators, trying to hold ourselves together while they asked us to prove that increased student supports were necessary.

Reminiscing about everything we went through and everything we learned in the process, we wanted to create something to honour the experiences we had while also passing on what we learned to future generations of activists. Somewhat jokingly, we threw out the idea of writing a book—we'd both written, published, and performed in various other media, so why not tackle something bigger? Evidently, we quickly stopped joking. Rather than only telling our own stories, however, we wanted to include the voices of other activists across Canada who were doing similar work and facing similar challenges. Hence, the idea of writing a book morphed into the anthology you're holding now.

Throughout this anthology, you'll find an array of stories, poems, and speeches written by student activists—both past and present—fighting sexualized violence on Canadian campuses. Sending out our call for submissions in 2021, the goal was to achieve as wide a range of stories as possible, representing the diversity of experience that exists across Canada, across campuses, and even within movements. We wanted to show the world the amazing work being done by students that is so often overlooked, and so rarely celebrated. The stories presented in this anthology come from twenty-four activists from seven provinces, writing about their experiences at fifteen different post-secondary institutions. Each of the stories are unique and demonstrate the diversity we were looking to achieve, yet by virtue of the work we do, also highlight the common experience of fighting for action and justice on issues of sexualized violence.

Across three categories—*What We Faced, What We Built*, and *How We Survived*—this anthology makes space for conversations about active protest, collective action, contentious movements, community care, institutional failure, combatting rape culture, creating solutions, and more. In the first section, *What We Faced*, our contributors write about and reflect on what it's like to confront post-secondary institutions and their troubling policies (or lack thereof) head on. Among others, you'll hear from the two of us, as well as from a few of our peers, about various movements that occurred during our time at St. Francis Xavier University (StFX); from Michelle Roy, who led a series of protests against sexualized violence at Mount Allison University in 2020; and from Caitlin Salvino, who founded the national OurTurn movement in 2016.

In *What We Built,* you'll read stories about how peer support programs had their start at various institutions, including StFX, Dalhousie, and the University of Toronto. You'll hear from Shelby Miller, who founded a near-national ribbon campaign in support of survivors; from Cameron Smith, who worked to rewrite Acadia University's sexualized violence policy and from Maddie Brockbank, who has led award-winning work, engaging men in conversations about sexualized violence prevention at McMaster. In *How We Survived,* you'll hear from the co-founders and co-chairs of Students for Consent Culture Canada (SFCC)—a national, student-led non-profit supporting student activists across the country—about how they integrate practices of care into their work. You'll read stories about recovery, about community care, about taking back power, and so much more.

Scattered amongst these stories and personal essays, you'll find a variety of poetry, as well as transcribed speeches from the women's marches, Take Back the Night events, and protests that our contributors have organized and spoken at. We don't believe that activism has any one form, so writing about it shouldn't either. In our own activist experience, creative work was a place of grounding, and a way to deal with the messy, complicated emotions that came with standing up for what was right; it was an alternate means of expressing what was often too difficult to process or say out loud. In many cases, poetry came first, and activism was a way of putting poetic imaginings into action. And so, it has a home here on our pages—offering a window into the hearts and souls of student activists from across the nation.

It would be unjust to begin, as well, without acknowledging those who have come before us. Activists have been speaking up against institutions for decades, fighting for policies where before there were none and then continuously fighting to improve them, and believing and supporting survivors since before there were specific platforms and hashtags created to do so. It was their bravery and commitment to justice that have made the activism detailed in this book possible, and through our own work, we hope to continue honouring theirs.

This work has never been easy. It can be exhausting, isolating, triggering, and at times, frustrating beyond words. Often, it can feel as if you're fighting a battle that can never be won, and yet, there are wins happening all around us. For many of us who are just leaving our campuses, we might not understand how much change we've made until we think back on what our campuses looked like four, five years ago—recognizing change, especially gradual, messy, high-level, complicated change that happens over the span of so many years, is not an easy task. Sometimes, in order to see the progress we've made, we have to stop and reflect on where we started, and on how far we've come. We hope that the stories highlighted here will help start you, our wonderful reader, on that path of reflection and recognition, and that you might find hope and energy in the collective memory and experience of our contributors.

This book is a collection of stories about real life experiences of activism. Each contributor's story is their own, and reflects their experiences, memories, and emotions. Others who were part of the stories featured here may have different experiences. The intention of sharing these stories is to bring awareness to the pervasiveness of sexualized violence in post secondary spaces, draw attention to the courageous actions of activists across Canada, and create a space for those activists to pass on their learnings to new and emerging activists doing similar work.

This Wasn't on the Syllabus

What We Faced

Stories of protest and collective action against rape culture, institutional inaction, ineffective policies, and more.

I Wonder

EMMA KUZMYK

Content Warning: Description of sexual assault and physical violence
To skip to the next story, turn to page 7.

I used to wonder
When the simple act of walking home made us
So small,
And wonder
Why she feels the need to pretend to make a call
To her fake boyfriend,
And wonder
Why this fake boyfriend has been used
So much,
And wonder
When these questions will be pulled back up
From under the rug,
And wonder
When they will respect our "no"s
More than the idea of being someone else's possession,
And wonder

When bringing this up will create more
Than just tension.

And then I began to wonder
Why it was that him having drank too much
Makes it okay,
And wonder
Why when she does the same, we tell her that
Well, she shouldn't have drank so much anyway,
And wonder
When we will finally start to shift the blame

And now,

I wonder
If you felt her heart break
When you broke into her
I wonder
If the halt of her breath ever made you wonder
If maybe you should halt as well
I wonder
If the impact of your fist
On her skin
Had any impact on you at all
I wonder
If hurting her ever made you hurt
As well
I wonder
If telling her that she was 6 years younger

Than your younger sister
Told you anything
At all
I wonder
If the strength that you used to hold down her arms
Made you feel strong
I wonder
If it was her complete lack of appetite
That fed into yours
I wonder
If her complete inability to respond made you pause
At all

I wonder.

I wonder
Why this has happened over and over
And only right now
Seems large,
I wonder
Why this fucked up justice system
Makes it so hard
To come forward,
I wonder
When we started to take plagiarism more seriously
Than sexual assault,
I wonder
Exactly who it is that makes that call,

I wonder
When this will stop.

Almost as much as I wonder
When we will start
To fight back.
I wonder
If we can raise our voices loud enough
To finally be heard.
I wonder
When every single one of us will stand
Behind her.
I wonder
When this silence that's been established
Will finally
Be disturbed.
I wonder

If it is now.

X-Resist: Responding to Institutional Inaction

Addy Strickland

The air in the hallway is tense with anticipation and nervous energy. We are silent, out of necessity, eyeing the X-Patrol officers stationed at the gymnasium doors as we shuffle closer—anxiously adjusting the teal ribbons pinned to our jackets and sweatshirts, readying cameras and megaphones. Half our group makes their way to the opposing entrance, and we wait until we see them through the opposite window to make our move. It's the loudest quiet I've ever felt, waiting in that hallway—you can almost hear the energy buzzing.

"Now!" someone behind me shouts, breaking the silence with what is still almost a whisper, and we surge into the gym from both ends—interrupting the university's open house with gusto. Another student, who was one of the driving forces behind the protest, takes centre stage as she shouts a list of demands into a megaphone, the rest of the group linking arms behind her. It's a powerful image of solidarity and dissent that will accompany national headlines for weeks to come. It is also just the beginning.

Shortly after the start of the new school year, news broke about a student who had left the university. She'd returned to campus excited to see friends and start classes, only to find out that the man who'd harmed her—who she'd been told had been suspended—had returned as well. What the university had failed to tell her is that despite being found responsible by the university's internal investigation the previous year, the man had issued an appeal, and the suspension had been put on hold.

The news sparked rage and devastation for a lot of people. On the tail of another noteworthy case the year before, the fire had already been started—most of us didn't know the woman who left, but we knew too many others with similar stories. We were tired of watching sexual violence get swept under the rug, tired of watching the university do too little to support survivors. Two days after the article came out, a professor in our Women's and Gender Studies department organized a series of meetings for concerned individuals to come together, share their own stories, and channel their rage into action. It was a powerful, emotional space. I remember sitting in the packed auditorium with tears in my eyes, listening as so many people stood up and said *it happened to me too,* and watching the overhanging grief transform into a plan. What came out of those meetings was an array of ideas for protests, a critique of the school's reporting and disclosure system, and the following message (copied verbatim from a follow-up email):

"WE WON'T STOP UNTIL CHANGE HAPPENS!!!!! THIS ISN'T GOING TO DIE DOWN IN A WEEK! KEEP PUSHING!!"

The conversation continued online, and plans for what came next quickly started to take shape. The university's upcoming open house was identified as a prime location for having our voices heard, with a guaranteed audience of prospective parents and students, as well as the university's president. In preparation for the event, the hashtags

#IStandWithHer and #IAmHer began to circulate on social media as survivors and supporters posted messages of solidarity with the woman who left and shared their own stories. Similar messages soon began to appear on residence whiteboards, and in windows across campus. Posters emphasizing survivors' rights to education and furthering messages of solidarity went up by the dozen, and volunteers folded, pinned, and distributed teal ribbons to anyone who wanted to wear their support. A list of demands, drafted at the initial planning meetings, was finalized.

It was a hectic few days for those involved—myself included. As plans fell into place, there were a lot of moving parts to keep track of, and not everyone on campus was friendly to the idea of protest. Soon enough, however, we ended up in the hallway outside of that open house. Earlier that morning, we congregated in "the pit"—an auditorium-like space in an old residence, temporarily home to faculty offices because of construction. Someone brought poster board and markers, someone else a Tupperware container full of teal ribbons. A friend from Toronto sent me twenty dollars for tea and Timbits, which were passed around as we hammered out the last few details of our plan. The weather was still reasonably nice for that time of year, and the short walk across campus to the rec centre helped the group shake off some nervous energy. After moving inside and waiting in the hallway for what felt like eternity, we ended up where I started the chapter: facing off against the university president in the middle of an open house.

The demands read were as follows:

1) We demand that survivors be informed and protected throughout the entire reporting and investigation process, including any actions that might be taken after the process is complete.

2) We demand that all decision-makers and contributors to the sexual violence policy need to receive education about sexual violence that is survivor-centred and trauma-informed.

3) We demand that the university make a financial commitment to sexual violence prevention.

4) We demand tangible models of assessment for concepts such as risk and foreseeable threat.

5) We demand a communication plan that informs the campus community of incidents of sexual violence and action taken.

6) We demand a reconstruction of the sexual violence policy that centres survivors and is done with expert oversight.

We didn't wait around for a response, and as we left the gym, the sound of the president's voice carried as he pointed out the teal ribbon someone had pinned to his lapel.

We made our way back to the pit, where campus security had revoked the keycard access of the professor who had let us in and helped coordinate the protest. Someone else managed to get us back into the building, and we settled into a circle on the floor—utterly exhausted, but still buzzing with the excitement of what we'd just pulled off—for a group debrief. Going around the circle, we shared what the action meant to us, and what change we hoped to see. While listening to everyone speak, I downloaded the protest photos from my camera, sent off an email to the media, and posted the images on Twitter. We were making national headlines the next day, and word from the remainder of the open house was that parents weren't too happy about sending their kids to a school that couldn't properly address sexual assault.

In the weeks following the open house, StFX organized a series of open forums for admin to "listen" to the voices of students, staff, faculty, and community members. They were, from the point of view of many, yet another excuse for administration to take a few performative steps in the right direction before going back to their usual means of operation: pretending they don't have a problem. Still unsatisfied with the university's actions, X-Resist interrupted the second forum dressed in a uniform of all black with teal ribbons and toting a sign declaring "WE ARE THE RESISTANCE" over and over again, representing the thousands of people calling for change. During question period, Kait was handed the mic, and presented the university's president with a hard copy of a petition that was launched shortly after the initial protest, now containing more than five thousand signatures. The number might not seem huge, particularly to those who attended larger universities, but for a school of just over four thousand students, it was nothing to laugh at.

There were other, smaller continuations of protest as the semester came to an end, but that open forum marked the beginning of a resolution, if only temporarily. Ultimately, it was the cumulative impact of not only our semester of resistance, but of the decades of anti-violence work being done on campus before our arrivals, that led to action on the part of the university. Later that year, StFX welcomed an external panel of experts to review our sexualized violence policy and implemented a much-improved version of the document. They introduced a permanent position for a trained individual to handle disclosures, reports, and support survivors. They finally added a resource list to emails regarding sexualized violence. At some point in the semester, the man whose return sparked the protests voluntarily withdrew from the university. These were all demands made by students, faculty, and community members.

Many of the demands on our petition were met, but many were not, and the university's response is still not perfect by any means. Two years later, the student who was initially suspended returned again to the StFX campus after being acquitted by a Nova Scotia Supreme Court judge. Despite a resurgence of protest (virtual this time, due to COVID-19), unfavourable media coverage, and the fact that they had, two years earlier, found the man responsible through their own internal processes, the school claimed they had no reason to deny his admission or enrolment. The new policy, at the time I'm writing this, while leagues better than the previous, still relies on legal jargon that is largely inaccessible to much of the student body. Training on receiving and responding to disclosures or on preventing sexualized violence still isn't mandatory for all staff, faculty, and students. Survivors are still forced to deal with systems that feel like they aren't built for them. There has been progress, certainly, but we are nowhere near where we need to be.

X-Resist was a breaking point, but it was also a turning point, and a starting point for something better. It was dozens, then hundreds, then thousands of people deciding they'd had enough—that they wouldn't put up with inaction and insufficient policies any longer. It was an interruption. The active protests and petitions happened over the span of only a few months, but the energy I felt at that first open house has lingered. Consistently, when issues of sexual violence have come up since, someone has put out the call, and people have stepped up—offering legal resources and information about support services, coordinating media coverage, circulating open letters and petitions, contributing to zines and newspaper features. In contrast to what happened at the open house, those smaller acts of resistance haven't been revolutionary, but they're a testament to the lasting effects that collective and contentious action can have on university campuses.

#MeToo

Kylee Graham

This poem was first published online in *Laurel & Bells Literary Journal*

'Cause you think you're so big and so tall
and us so scared and so small
but we're not
we're done hiding
we are rising
Does our truth hurt?

Hurt like those words
and your hands
their stares and demands
you did this to yourself
It couldn't possibly be their
boss
friend
brother or lover
as long as they were admired and covered
by the strength of cowards

You showed us that there's power in numbers
well then I'd be scared because while you all slumbered
on your thrones of entitlement and institutionalized security
we've been building bridges out of each other's despair
climbing mountains of self-worth
you were so unaware
of us pulling our sisters and brothers up too

Our voices now loud enough to shake your foundation
and cause you to fall, because without hesitation
we were forced to thread shame into the ends of our hair
and carry it with us

but not anymore

This conversation is so long overdue
our time has come, we know this is true
as there are skeletons willing to rise from their grave
if it means justice finally coming our way
and shining light on all those who thought they could
take what was not theirs

Now we are here and our numbers are strong
we will build our own empire out of what was done wrong
Our first ruling order is not a request
you WILL understand
no doesn't really mean yes
it doesn't matter the length of my dress
your position doesn't make my autonomy mean less—

My body is not some quest for you to conquer
We are tired of shrinking ourselves just for you to be comfortable

Time's up

Your rule is over, this is our kingdom now
and so we ask
Does our truth hurt?

The Poet

ANONYMOUS

The poet
sees her school in the news
reads about three charges
of sexual assault
listens to a male student say
"I feel safe here"
as tears stream down her face
listens to her friends say "me too"
and thinks "no more"
pens a poem.

The poet
sits nervously on stage
clutches her notes
as she addresses the outraged
in gratitude
calls for action to be taken
and prays that it will
hopes it won't take long

but understands that it will

pens a poem.

The poet
realizes that justice
is a lot like poetry
because both are always messy
and always hard
decides that poetry is rebellion
that justice is rebellion
and that both are always worth it
calls herself a rebel with pride
pens a poem.

All of the Noise

Anonymous

Content Warning: Moderate description of rape and ensuing legal process
To skip to the next story, turn to page 25.
Disclaimer: all names in this story have been changed to protect the identities of those involved.

The first time I ever said "I was raped" out loud was because my father thought some boy had pictures of me. I didn't mean to say that, especially not to him. I hadn't even fully admitted it to myself yet. Not really. I knew what happened was wrong, but rape? That couldn't have been what happened to me. Not by somebody who was supposed to be my friend. You see stories in the news, but you never think it will happen to you.

On Christmas break, I decided to talk to my mom. I remember telling her how scared I was, after it happened. I was scared to leave my dorm room, but I was also scared to be there. I had a double room to myself, so I tried switching beds, but it didn't help. It just changed the view when I watched that night play out over and over in my head. I'd see it in flashes, but I could never fully remember. I was scared to see my friends because they were all friends with him too. I remembered times I'd stop by their rooms and be asked not to come in because he was there. I was scared to be alone; what if something happened? I was scared to not report, as I just wanted to feel safe again, but I was more scared of reporting. I'd heard the stories, read the statistics. On top of all that, taking into account I had a hole in my memory, I didn't think I had a chance of obtaining justice.

When we returned to school in January, I had more of a grasp on what had happened to me. I was fucking angry, and rightfully so. I confronted Jacob via text.

He wanted to finish the conversation in person. I think I was hoping that sending those messages would give me some closure. It didn't. Instead, I locked myself in the bathroom and began hyperventilating. He just wanted to make sure I wouldn't tell anyone. At the time, I had no intentions to, but what he was focused on, himself and not how I was affected by his actions, shocked me.

A few days later, after an incident where I had to go to the hospital, I started to open up to a residence staff member. First, I made a statement to the school without going to the police. Time went on, and I decided to make a report. I'd had enough. I ran into him constantly, and I was tired of living in fear. The school opened an investigation into my assault and found him responsible. They decided that he would be suspended and not welcome on school grounds the next year. Unfortunately, reporting him didn't make a huge difference for the current school year. I didn't want to switch residences, as I'd made other friends by then, and the school refused to move him out of the residence for a long time. There were supposed to be restrictions in place. He was not allowed on the fourth floor, especially the lounge. I found out later that the residence staff were never informed of any restrictions, or even the fact that an incident had occurred.

I remember getting the news that he had appealed the school's decision. They told me it would take a couple days, but it took nearly two weeks. I had people telling me that he would win the appeal because 'his family are all alumni' because 'he's their music prodigy.' I was hearing all these reasons that the school would overturn their decision and not one of them had to do with my case. That's when I decided to go to the RCMP. Once I got to the station, I gave my statement and went home. It was all so surreal. I just go home after unloading all that? It wasn't until I got the call that he'd been brought in and charged that it finally felt real.

I spent my summer doing anything to distract myself from the upcoming school year and preliminary inquiry. I decided to go back to school to try and start fresh. I wouldn't say I was excited to go back, but I was certainly hopeful. I had reported to the school and to the RCMP, and Jacob had been suspended for the year. This was my fresh start. I'd switched to a new residence to have a more social experience. I was in contact with a student involved in the weightlifting club and planned to join. I had started new medication and set up appointments at the hospital and women's centre to stay on top of my mental health. I really thought I'd put everything in place to have a kick-ass second year. I may have had to avoid a certain fast-food restaurant because Jacob was living in town and working there, but that was okay. I always had campus as my safe space. This campus, this community, this family. I chose it. I chose to return despite my assault the previous year. I chose to move forward and heal. I wish the school had given me that chance.

On the first day of classes, and for the first time since returning to the province, I felt excited. But then I heard through a friend that Jacob had been seen at the radio station on campus greeting new students. I was sure that the school had made a mistake and that they would fix it. How could this not be monitored? I packed my bags for class and went over to the residence life office to inform them about Jacob. Someone brought me in to talk to the director, Katherine. I started to recount what

I'd heard and the look on her face made my stomach drop. She started off with, "There's been a miscommunication, I'm sorry." My heartrate started to speed up. She continued, "His lawyers got in contact with our legal counsel, and he's been permitted to take classes this year."

I still don't think I have the words to describe how I felt in that moment, but I'll try. It hit me all at once. I was scared. I was angry. It felt like my heart was breaking. I felt insignificant. This school that was supposed to protect me, be my community, but had betrayed my trust and treated my assault like a joke. I got up to run outside because I felt a panic attack coming on. Katherine shouted as I was running out the door, "He's only allowed on campus for classes," as if that's fucking consolation. I bolted out of the office and called my mom. I was crying. Shaking. Yelling. She could barely make out what I was saying. I was utterly devastated—my university cared so little about my safety. My mom told me she'd book me a flight home for the next morning, that she would never leave me somewhere I would never feel safe. Before I went to pack my things, I stopped into the residence office one last time. I told Katherine I consented to the sharing of information with my mother and that, "No, I will not be staying to handle my academics. You guys are going to do that, as well as reimburse us. I'm going home." It broke my heart, but I left the university. I left the city. I left the province.

When my mother and I talked to a reporter, I remember them telling us that it was possible none of the news outlets would pick the story up. We weren't sure anything would come of it. When I woke up to multiple news stories and messages asking if it was me in the news, if I was the anonymous survivor, I was so overwhelmed. I turned my phone over and cried for a long time. I was thrilled the story was gaining momentum so fast. However, seeing my story all over the news was a lot. Constantly reading and reliving what happened to me was not good for my mental health. Then, other stories started to come out. About students who had experienced similar situations. Students who were tired of the campus culture. Students who were starting to speak out. There was such an out-pouring of support, not only for me, but for all survivors and members of the community. That's when I began to realize that as hard as it was going to be, it was the right thing to do.

Even with all the noise being made about my case, I still wasn't ready to face what had happened. I tried to avoid thinking about it, but the up-coming preliminary inquiry kept nagging at me. My anxiety was through the roof. I'd been asked earlier if I wanted a screen in front of Jacob at the hearing so I didn't have to see him. I told the Crown, no, I wanted him to have to look at me and see what he'd done. I was offered a support person to sit beside me while I testified instead. I reached out to an individual from the city's women's centre, and she was amazing. She used grounding techniques like rubbing her feet on the ground to bring me back to the room when I would get too in my head. I got the news that we'd be moving on to trial. This was great, as that's what I wanted, but I also realized the amount of time and energy this would take and that this was only the beginning.

It took what felt like forever to get to a trial date. When we finally did, I was scared. I'd spent the last couple years trying to not think about the assault. Then I had to go over every detail of that traumatic event that happened nearly three years ago. I hated preparing for trial. Reading and re-reading all those transcripts. My statement to the university. My statement to the RCMP. What I had said in the preliminary. The Zoom calls with lawyers. Morning, afternoon, night, I was reading about what happened to me or playing it in my head. Here was the worst thing that has ever happened to me and in order to get the justice I deserved, I had to continue to relive that moment.

Those couple of weeks between the trial and verdict were like a vacation. It was the first breath of fresh air in a long time. I had said my piece, and it was out of my hands. All vacations end, though. Getting the call with the verdict crushed me. I'd gotten my hopes up, though everyone had said not to. I had expected a follow-up article due to the case being highly publicized. What I hadn't expected were the Judge's comments. I expected somebody of her status to understand that her words have an impact and consequences. It didn't go unnoticed that she decided to omit Jacob's text messages in evidence. She did, however, feel the need to include that he apologized.

I'm still trying to deal with the aftermath, and I'm learning how to be okay. It's hard because what happened to me and what happened at trial is never going to be okay, and I can't change that. I just have to be okay with the fact that it sucks and let myself be sad about it. Reading back and reflecting on all that's happened, I know that as hard as it's been having my case publicized, I'd do it all again. It was not an easy road, and it didn't end the way I had hoped, but I am proud of myself and all that has come of this.

White Woman's Work

Sufia Langevin

I leave this work to the white woman
She is more likely to be heard, believed, and helped
In white woman's hands, the task is safe and held
Far from my reach
Our institutions simply aren't ready
Not ready to hear about the intersections of race and sexual violence
Not ready to know that women of colour are more likely to be victims
Not ready to hear and support them in their reports
No one wants to have these conversations
Not about fetishization and exoticism
Not about the "conquest" of a woman of colour
Not about interracial rape
The only time race is mentioned
Is not to highlight vulnerability or risk
But to demonize men of colour
We have the short end of every stick
To be silenced by perpetrators is hard, but expected
To be silenced by allies, who share our goal of protection?
How can we be expected to fight that,
With so much on our backs?

To support only white women is seen as the first step
The rest of us will be helped once they are saved
In a never-ending battle, if you support your most vulnerable
Will you not have helped your most powerful too?
How do we make progress?
In a PWI[1], unseen, unheard, and hurting
I leave my safety, foolishly,
To be white woman's work

---

1. PWI stands for "Primarily White Institution," used to describe academic institutions
where the majority of staff, faculty, and students are white and have historically been white.

The After

Rebecca Mesay

In[1] the stories we read in school, we would hear about the main character overcoming tribulations time and time again, until finally at the end of the story, they would fulfill their purpose and be allowed to live in peace. This, of course, is not reality. These stories rarely tell us about the "after," what happens in the days, weeks, and months following these difficult, life-changing experiences. I think this sometimes makes us forget about the "after" in real life too.

In 2018, I published an article in *The Xaverian Weekly* titled, "An Open Letter to the X-Men Basketball Team Captain." It was an impact statement that described how my life had changed after an incident with the aforementioned captain. I wrote the statement at the beginning of April 2018 in a twenty-four-hour Tim Hortons, when I was supposed to be writing a paper. At the time, I had pursued all my options for holding this person accountable and the process had reached a point

---

1. As I begin this conversation, I would like to preface by stating that this is the type of discussion I typically reserve for debate within the Black community. I am pulling the veil back on my experiences for the sake of transparency and mainly in hopes that young Black women who have experienced or are experiencing what I am about to describe, will benefit from me talking about it openly. My aim is not to invite criticism or judgment from people outside of my community for what happens within my community.

of stagnation that made me realize he was going to escape almost all responsibility.

In the aftermath of this incident, I thought I had done everything right; I had reported it to the university and then to the police. I had filed my police report, been patient, offered witnesses, and communicated weekly with the case officer, but it wasn't going anywhere. A small part of me thought, *I have done everything I can so he cannot harm anyone else; just let the system do its thing.* Then another, larger part of me would respond in indignation, *When has the system EVER protected someone like you? And what about how your life was forced to change?*

So, I wrote about what it was like—the fear, stress, and anxiety—and about watching the systems fail me. I wrote about the toxic, male athlete culture that allowed a person like the captain to thrive. My statement not only expressed derision for how the system was treating me, but also for how it had treated those who came before me, and how it would continue to treat those who came after me. The year had left me tired of seeing and hearing about violence against women, especially because it went largely unchecked. It was pervasive in our student body's social scene and also existed in more nuanced forms outside of that sphere. It simply takes one glance around any campus to understand how these power dynamics exist in a way that conspicuously protects certain people while leaving others entirely vulnerable.

What I thought was going to happen versus what actually happened when my letter was released could not have been more different. The article was posted on April 24, 2018, at approximately 2:00 p.m. I was sitting in the Tall and Small Café, palms sweating, continuously checking *The Xaverian Weekly*'s website waiting for it to appear. Finally, the editor texted me ... it was up. I anxiously refreshed the website; there it was, in black and white. I thought I would immediately feel liberated, but I was nervous about how it would be received. I looked around, wondering if anyone could sense my disquiet, but it seemed the world was still spinning. So, I stayed in the Tall and Small and tried to work on my paper, even though I was too jittery to really focus.

The world paused for a moment at 2:52 p.m. This was when I received my first message. It was from a young woman one year above me. She commended me on my statement and said that it had made her reflect on her own experiences. She asked me if I could go for coffee the next day. After this first contact, there was half an hour of almost nothing. Then the world stopped spinning—for real this time. I started receiving calls on my cellphone, one after another after another, from journalists across the province. Simultaneously, I was getting a torrent of text and social media messages from people far and wide. I didn't understand right away how the journalists had gotten my personal number, and then realized too late that it was on The Union website under my profile as a student leader. The following year when I was Student Union President, I set a guideline with my team to only put their office phone numbers on The U's website.

At this point, I started to understand that it maybe wouldn't just be the twelve people I had envisioned in my head reading my article. It began to feel overly warm in the Tall and Small, so I texted one of my mentors telling her what was happening, and she told me where she was. By coincidence, she was getting her hair done not far from the cafe. Despite my stressed state when I entered, the hairdressers welcomed me with open arms, and their funny banter helped lighten my mood. It truly was the perfect place for me to be in that moment, among warm and kind-hearted people. And really, who would think to look for a coily-haired Black girl in a white folks' hair salon? It was the perfect hideout. I stayed there the whole afternoon with my mentor as I tried to process what was happening.

People were reading my impact statement. *A lot* of people were reading my impact statement. I was getting tagged on Facebook by family, friends, and strangers. I looked at the shares on the original link, and the number just kept getting bigger and bigger until I couldn't believe it anymore. I was receiving an onslaught of text messages, Facebook messages, and emails, again from family, friends, strangers, and even some professors. People from across the province, the country, and in some instances, from across the world, were reaching out. I was in disbelief. Was this even real life? The messages I got were so overwhelmingly supportive—friends and colleagues reaffirming that they were there for me, people telling me that I was courageous and that they wanted their children to be like me. It was so much to take in, and as much as I tried to respond to each person, I knew it would take me days to get back to everyone.

Two days after the article was released, a former member of *The Xaverian Weekly* reached out to me with the statistics on the piece. I did a double take when I saw the number and then felt my face flush. It had received over 49,000 views. By the end of the week, that number would be closer to 61,000. What would this all mean? I simply did not know.

On the day the article went out into the world, and in the weeks and months following, I would receive disclosures from women around the country. There were even women who now lived on different continents that reached out. The disclosures came from young and old, from mothers, grandmothers, friends, and teachers. I was reeling. Some of these disclosures included accusations against certain varsity teams going back *decades*. I listened to repeated stories of coaches, some well-known and others not so much, condoning their players' behaviours, failing to report violent or inappropriate incidents to administration, and not complying with the simplest of requests made by survivors to change the culture of their teams. After hearing from so many people, I couldn't help but wonder how many women could have been spared pain, finished their degrees, or positively impacted their communities had there been any *real* consequences for the players who perpetrated these behaviours and for the coaches who fostered environments that allowed these issues to go unchecked.

It was from some of these very coaches and players that I would receive the harshest criticism and endure the most disrespectful conduct from after the statement was published. I was not surprised by it—the guilty always show their hand in the end; but I simply marveled at their arrogance. These people were fully aware of how their actions had contributed to what happened to me, as well as to all these other women. And yet, instead of keeping their heads down and hoping no one would point them out too, they got on their soapboxes and claimed that I must have antagonized the captain and that his response was warranted, or that I was making too much of the situation. It has always intrigued me how previously incurious and unambitious men suddenly become investigators, judges, and lawyers when faced with a situation like mine. I understood that the reason for their defence of a man so clearly in the wrong was because they were afraid their own crimes would come to light. The whispers in the corridor of a university and the quiet revelations after a night-out are powerful. I knew well what lurked in the closets of my loudest detractors. I think they may have feared me. If a powerful captain could be held accountable, what was keeping them from being liable next?

To fully understand the treatment that I received from the male athletics sphere at that time, it is important to contextualize what the environment at StFX is like for young, unambiguously Black women. In a majority white town and university with maybe two to three hundred Black students, there is a heightened visibility for Black people. In Antigonish, like in other small university towns, male athletes on team sports are treated like deities on and off campus. By virtue of these two realities, Black male athletes become amongst the most visible and well-known members of our campus community. Through their own admission, this makes life easier, especially in social settings. There is ease of access when entering establishments, going to parties, and meeting women. And as uncomfortable as it is to say out loud, they namely have easier access to white women. This fact is also true for white athletes and non-Black athletes of colour. This phenomenon is in part explained by sheer numbers; there are significantly fewer Black women on campus than white women (less than 100 Black women and approximately 2,500-3,000 white women). Furthermore, deeply seated misogynoir (a bias that intersects misogyny and racism) and classism dictate that white men do not date Black women. And certainly not on a campus like StFX, where whiteness and wealth often walk hand in hand. I cannot describe to you how far outside of the norm white men dating Black women was at StFX during the time I was there, especially a white varsity athlete dating a Black woman.

In contrast, what then explains how Black men, especially Black male athletes, treat Black women at StFX? An early and imperative disclaimer: not every Black man or Black male athlete at our university has treated Black women badly. What I am aiming to point out is that there is an underlying culture that exists among certain Black athletes where shunning and vilifying Black women is not only the norm, but actively encouraged. Sometimes it does not even have to be said, as actions always speak louder than words.

The reason for this phenomenon is complex and multi-faceted, including factors such as colourism, classism, and internalized racism. The discussion of these systems of oppression is nuanced and complex; regardless, there is another reality that is important to point out: Black women typically represent and uphold the values of the communities that Black men come from. During the time that certain Black men are athletes at StFX, they reject these values and are unwilling to uphold the standards that would be expected of them otherwise. Therefore, these Black men do not date Black women because Black women would hold them accountable for their actions. To top it all off, the Black men who have these beliefs and who engage in these behaviours will never admit it, but instead use coded language such as "Black women are difficult," "I'm not attracted to Black girls," or, popularly, "It's just a preference." Do not be fooled, a preference does not repudiate everything outside of its category—what they are showing is internalized racism.

The realities that I described above connect to how I was treated by the male athlete sphere in the aftermath of my article because their response was aligned with how they already treated and thought of Black women. This behaviour also mimics how Black women are treated in the larger Black community. I was a Black woman who had faced violence coming from a Black man and because he was Black, I was supposed to have stayed quiet about how I was treated, because Black men are already treated unfairly by the world. The idea of Black women "being difficult" was created to inherently undermine Black women, and more importantly, to promote not believing them if they ever decided to come forward. Above all, this is intended to gaslight Black women into thinking they have not been hurt in the first place. It is clear how these attitudes and stereotypes shaped the narratives coming from the men on the soapboxes. The issue with these stereotype-based narratives is that the people who are inclined to believe them are also inclined to act upon them.

In the days and weeks following the publication of my letter, my friends sent me posts of people who were trying to undermine what I had written. I think the popularity and resounding support of the statement probably deterred more aggressive public stances, seeing as most of the posts used coded language and did not make direct reference to my statement. In contrast, there was one young man from a cohort of football alums making some of these posts, who messaged me directly. I was suspicious of his intentions from the beginning of the message, so I perused his Facebook profile. Sure enough, the third picture was of him and the very captain in question. At the conclusion of his messages, the recent alum asked me if I could tell him what had happened the night of the incident. I rolled my eyes and debated responding to his query with the picture of him and the captain, followed by, "This you?" I wasn't interested in taking the conversation further, so I simply responded that I had nothing more to say publicly.

As you can imagine, some people with direct relationships to the captain had in fact responded openly and intentionally to my statement. In the meal hall on release day, one of the captain's friends who had been present at the altercation started telling people that I was lying. My friends overheard, confronted him, and asked him how an *impact statement* could have been a lie. They also pointed out that he had previously acknowledged that an altercation had happened, and that he himself was one of the people who had intervened to prevent me from being harmed. That day, he was saying things like, "Why do Black women gotta do this to Black men?" As I said before, these types of attitudes are directly connected to how Black women can be harmed in and by their own communities.

A few days after April 24, I was out with some friends at the bar in an attempt to return to some semblance of normalcy. I had expected it to be a relatively dead night, with most students gone for the summer. Everything was okay for about fifteen minutes, until two Men's Basketball leaders walked in. I saw them and I knew that they had seen me. This was not going to end well. To offer you a synopsis, other than when I was in the washroom or when they were trying to pick up girls (which they seemed too drunk to do), they were no further than a metre from me and they used their height and ability to take up space to make their presence known. If I was on the dance floor, they were on either side of me, blocking me from getting to my friends. If I was sitting in a booth, they were standing conspicuously close to it, and even toasted their captain over my head at one point. After finally making it through what ended up being an awful night, I crossed the street to the pizza place. Within ten minutes of my arrival, they also entered the establishment. The captains came in and started to speak loudly to a friend of mine at the pizza counter, telling him that I was "salty." I had given them little to no response the whole night, knowing that they wanted to anger me. It was only by reminding myself repeatedly of this fact that I did not, for the most part, say anything to them. I walked home weary and frustrated, thinking that I should probably prepare for that type of behaviour from the rest of the team when they returned in September.

As part of my case's whole debacle, the officer who processed it had encouraged me to participate in a Restorative Circle organized by the John Howard Society. I was told that because the captain was a first-time offender and because the Crown was unlikely to take the case, this was one of the few options available to me to ensure my report remained on record. This circle was supposedly part of a program they were developing for the captain to help him deal with his anger and address the underlying misogynistic attitudes he had towards women. Dear reader, let me say: don't ever participate in a Restorative Circle with someone who is facing consequences for violent crimes against women. Frankly, I don't even know why this is an option for adults who are offenders. No kumbaya is going to change what they did or what happened to you. I only did it because I didn't know any better.

Both the offender and the harmed party got a support person (yes, you heard that right) and the other participants included the case officer, the John Howard facilitators, a university official, a member of the Naomi Society, and a probation officer. The support person for the captain worked in the Men's Basketball program. In the circle we were told that each person had the chance to speak, uninterrupted, and then the next person could talk. During his turn, this individual took the opportunity to yell at and lambast me. In his rant, he lauded the achievements of the captain, saying that he was a member of the national team and recognized in the AUS. Then the person pointed at me and said that I did not know about the team or its players (not true, seeing as I had volunteered as one of the team's study hall coordinators the year prior), and that I should not expect the organization's members to know what their players were up to off the court on weekends. I did not break eye contact with him the entire time, and then it occurred to me—this man, several decades my senior and employed at StFX, was fundamentally unhappy with his life. Why else would he be so easily pushed to anger that he would rage at a twenty-one-year-old woman, during a Restorative Circle of all places, and risk his career in front of a university official? In later discussions, a friend would offer that maybe it wasn't that he was unhappy with his life. Maybe he was completely satisfied with his existence, and he did what he did and said what he said, because he knew that his privilege as a man, university employee and member of the athletics realm at

StFX, would protect him and permit this kind of behaviour with little to no consequences. Perhaps he knew there was little risk to him and his position, which encouraged him to be as bold as he was during that restorative circle. After all, he remains both employed and involved with Men's Basketball and will continue to serve as an "example" of acceptable behaviour for generations of StFX basketball players to come. In my article, I stated that the behaviour of players was often condoned by the university's athletics sphere. Whether this person realized it or not (and I am inclined to think he didn't), he had just proved my point *exactly.*

There were a few more incidents like this, mainly from the same types of people, for the remainder of my time at StFX. Usually, it bothered me in the moment, but I did not, or at least I tried not, to hold onto those instances for very long. Of course, the process of moving on and healing is much more complicated than that. But when it seemed too difficult, I would focus on the tens of thousands of people who had read and supported my article, and I was comforted to think that people cared. Even though most of my critics had come from the athletics sphere and basketball in particular, some of the most touching messages that I had received came from members of that same basketball team. Unexpectedly, a year later, I even had a conversation with one of the team's leaders who had been following me at the bar. He took the opportunity to apologize for his actions that night, and expressed how deeply sorry he was for what he had done.

When I think about the 2017-2018 school year, I think most often about the things that I lost. It had been a difficult year at StFX, with multiple high-profile assaults and the arrests of various varsity athletes. And yet, a year of pain and loss for so many of us would become the foundation for our advocacy against sexualized and gender-based violence on our campus. The following year, another high-profile assault would emerge, and the activism that StFX students led during that time would again make national news. The bystander intervention and sexualized violence prevention programs, the introduction of a new sexualized violence policy, the town halls and feedback forums—and the shift that has happened at StFX in the last several years would not have been possible without the tireless efforts of StFX students.

Without exaggeration, I could probably write a book about my years at StFX. The stories that touched me that year and the ones that I heard about after publishing my letter will always live with me. At its core, my statement discussed one person's experience, and yet it resonated with so many people because it echoed what women at StFX and in universities all over the country had endured for generations. Before writing the piece, while I was dealing with the incident and the case that followed, I felt so alone. I kept a lot of things to myself, hoping that if I pushed them down far enough, I would forget about them. I swiftly found out that this is not how emotions work. I was only able to move on after I had fully acknowledged each part of what I was feeling. In the months before I wrote the impact statement, I hadn't truly been living, and though the letter didn't solve all my problems, it did allow me to finally stand up for myself on my own terms. I never could have believed what it would become or how many people would see it. After all, my letter had one simple message: what happened to me was wrong and it should not happen to others. The responsibility to change systems should not just fall on activists and survivors, it falls on every single one of us to act and to move these systems forward each and every day.

The Home Stretch

Anonymous

The following speech was written for and performed at Take Back the Night on September 26, 2019, hosted by St. Francis Xavier University and the Antigonish Women's Resource Centre and Sexual Assault Services Association.

———

I didn't wake up one morning and decide that this is the issue I wanted to advocate against. It punched me in the face and pulled my hair, and I felt that my only option was to punch back. And now I'm left feeling like I may have been punching a bit above my weight class.

I'm left feeling exhausted.

I have a feeling that there is a similar narrative around most activists, because of course we want to fight against things that we care about, and we usually care about things because we've been directly impacted, whether it be a friend, a family member, a teammate, a colleague, or ourselves. And engaging in a conversation or in work that emotionally drains you, that re-traumatizes you, that forces you to use every ounce of your energy to try and use logic when discussing an act that is so illogical is exhausting.

I know that we are tired. And how can we not be? We have to fight to have our voices heard and then we have to try not to stutter. We have to bring people inside of our trauma to get the accommodations we need. We have to listen as people in positions of power refer to sexualized violence as a "hot button topic" when in reality it's the lived experience of millions. Our trauma, our victimization, is not a "hot button topic," it's a fucking tragedy and it's one that's been going on for far too long.

It's no wonder that we're tired, and we have every right to be. But I want to believe with every ounce of my being that we are in the home stretch, that soon there will be rest.

And until then, I want safe spaces and rallies. I want those times when you know that you're preaching to the choir because it's those things that rejuvenate us and allow us to come back with a new sense of purpose, a new hope. It's those little shreds of optimism that make their way into the darkest days that allow us to keep going.

And so I know that we are tired, but tonight we will chant loudly, we will march, and we will continue to support one another. We will keep fighting, because even if we're tired and we don't feel like we're making a dent, there are changes happening all around us, there are communities forming and survivors finding their voices, people are speaking out and speaking up and others can no longer hide in their ignorance, they can't pretend they don't hear us because we're being too loud, so we're going to keep being loud until there is no room for anything but change.

I know that we're tired, but we're in the home stretch.

What Resolution?

HEATHER CHANDLER

Content Warning: Mild description of sexual assault
To skip to the next story, turn to page 49.

When I was in my fourth and final year of my undergraduate degree at Mount Allison University in Sackville, New Brunswick, I was sexually assaulted. It happened on November 23, 2012, by a member of the Mount Allison football team, a factor which played a large role in how the incident was dealt with by various members of the university community. This became apparent almost immediately after the assault took place, when I walked across The Pond (the campus pub) to a student security staff member, who was a fellow football teammate, and pointed out my assailant. He looked at his friend, then back at me, and told me there was nothing he could do about it.

This same student security staff member would later go on to post my story on Reddit—with the misinformation that I had accused his friend and teammate of rape[1] —in an effort to garner sympathy for himself when it was obvious that he'd failed in his job of keeping students safe. I'd like to think that if I'd sought his help after being raped by his friend, his answer would have been something other than, "I can't help you." But unfortunately, this was exactly what he said to me when I approached him. He directed me to the Event Security Student (ESS) Coordinator, who took a description of my assailant and said that he would review the CCTV footage. I wasn't offered the option to review the footage myself and was later told that the tapes were too dark to make anything out, which begs the question: why bother having surveillance equipment if it isn't useful?

Four days after the incident, I contacted the Head of Student Life (HSL) with my complaint and was told that she was waiting on the incident report from The Pond before moving forwards. I expressed my wish to have the incident dealt with before the end of term.

Two and a half months later on February 13, 2013, I sent an email to both the Head of Student Life and the Sexual Harassment Advisor (SHA), as I had yet to hear anything regarding my complaint. I asked to be informed about the proceedings, and to meet with the SHA, as we'd planned to do in January. The HSL responded, citing the Event Security report and stating, "To date I also have not received other complaints about this individual." She informed me that there was not sufficient evidence to move forward with a complaint. I wrote back, stating (for

---

1. Sexual assault falls under the umbrella term of sexual violence, defined by the World Health Organization (2021) as: "any sexual act, attempt to obtain a sexual act, unwanted sexual comments or advances, or acts to traffic, or otherwise directed, against a person's sexuality using coercion, by any person regardless of their relationship to the victim, in any setting, including but not limited to home and work." Sexual violence includes rape, defined as physically forced or otherwise coerced penetration – even if slight – of the vulva or anus, using a penis, other body parts or an object.

the second time) that the security staff had seen my assailant's face when I pointed him out, as well as the fact that my boyfriend had been with me at the time of the assault. The Head of Student Life told me that with this "new information" she was willing to continue her investigation. The SHA was cc'd in this email correspondence but still had yet to contact me.

For many years afterwards, this particular line has stuck with me—"I have also not received other complaints about this individual." I can't fathom ever saying this to a survivor while referring to their assailant. The statement is absurd in many ways. It's been documented, and has been for some time, the low percentage of sexual assaults that are ever reported, and the even lower percentage of which that are actually prosecuted. The Canadian Women's Foundation has compiled statistics showing that in 2014, just 5% of sexual assaults were reported to police.[2] The idea that a lack of prior conviction somehow exempts this individual from the consequences of their actions, while at the same time completely discrediting my experience, is abhorrent.

On February 20, I informed the HSL that I had set up a meeting with the Mount Allison Student Union President to talk through Mt. A's policies regarding sexual harassment and assault and asked if she knew a better way to contact the SHA. The SHA emailed me the following day to set up a meeting.

On February 22, the HSL emailed me again with the following, "I have solicited witness statements from the persons you identified. There is sufficient information, and I am prepared to move forward with the complaint. As the victim, I wanted to confirm what resolution you are

2. "The Facts About Sexual Assault and Harassment." Canadian Women's Foundation, last modified June 1, 2022.

seeking in this case (charges, education, etc.)?" This was the first time in months that I felt as though my complaint was finally being acted upon. It was still another few weeks before I had my very first meeting with the Sexual Harassment Advisor, at which time I had to remind her of significant details regarding my complaint, including the name of the perpetrator. She initially tried to convince me that what I had experienced was sexual harassment and downplayed my assault even as I described it to her. To be tasked with defending myself to the one person at the university who was supposedly trained in this area of counselling was degrading and left me feeling as if she couldn't wipe her hands clean of the situation fast enough. When I remained steadfast in my assertion that what I was subjected to was both physical and sexual assault, she subsequently proposed three recommendations:

1. that the individual be banned from the Pond;

2. that the individual receive education on sexual assault from the Sexual Harassment Advisor;

3. that the individual's football coaches be made aware of his actions.

On March 20, I was asked into my first meeting with the Head of Student Life to discuss the results of her investigation. She told me that there was "insufficient evidence to move forward with the complaint." I asked if the recommendations that the SHA had included were still available for resolution of my complaint and was told that they were. The next day, however, they went back on their word. I sent a follow-up email to the HSL and the SHA to inform them that I was planning on celebrating with my rugby team at the Athletic Banquet After-Party at the Pond. I wanted to confirm that the perpetrator would not be in the vicinity, since the recommendations were still in place. To this, the HSL responded, "What I am faced with is inconclusive evidence. This means that the information that I have isn't adding up to a cut and dried situation. There are missing pieces and until these pieces are determined, I am unable to lay charges. That is not to say that charges will not be laid but at this time, to act is premature."

At this time, to act is premature. At this time, after he has already assaulted one known victim at the very location that I am hoping to attend again, it is premature to ban him from said location. At this time, to give the victim the benefit of the doubt, and possibly prevent other people from becoming victims of his, to act is premature. At this time, after I've already offered you resolution through charges and education, I've now decided that to act would be premature.

In reply, I asked her to explain what had changed between February 22 when charges and education were offered, and this point, when nothing was being offered to me in terms of resolution. As of March 22, after I had sent two requests for clarification around the complaint process, I was invited to a meeting with the Head of Student Life. Due to the heavy work burden associated with the time of year, the amount of time this process had already taken up, and my diminishing mental health as a result, I declined the offer to meet. I sometimes look back on this decision with regret. I sometimes wonder if one more excruciating meeting, where I fought to have my complaint acknowledged, validated, acted upon, and was made to rehash and relive the experiences and frustrations, would have made the difference. But I'm confident that it wouldn't have. The way that my entire complaint process was handled clearly evidences a lack of student advocacy and an inherent incompetence on the part of the individuals entrusted to foster student well-being and safety. I did what I had to do to protect my own safety, and I stepped away from the complete absence of support and transparency showcased by the administration. I was lucky enough to have an incredible mentor in the form of a professor, who acted as a sounding board, an advisor, and someone who would listen without judgment. In short, she embodied the roles that every administrator who I approached for help should have, and where they were unable or unwilling to do so, she helped me when I needed it most.

I detailed my experiences in a letter to then-president Robert Campbell. I wanted to highlight three major points of concern:

1. As in cases of physical assault, the security staff member that I initially approached on the date of my incident should have immediately followed up on my complaint.

2. In an email on February 18, the Head of Student Life informed me that she had interviewed the individual who assaulted me. I do not understand why I wasn't offered the same courtesy, or kept informed of my complaint. On the basis of Mt. A's Policy, #1003: Policies and Procedures with Respect to Sexual Harassment: "A complainant has the right... d. to be kept informed of the status of any proceedings under this policy, and e. to receive the results of the investigation in writing."[3]

3. On several occasions, resolutions to the incident were offered, and subsequently rescinded. The HSL initially offered to press charges in the email dated February 22, but this offer was later withdrawn without clear reason as to why. In our meeting on

---

3. "Policies and Procedures with Respect to Sexual Harassment." Policies and Procedures, Mount Allison University. retrieved February 2013 from https://mta.ca/about/leadershi p-and-governance/policies-and-procedures.

March 20, when I asked if the recommendations that the SHA provided would still be in effect, the HSL said that they were. When I tried to confirm this, so that I could feel safe while attending a university event on the university campus, I received an email from the HSL on March 21 saying that "nothing would be done" and apologizing for "any misunderstanding."

My experience with the administrative process around my complaint of sexual assault left me utterly frustrated, confused, and feeling re-victimized. My complaint was not dealt with in a timely manner, my statements were not properly reviewed at times, nor were they taken seriously. I waited months for the university's Sexual Harassment Advisor to schedule a meeting—which I was ultimately forced to initiate. Overall, the university processes around the Sexual Harassment and Assault policy emerged as inefficient and unclear.

Mount Allison, what have you done in the intervening years to make your campus safer for your students? My recommendations at the time included that there should be a student advocate made available specifically to assist complainants through the complaint process for sexual harassment and assault at Mount Allison University. They included frequent, effective training programs for staff who could be front-line responders in the event of sexual harassment or assault of students. For example, the security staff at The Pond would need this kind of mandatory education on sexual violence for the safety of students on Mt. A's campus. As long as incidents like the one I experienced are allowed to occur without repercussions from the university, sexual assault on this university campus and others will continue to be a serious and insidious problem.

Sometimes I find myself thinking back to ten years ago, sitting in a dingy student apartment, full of anger, confusion, and disgust. At the time, those feelings seemed insurmountable. They clouded the final year of my undergraduate degree, stole my happiness, and forever changed the memories of my time at Mount Allison. A defining memory of my Convocation weekend is sitting across from my father in a restaurant in Amherst, trying to find the nerve to tell him what happened. I have yet to return to Sackville, New Brunswick.

This experience is not isolated, but it is isolating. Find your support network. Tell your parents, your sister, your close friends. This experience had repercussions that I am still dealing with. For years, I held onto my anger and used it for protection. Anger can be a great motivating force, and it can also sap the joy from your everyday life. Learn to redirect it, focus it, and use it as fuel. To those of you fighting similar battles, I applaud you. This takes guts, it takes strength, and it takes stamina. Keep going.

Is my Campus a Brick Wall? A Conversation About My Experience with Sexual Violence at Mount Allison University

MICHELLE ROY

Content Warning: Mild description of sexual assault
To skip to the next story, turn to page 66.

This paper is based on my individual personal experience, and for the safety and privacy of others, all names or identifying factors (to an extent) have been removed.

———

In 2020, Statistics Canada announced that 71% of students at Canadian post-secondary schools witnessed or experienced unwanted sexualized behaviour. Likewise, they reported that 91% of women and 92% of men who witnessed these behaviours chose not to intervene or seek help.[1] Statistics often feel like impersonal data that doesn't relate to you. I will admit that I felt this way when I first came to Mount Allison. I knew sexualized violence was relevant at universities—after all, I watched tons of *Law & Order: SVU*. In the end, I was going to a small-town university in New Brunswick, and sexualized violence only happened at big universities. Right?

My mind changed quickly. Within a few weeks of starting school, a friend of mine was raped in the middle of campus at night by another student. Later in the semester, someone very important to me was sexually assaulted in her dorm room. It quickly seemed that everyone around me had fallen victim to sexual assault. I began my journey of actively listening to the experiences that students shared with me, and those statistics started representing people I knew and loved.

At the end of my first year, I was faced with the situation of a student who had assaulted multiple women on campus, including unwanted sexual behaviour directed at me. A number of us got together and reported him to the university. The perpetrator was suspended, and we went home for the summer feeling satisfied. We would later find out that he had successfully appealed the decision and would be back on campus as a full-time student in a larger residence. For most of us, it felt like we had been told, "We don't believe you, and we don't care about your safety" by the administration that had promised to protect us.

I ended up getting raped three more times while at Mount Allison. Not that it matters to the validity of my experience, but in the incidents, I was either unconscious, screamed no, or was sleeping next to someone

---

1. Marta Burczycka, "Students' Experiences of Unwanted Sexualized Behaviours and Sexual Assault at Postsecondary Schools in the Canadian Provinces, 2019," Government of Canada, Statistics Canada, September 14, 2020.

I trusted. On top of that, I faced dozens of sexual assaults and unwanted sexual behaviours. They were all moments that snuck up on me and where it felt like there was no way out. I tend to keep my personal trauma outside of my activism, but it is a strong motivation. I am no one special. I am just your average student, and I am one example of the hundreds of other students who have had similar experiences while attending Mount Allison.

I had been an active advocate for sexualized violence prevention on my campus for years but only realized how grave the situation was after one specific event. One of my best friends had lived a "privileged" life. I look back now and realize that, in a way, I envied that she had never experienced the trauma I had. I always felt like she had an advantage over me. Then one night, I fell asleep, and my phone fell off the bed. I woke up to a dozen missed calls from my friend, who had no idea what to do minutes after her assault. Those phone calls led to police interviews, eight-hour physical exams, and her clothes and sheets put into a bag, never to be seen again. All of this for one prosecutor to decide her rape wasn't "good enough" to be brought to court. It was now official: all of my friends had been sexually assaulted while attending Mount Allison University.

In 2020, Statistics Canada announced that 71% of students at Canadian post-secondary institutions witnessed or experienced unwanted sexualized behaviour. I look at those numbers differently now. The number is no longer irrelevant to me. It means 1,491 students at Mount Allison out of the 2,100 in attendance have experienced sexualized violence. In an average first-year class, that is twenty-nine students in a class of forty-one. In an average upper-year class, that is ten students in a class size of fourteen.[2] For most of us, it was all of our friends and peers.

After this point, my activism on campus became a central theme in my life. I woke up and breathed sexualized violence on campus. I wrote an article condemning the sexualized violence policy, I joined committees, organized three Take Back the Night events, and actively spoke up on social media. Routine responses were sent to me and everyone else concerned: "Mount Allison treats any case of sexual harassment or assault extremely seriously."[3]

Things felt different when my professor put me in contact with a first-year student. The story was too familiar to the many others I had heard. She was confused and scared, and all I could think about while standing in this office in Hart Hall, a former crucial building for the Ladies Mount Allison College, was of those women who had paved the way for us to be here today. They faced the same fate. An eighteen-year-old with dreams and passion entered an institute that promised to protect her, and she left traumatized. I could not picture leaving Mount Allison knowing that the cycle would continue for other bright, passionate women to have their spirits crushed by violence.

I had graduation photos booked the next day. I took a photo in front of the university's welcome sign in a cap and gown with a poster that read: "Mount Allison supports rapists #mountiepride" and "Mount Allison silences survivors." I posted the photos on Instagram with the following caption:

---

2. "Facts and Figures," Mount Allison University, n.d.

3. Zane Schwartz, "Canadian Universities Are Failing Students on Sexual Assault," Macleans, March 1, 2018.

I refuse to leave Mount Allison University without acknowledging the harm the Mount Allison institution has caused. It all started in 2016. I came to know of an individual who had assaulted roughly a dozen women in residence. Although women came forward, the university decided to allow him to continue attending campus AND remain in residence, where the next year he would be given the opportunity to assault a dozen more women. I quickly realized that Mount Allison University would not protect their students, but instead protect the rapist that attended our classes and walked our campus.

The next few years were really hard. I became known has an activist and students started pouring in, telling me personal experiences where their rapist was allowed to continue attending Mount Allison, despite many women coming forward.

Mount Allison loves to tell us how low their rates of sexual assault are. I want you to know, that is a lie. Ask the women around you, sexual assault at Mount Allison University is as common as attracting a common cold. Personally, I know more victims of sexual assault on this campus than students who have not been impacted. I can go to Ducky's on a Saturday evening and name more than a handful of men who got away with sexual assault at the bar, preying on a new target. In all honestly, in my last five years attending Mount Allison University, I have met approximately fifty victims. I have never seen a rapist be expelled.

As I become an Alumni, I will forever stand by my choice to let everyone know that MOUNT ALLISON IS NOT A SAFE INSTI-TUTION. MOUNT ALLISON PROTECTS RAPISTS. MOUNT ALLISON SILENCES VICTIMS.

I came to Mount Allison University knowing it was the under-graduate university. I left Mount Allison University knowing it was the university in ignoring sexual violence.I spent the last five years begging the university to revisit how they approach sexual violence, and they continuously refused. So here is the truth! Fuck you Mount Allison University!

#mountiepride am I right?

It was a few minutes of my time, and, at most, I expected a small response and an email from the administration. Today, that post has nearly seventeen-thousand likes. That is more than eight times the Mount Allison student body and more than three times the population of Sackville. It was shared across the nation, even the world, and made national headlines.

Following the viral post, a number of students wanted to show their support beyond social media. With the help of the Mount Allison Students' Union (MASU), I was able to organize a protest where four-hundred students, faculty, staff, alums, and community members came together in person, and hundreds more watched live online. It was a life-changing moment that showed the Mount Allison administration that we would no longer be silenced and that we demanded change. The amount of media attention no doubt scared the administration into listening.

The first time I heard from the university regarding my now-viral Instagram post was in a mass email sent to all students on November 9, 2020, titled *Concerns over Sexual Violence at Mount Allison*. In a quick summary, the posts, comments, and personal stories shared online were acknowledged by the university, and they reassured students that they were being heard and that they understood not enough was being done for survivors. The President's Cabinet concluded that they would commit to an action plan by the end of the week.

On November 11, 2020, the day before the protest, I had a meeting with some of the higher-ups in administration and the university president. I offered my recommendations based on my experience so far and called for the immediate removal of our sexualized violence prevention staff member. Most of my recommendations were part of the campus plan that was announced the following day.

On November 12, 2020, another email was sent to the student body alongside a public statement from the university. The university acknowledged that they had let down students and apologized for the harm they had caused. They pledged to students that they were in the process of change. They announced a plan in which they committed to:

1. Increase resources focused on sexualized violence prevention and response

2. Immediate changes to sexual assault intake and counselling services

3. Establish a Sexual Violence Prevention Working Group at Mount Allison

4. Initiate a third-party review of Mount Allison's sexualized violence prevention model, resources, policies, and procedures.

Many more emails and statements were soon sent to students, all of them related to the steps announced earlier. The most crucial components were that a working group was put together and I was announced as co-chair alongside a faculty member; an outside resource was brought onto campus in the interim, named Crossroads for Women; and a third-party group was selected to review procedures and policies on campus, The Canadian Centre for Legal Innovation in Sexual Assault Response (CCLISAR).

When the Sexual Violence Prevention Working Group (SVPWG) was formally announced and they asked if I would become co-chair alongside a faculty member, there were several reasons I hesitated. Sara Ahmed's concept of the "brick wall," where she defines the institution and its administration as a literal brick wall standing in the way of change, immediately shot into my head. Before making any decisions, I spent some time reviewing Ahmed's *Living a Feminist Life* and put together a series of summarizing quotes to share with the administration. I felt that if they were able to acknowledge the concept, they could actively work against being an institute that uses its community's hard work as a sign of progress rather than requiring direct action on their part. I mandated that all members of the SVPWG would have to read Ahmed's chapter on the "brick wall" theory, participate in a presentation, and be a part of a greater discussion about what this meant for our working group.

It was clear that my presence on the SVPWG was necessary for the university to give the illusion to the community that they were sincerely making an effort to change. It was pretty simple: the students and alums had grown to trust my input and represent their interest as members of the community whose safety and lives were put at risk by the university. Without my approval, it would have been far less plausible that they had student interests in mind. For the sake of honesty, I am not sure how it made me feel. In one sense, it gave me an upper hand, a sort of power to hold above the university. In another, it gave me a sense of being used, that I was just another marketing tool in rebuilding their image.

Early in her novel, Ahmed explores her theory of willfulness and the "wilful subjects." She explains that feminists are often labeled as "wilful subjects," where willfulness is defined as: "asserting or disposed to assert one's own will against persuasion, instruction, or command; governed by will without regard to reason; determined to take one's own way; obstinately self – willed or preserved."[4] Diversity workers in institutions, she writes, must appear "willing" in order to be willful.[5] It was evident that the most effective way I could create change at the institution was by appearing "willing" through relationships with the Mount Allison administration, and so I built a close relationship with other members of the SVPWG and the Mount Allison administration in an effort to seem willing rather than wilful.

Our first order of business was putting together our mandates. Those included:.

- Recommendations for the new position for sexualized violence prevention and education and survivor support services.

- Recommendations for training and strategies for support of survivors (includes interim recommendations for sexualized violence and harassment investigations and sanctions on campus).

- A report on recommendations for campus-wide education and training to reduce sexualized violence within the campus community.

---

4. Weiner & Simpson, 1971, as cited in Sara Ahmed, *Living a Feminist Life*. (Durham: Duke University Press, 2017), 65.

5. Ahmed, Sara. *Living a Feminist Life* (Durham: Duke University Press, 2017), 101.

- Final recommendations on campus policies and investigations derived from the third-party review.[6]

The first step was a discussion on the historical data of disclosures of sexualized violence on campus in order to give the group a better understanding of the problem. Tensions between the administration and myself were evident. I was clear—Mount Allison procedures were created to keep the number of reports lower, which resulted in fewer students disclosing and not fewer sexual assaults happening. For a while after this meeting, I struggled to speak up. It became clear that opening the room for discussion and arguments made me uncomfortable. At the end of the day, I was still a student, and the administration, whether they wanted to or not, had a certain authority over me that frightened me. It took a lot of personal reflection and inner battles to remind myself that I had worked hard to be in this position, and I would not let fear control my behaviour.

The next month was dedicated to discussing the new position we were hiring for. There were many questions I never even considered: should this person be a crisis intervener or outreach coordinator? What type of education should this person have? What type of training should be offered to them? It felt like every time we agreed on something, at the next meeting someone would want to discuss it further. The process took a month longer than expected and highlighted the importance of discussion among peers. I stand by the recommendations we made as a group.

A concern that followed me was whether implementing a new sexualized violence prevention program and position would make a difference.

---

6. *Sexual Violence Prevention Working Terms of References.* Mount Allison Sexual Violence Working Group, January 21, 2021.

Ahmed explores how diversity workers create similar programs and positions that are later used against them. She tells us, "A program developed in response to a problem is assumed to resolve a problem. When the problem is not resolved, the resolution becomes the problem."[7]

This was something I had already seen the administration do. As soon as the Instagram post began going viral, the Sexual Assault and Harassment Response and Education program (SHARE) —the original sexualized violence prevention program and corresponding position on campus—was erased from the website and, in reality, erased from campus culture. The administration quickly blamed SHARE and the SHARE coordinator for the problem instead of taking accountability for their role in what went wrong. Admittedly, the SHARE program could have been successful on campus if the administration funded it properly, gave it access to resources, and relinquished some control over its actions.

At the time of writing this essay, the new program has yet to be implemented. I fear the same thing may happen, and that the new program is not about change but about rebranding Mount Allison's tarnished image. We worked our hardest to avoid the problem through dozens of recommendations, but whether those recommendations are ever fully implemented is up to the university. Putting a new label on a soda can does not change what is inside the can, only what it appears to be.

We recommended, with the help of Concordia University in Montreal, mandatory training for students and student leaders, to be completed online. The training would go beyond consent but still touch on bystander and sensitivity training. As mentioned above, I was happy with

---

7. Ahmed, Sara. *Living a Feminist Life* (Durham: Duke University Press, 2017), 100.

our recommendations, but the implementation now falls on the administrators, who have yet to acknowledge our hiring recommendations.

And so, our hopes rested on the recommendations of CCLISAR, a team of three lawyers hired by Mount Allison to review policies and procedures around sexualized violence on campus. The SVPWG had a say in their hiring, but in full transparency, I felt overwhelming pressure to agree to the group due to the short time frame. As I tried to research the group, I kept being reminded by the administration of the urgency to make an immediate choice. In the end, I agreed, despite not wanting to.

I made a joke at the beginning of the process to my co-chair, saying, "The only red flag that would set off an alarm for me would be if they had worked with StFX." I am sure you can imagine my disbelief when I looked over their website to see that the only undergraduate university they had worked with was ... you guessed it ... StFX. I would love to bring up formal statistics and evidence to prove my claim, but universities are notorious for finding loopholes to make their numbers seem much lower than they are when it comes to sexualized violence, and in full transparency, I do not trust any statistic provided by a university. As a student, I can say that StFX has the absolute worst reputation in Atlantic Canada for its lack of effort in protecting students from sexualized violence, instead, their efforts seem to be focused on protecting assailants, and I am sure a majority of students would agree. But again, I felt great pressure from the university to agree to CCLISAR being announced as the third-party investigators.

At the beginning of the process, I was under the belief that the SVP-WG would have a close relationship with CCLISAR and that I would be formally interviewed in my experience as a student. This did not happen. In my first meeting with them, it was clear that the relationship was unequal. I was not seen as a peer but rather as a student in a room full of higher-up academics. I felt small and unable to speak up. My co-chair, as always, was absolutely amazing at getting our points across, but I sat there mostly silent and red in the face. This pattern became evident throughout the entire process. There was an unequal relationship between students and everyone else involved, and only my co-chair, a faculty member, made an effort to eliminate the inequality.

After our initial meeting, we expected to have bi-weekly check-ins. After weeks of waiting for responses from their team on our emails, we had two meetings. I made an effort to get students to participate in their interviews, only to find out they had not been contacted.

In late July, CCLISAR published their final report on the investigation against Mount Allison University. I had been a part of the review of the draft a month prior and had begged a group of lawyers and administrators to re-examine how much power they had given to the Vice President of Student and International Affairs. I argued that giving the ultimate decision power to one person on the administration was how we had gotten into this position to start with. We had students wearing shirts saying "FIRE (Name protected)," for god's sake.

In the end, as expected, they didn't listen to me or any of the other students. I knew the only way justice would be carried out on our campus was if sexualized violence was addressed and adjudicated by a team of people curated for the specificities of every case.

I felt silenced, unheard, and small while working with CCLISAR. I cried for hours after our last meetings, feeling as though any power I had was slipping through my fingers. I was no longer needed by the university as a pawn—they were no longer interested in listening to me. I was no longer a threat and could be muted just as easily as the sound of *Jeopardy* playing in the background on a television. I was no longer relevant to their image, so I became disposable.

———

There were other challenges that came up over the course of my activist journey as well. Communication was a big one. Communication between the SVPWG and other groups and key people on campus was, as described above, exceedingly difficult. Communication with the president of the university was extremely difficult as well. Although the working group was created under his name, he had little to no involvement. Dozens of emails were sent to his account and to his reception desk, and responses came weeks later or not at all. When meetings were scheduled, I was expected to meet on his time, which meant I was forced to miss classes. It embarrassed me significantly to be excused from my seminars and lectures despite his receptionist having access to my calendar. Similarly, although hiring recommendations were sent to the president on March 15, 2021, as of April 26, 2021, we had received no sign that the university was actively reading our recommendations or searching for someone to fill the role.

This silence on behalf of institutions, which pushes students and faculty to create systemic changes on their campuses themselves, is another tactic Ahmed describes in her brick wall theory. Dozens of meetings can be held, and dozens of recommendations written, but unless the institution acknowledges the work, nothing can progress. In the case where replies are sent in an untimely matter, progression is so slow that it could be deemed as no progress.

Student engagement was another issue I encountered. Getting students and alums together for a protest was great, but keeping those students engaged was much more difficult. Students wanted immediate change and had little understanding of how the process worked. I felt a constant pressure to reassure the public that changes were in the works, but they slowly stopped engaging with the material I posted on social media. My initial post had seventeen thousand likes, and my latest post relevant to Mount Allison's procedures only reached 139. My power and authority over the Mount Allison administration strongly depended on the community standing behind me. Students demanded work from me without getting involved or helping.

The institution is often referred to as the "brick wall," but, in many cases, I believe that students are no different. The best way to describe the feeling of reaching out to a student body who has lost interest in the subject is like screaming at a wall. Some days, I felt the lack of engagement was similar to the bystander effect. Everyone began assuming someone else would take action, and, in return, stopped doing anything at all. This is not meant to attack the student body or give them responsibility for any part of this, but it is crucial that they understand the power of every like, comment, and share.

The lack of engagement from students, I believe, is a consequence of an evolving culture. Most students at Mount Allison have a case of performative activism, and though comparable in some ways, they don't necessarily fit the profile of Ahmed's brick wall. The problem was that when the protest was no longer at its peak, students lost interest. This became a barrier to further change.

In the spirit of being forthright and sincere, media was also a barrier—and downright annoying. My emails, DMs, and phone were constantly blowing up with media requests. It seemed like any small story relating to sexualized violence in Atlantic Canada required comment from Michelle Roy, fifth-year history student at Mount Allison University. I was persuaded to participate but had a difficult time juggling my responsibilities as a student. Likewise, I generally hated speaking on the record. I did not feel like the expert they made me out to be, and I constantly feared saying something wrong or out of context. While I wanted to speak out against the system that allowed Mount Allison to create a culture where sexualized violence flourished, I was not interested in condemning individual members of the community, something that was often pushed on me. I often felt that the media was more interested in a headline than sharing my story, and that sexualized violence did not matter unless it had enough likes on Instagram.

———

Is Mount Allison my brick wall? I still do not have an answer. Some days I felt loud and powerful, and other days I felt small and disposable. Most days, it felt impossible to believe that Mount Allison was my brick wall, but the evidence says otherwise.

In writing this piece, I often referred to the administration as the "Mount Allison administration," but this is an attempt to put the individual personalities of a dozen employees under an impersonal, almost evil-sounding, umbrella. It feels easy to be angry at an idea rather than at the people I have spent the last five years growing with. Saying that Mount Allison will most likely not implement any changes (or very few) once I graduate feels like an attack on the people that make up said administration, but it's the truth. I truly believe that most of the administration is so deeply enveloped in the culture that they have no understanding of the harm they continue to perpetuate.

The entire experience made me question my understanding of community. I was always told Mount Allison University was one giant community, where people would support and help each other. But looking more closely, how are community and business differentiated? Why are we told to be part of a community where the leaders make us feel like numbers and dollar signs rather than human beings? In this community, we became victims instead of graduates.

This piece is an examination of how the personal intersects with theory, how theory is present in our lived experience, and to confirm that these experiences are valuable and deserve to be heard and shared. The voices of survivors must be heard and shared to create a safer space in academia.

Chanel Miller, a brilliant artist and writer, is the survivor of the infamous Stanford Rape. She spent years anonymously telling her story in the media and in 2019, released her memoir *Know My Name*, which revolutionized the way that personal experience can become evidence of theories and concepts within academia. It is also a memoir that inspired me to become the activist I am today, and for that, I am forever thankful. I leave you with her words: "You took away my worth, my privacy, my energy, my time, my safety, my intimacy, my confidence, my own voice—until today."[8] The reality is that my rapists took almost everything from me, and Mount Allison University took the rest. For the remainder of my life, the Google search "Michelle Roy" will lead to dozens of articles about my experiences with sexualized violence. I do not believe that Mount Allison will make the changes required to keep students safe, but they can never stop me from speaking my truth.

---

8. Miller, Chanel. *Know My Name*. 2019 (Viking Press, New York), p. 310. Used with permission.

An Imaginary Letter from a University to Survivors of Sexualized Violence

Johannah May Black

This is what they might say
if they had the courage to respond at all
or if they had the compassion
or whatever else it is that is lacking.
So much is lacking.

They might say,
"We are sorry we have failed you."
"We are sorry for allowing this harm
to continue and continue and continue
again and again and again."
"We are sorry for all the times that we will continue to fail so many of
you."

"We know that you are more than one."
"We know that you are so many
invisible women
invisible survivors

sitting with silence—
silenced."

"We know we are not innocent,
we are not even neutral."
"We have supported those who cause harm,
we have lauded them,
awarded them,
shielded them from you, invisible survivors."

"We are sorry for all the ways that
our campus culture leaves you vulnerable
to disposability."
"We have treated all of you
as though you were
expendable,
trivial,
dispensable,
replaceable."

"Because we care,
we will offer more than a phoneline
for you to call if you feel triggered
by the daily onslaught of rape culture in the news."
"Because we care,
we will offer more than a sterile campus therapist's office
or the torture of facing a nurse with a rape kit."

"In this imaginary dream world of ours,

where universities write letters of apology
to all the survivors of sexualized violence they have failed,
we will instead commit to supporting you,
to lauding your courage and your strength,
to awarding you for continuing on in the face of this violence,
or for deciding to prioritize your survival and dropping out
because sometimes leaving is the only choice available,
and we will do our best
to shield you from
all of the people who will throw back
courtroom declarations of innocence
and the recycled rape myths of defence lawyers
and the ignorant jeering of online misogynists
in your faces."

You deserve better.

What Would Gracie Think?

MICHELLE ROY

Content Warning: Moderate description of sexual assault
To skip to the next story, turn to page 75.

The following speech was given at a protest that took place at Mount Allison University on November 12, 2020.

———

Grace Anne Lockhart, better known for her nickname, Gracie, graduated from Mount Allison University in 1875 with a Bachelor of Science and English literature. Gracie was the first woman in the entire British Empire to receive a bachelor's degree, something Mount Allison prides itself on. Gracie, no doubt, helped pave the way to break down gender barriers in post-secondary education. Look around you today. Take a second to reflect—do you think Gracie would be proud of what Mount Allison became?

A lot of people have been asking me how this story starts. Well, honestly—it goes back fifteen years. I was seven years old when I was sexually abused by a stranger in my own bedroom. This was the day I stopped being a child. I blamed myself immediately. I wondered why I hadn't stayed at my grandparents that night, or why my robe was so short—for context, I was wearing a Ruggrats PJ robe. I spent the years to come hating myself for not standing up sooner and running away. My mom watches the news every single night, and I slowly started understanding that this happened to other people. The more I educated myself, the more I wondered: why did I live in a world that created an environment where I was able to blame myself for something that had happened to me as a child? I wasn't born an activist—neither did I have a moment at Mount Allison that flicked a switch. Sexualized violence in our society was—and will—always be something I was concerned about and would speak against.

That's why a situation at my first year at Mount Allison troubled me deeply. It was Halloween night, and my female friends were away. I decided to go to a party with my football friends—who, to this day, are some of my best friends. I am going to be honest about an embarrassing fact I did not mention in my now-viral post. My boyfriend had broken up with me that night and I wanted to make him jealous. I figured the perfect way was to flirt with his roommates' brother—that would for sure get his attention. So, I flirted playfully. In all honestly, my friends and I were mostly laughing at him. Then things took a weird turn. It was in the basement of some house I can't remember. He pushed me against a bar and tried kissing me. I turned my face, but that didn't stop him. I couldn't get away until a bystander grabbed him and pulled him off of me. I laughed it off—confused and scared—and continued with my night. I stopped talking to him after it happened.

Later that night, I was standing outside. There were a bunch of boys from the party around me. I was dressed as a bunny—which included a very tight black dress. I was talking to my friend when, all of a sudden, he came behind me and lifted my dress. My dress was tight, so when he lifted it, it stayed up. I was basically naked from the bottom down for everyone to see. He proceeded to slap me, hard, and ran away with a smirk on his face. I could never forget the amount of humiliation and shame I felt that he had done this in front of all my peers.

I told all my friends about it. I warned them all—stay away from, let's call him B. For the record, his name does not start with B; I just like the letter. I started warning my friends of B's behaviour, and I started discovering stories of B assaulting multiple women. This went beyond sexual harassment into full-fledged sexual assault. Many of them came forward to the university and were quickly scared into not filing a formal complaint, myself included. Although dozens of women were victims of B, only one complaint was made formal—which forced B to be investigated, found responsible by the university, and removed from campus. We left for the summer feeling satisfied. Fast forward a couple of months—it's still summer—B had appealed his case, and for some reason, the student administration decided that although they had heard dozens of stories from B's victims, he was no longer responsible. He came back for the fall semester. He was moved into another residence, a bigger residence, where he would be able to prey on more women.

I started speaking up about the experience. Slowly, more and more similar stories were shared. I could no longer pretend that this was not an issue at Mount Allison. I started speaking out online, I went to student forums on sexualized violence, I volunteered with groups, I joined societies, and I even wrote articles about it all. Nothing changed. It was always "Let's meet to talk Michelle ... Okay, we heard your concerns." And then nothing ever happened. I spent four years actively speaking out.

Last week, my professor wanted me to meet a first-year student. In all honestly, I just thought this student was impressed by my research projects and wanted my academic advice. I bragged to all my friends all week about how smart I was. But it turns out my professor knew I was an advocate against sexualized violence at Mount Allison—and this first year approached me with a story that horrified me. I first want to say, this is not my story to tell but very similar to mine from 2016. I remember her asking me what to do—I was staring out the window into Avard Dixon—and I felt hopeless. I could not tell her what to do. I saw the light leave her eyes when she started talking about how excited she was to come to Mount Allison and get a degree. She had come onto campus with so many ambitions and dreams and instead was faced with victimization and trauma. This was the case for many first years.

The most popular question I have gotten so far is, "How did you come up with this idea?" I tell people it just "came to me" but I fail to mention that it came to me at 11 p.m. after finishing a bottle of red wine. I messaged all my friends, expecting them to say what they normally say to all my drunken ideas, but was instead met with encouragement. My grad photos were the next morning, and I knew I could not wear the Mount Allison graduation gown proudly, knowing what was secretly happening behind closed doors. Don't worry, I did not make the poor photographer take the photos. My best friend Kaelyn took the photos on my iPhone while my other best friend Emma kept watch for anyone walking by. I posted them that day.

I never expected the response I received. I just knew Mount Allison followed my social media. Today, the post on Instagram has over sixteen-thousand likes. That is three times the population of Sackville and eight times the size of the Mount Allison student body. People started flooding my messages with their experiences with sexualized violence at Mount Allison. I quickly realized the problem was much bigger than I believed. And I want to take this moment to thank every person who messaged me—if you decided to go public or keep your story between us—every single one of you made an impact. I keep saying, "I am not the brave one; you guys are." All I did was take a photo, but it's you guys sharing your stories that lit the fire of this movement.

As mentioned in another speech of mine, according to the Canadian Federation of Students in Ontario, one out of five women will report being sexually assaulted while at a post-secondary institution in Canada. These numbers are reported to be three times higher for Indigenous women, women of colour, women with disabilities, women who are new to Canada, and people who identify with the 2SLGBTQ+ community.

Since I became a student at Mount Allison, the number of people impacted by sexualized violence seemed much higher. Not experiencing sexualized violence seemed like a privilege most students on campus would not be granted, instead of a basic human right.

I am here today to acknowledge that Mount Allison University has a serious problem with sexualized violence. I am here today to acknowledge the harm that the Mount Allison administration has caused to students. I am here to hold Mount Allison accountable. Remember—there is no community without accountability.

I do not want to hold only Mount Allison accountable for their failure to protect students but also other universities. UNB and STU students, Mount Allison students stand by you as well. I am here to acknowledge that sexualized violence is a behaviour in which universities foster and encourage. Sexual assault is much more than "unacceptable behaviour;" it is a crime!

Today, we are here to take back our campus. We are here to take back the streets we walk on, the classrooms in which we learn, the library in which we study, the residences we live in, and the fields on which we play.

Before I end this speech, I want to take some time for some self-reflection. Recently, I wrote a feminist manifesto for a class assignment and spent a lot of time reflecting on what it meant to be a feminist and activist. I came to the conclusion that a big part is accepting that you may have been wrong at one point. I want everyone to take some time during this protest to reflect on what role they may have played in perpetrating the rape culture at Mount Allison. Did you laugh at a bad joke? Did you not believe a survivor? Did you protect your friends and teammates? The list could go on. I ask that you acknowledge the harm you may have caused—and take on the role of someone who is dedicated to ending rape culture on your campus and all around you!

I am here to say to Mount Allison Survivors, WE BELIEVE YOU!

Rape Culture

KYLEE GRAHAM

Content Warning: Moderate descriptions of sexual assault and harassment
To skip to the next story, turn to page 79.

Dear_____,

Thank you for flicking my bra strap
Thank you for hugging me a little too long
Thank you for that locker room boys' talk
Thank you for calling me "that type of girl"
Thank you for grading us
Thank you for the lingering gaze
And
                                  hands
Thank you for sexualizing my 12-year-old body
Thank you for calling me a slut
                        because I kissed a boy
And
                        because I didn't kiss you

Thank you for commenting on my body in front of your friends

Thank you for grabbing my thigh

Thank you for whistling at me

                  because I was wearing shorts

                  because I was wearing pants

                  because I was wearing my parka

                  because I was wearing two parkas

Thank you for referring to me as a porn category

Thank you for hugging me at work while you shake my male coworkers' hands

Thank you for sending me that unwanted dick pic

                  because you

              "liked my picture so much"

Thank you for grabbing me while I danced with my friends

Thank you for yelling

                  "hey baby"

                  "nice ass"

And

              "I'll show you something to smile

                                  about"

Thank you for saying that I

"owed you"

                  because you bought me dinner

                        because we were dating for 6 months

Thank you for sending my naked pictures to your friends

And

                      posting

them online

Thank you for touching me when I was passed out
    Thank you for ignoring the guy touching me when I was passed out
    Thank you for not telling on your

                        boss

                                        co-worker

                    coach

And

                    friend

Thank you for coming onto me after buying me that drink
    Thank you for spiking that drink
    Thank you for undermining my decision
    Thank you for ignoring my
"no"

                                      "not right now"

                    "maybe later"

And

my

                    c r y i n g

Thank you for forcing yourself on me

because we flirted
because I was alone
because I was alone at night
because we were friends
because I was drunk

because I smiled back at you

because I didn't smile back at you

because we were together

because I broke up with you

because I rejected your advances

because we did it before

because I "wanted it"

    I say thanks,

    because you're supposed to say thank you for the things we ask for

Right?[1]

---

1. This poem was first published online in *Laurel & Bells Literary Journal*.

Sudden and all at Once

Kylee Graham

My start into activism was not gradual. It was sudden and all at once, almost as if by accident. If you asked some of the boys from my high school, however, you would learn that the real beginning was not an accident at all. But this story isn't about that. It's about *my* beginning, the beginning of my own healing journey and of a journey of resistance against sexualized violence in Canada.

It was March 2017, the end of my third year of biology and psychology at Acadia University. I was in the process of finding myself after experiencing a mental health breaking point a few months earlier. Up to this point, I had only been vocal about feminist issues on social media, and had attended a few women's centre events, but had yet to take any noteworthy action against sexualized violence myself. It was during the height of unrest surrounding Judge Lenehan's acquittal of Halifax taxi driver Bassam Al Rawi, who was accused of sexual assault, that I took meaningful action. The case was highly publicized due to the overwhelming evidence of assault and the infamous line from Judge Lenehan, who stated that "clearly, a drunk can consent." Following the release of this statement, protests sprang up across the country as people demonstrated their disgust over such ignorance, victim blaming, and blatant incompetence in correctly applying the definition of consent.

I watched as other cities planned protests, waiting for something to happen at my own institution, but nothing did. I was dismayed by this fact, as I wanted to show my physical support for the survivor who went through hell, as well as demand a retrial and consequences for Lenehan's violent and dangerous statement. This is where I give you my first piece of advice: if you see a need for something, for change, do not wait for someone else to organize or speak up, because more often than not, they won't.

Without much thought, or even planning, I emailed the entire student body and faculty at Acadia detailing the need for a local protest. Given that the judicial review of Judge Lenehan's comments were being held in Kentville, N.S, a short drive from Acadia, we needed to apply pressure. I emailed other professors and people in the community based on their known involvement and passion for feminist issues, most of whom I had never met, letting them know what I was doing and asking for help. The support I received was incredible, and students and community members became integral to organizing the protest by emailing important local political representatives, designing and distributing posters, and circulating a petition. With this help, I was able to focus on getting free transportation from Acadia to the courthouse by asking campus groups for donations. Luckily, I had an amazing psychology professor, Dr. Randy Newman, who advocated for funds through the women's faculty association to help secure this. She also took time in her classes to highlight the importance of this protest and encouraged students to go, which was a radical thing to do at the time, given that the protest was before the #MeToo movement. To this day, she is still one of my biggest role models, and I can never thank her enough for her support.

The downside to fighting against any established institution or status quo is that there is always pushback. Emails came in from students questioning the use of student union funds for transportation to the protest, as not all students were "*in agreement to the overthrowing of the presumably lawful, educated and deliberate decision ruled by the judge, just to bolster potential numbers ... We should be wary about trying to tear down our long-standing institutions for an ill-thought backing of a very emotionally involved cause.*" I quickly realized that the people who had a problem with this protest and who said such entitled and privileged things were only revealing what type of things they deemed ethical, moral, and right. So here is my second piece of advice: fight the good fight, and do not let anyone distract you from your goal. Shut them down quickly, but do so without instigating more resistance, so you can focus on what is important.

Over the course of six days, I lined up speakers for the protest including community educator Frank Heimpel from the Avalon Sexual Assault Centre, Tessa James, the head of the Women's Centre, and the Raging Grannies, a local singing group. Over a hundred people attended, which was quite a turnout at the time. People still thought calling someone a rapist was too strong. You did not speak out about sexual assault, let alone bring it up to your friends, family, and classmates, and you definitely did not organize and attend a whole protest about it. The words "sexualized violence" were seen as dirty, and "rape culture" was only whispered in feminist circles and gender studies classrooms. In reminiscing about the protest, I realize just how much the #MeToo movement has done, not only for the empowerment of survivors, but also for producing a substantial cultural shift where people are now comfortable discussing sexualized violence. If a similar protest were held today, the turnout would be even higher. The fact that it was seen as a radical thing to do back then, makes it even more important that we did it. We started the conversation about sexualized violence at Acadia University.

Frank Heimpel said during the protest, "We can say today, to this survivor, and to all survivors of sexualized violence and abuse, we believe you." And they were right, it was not just about that victim, it was about all victims. There had been multiple cases of sexual assault mishandled at the very same Kentville courthouse that year, one of which pertained to an Acadia student. Hearing "clearly a drunk can consent" as justification for an acquittal despite such strong evidence invalidated and re-traumatized almost every victim and survivor who had been sexually assaulted, but especially those who were assaulted under similar circumstances. And that is why we were there, so that no victim would ever be belittled, abandoned, or invalidated ever again.

The moment that stuck with me the most from this protest was when a family from Bridgetown came up to me at the end to say thank you for organizing. They had driven forty-five minutes for a space to put their anger and anguish, a place to show their little girl the importance of standing up against what is wrong. That right there made it all worth it, to have people tell me how much they needed this, because I completely understood, as I needed it for a long time too.

When I moved to PEI for vet school in 2018, I didn't know how to become involved in feminist issues again. I was leaving a community where I had connections and was working to address the culture at my institution. I had finally found like-minded people who were passionate and had the commitment to make lasting change. So, when I moved to

PEI and left that all behind, I felt lost. Luckily, or maybe unluckily, these issues and the community to address them found me.

Something I've done since my first year of university is work out at the gym. I got into weightlifting for my mental health, and it was something that I continued in vet school. One evening, when I was in the middle of my first midterm season, I headed to the gym to forget about dog anatomy for a while. What I encountered instead was a product of rape culture: the control and judgment of women's bodies and who is deemed worthy of respect based on how they present those bodies. I posted what had happened on Facebook in an attempt to find like-minded individuals like I had found at Acadia. Little did I know it would soon go viral, garnering thousands of likes and hundreds of comments and shares, and requests from *The Daily Mail*, Yahoo, and what felt like every other news outlet for an interview. Below is the post detailing that event.

"So today I went to the gym, just like I do about 4 or 5 times a week. Today I wore a cropped workout shirt to the gym, like I do all the time as do many other women, because it's more comfortable for me than wearing two layers or loose, long clothes that can move around and get in the way when working out (plus I might as well admit, I feel good wearing cropped shirts, which should be the point of clothes).What was different about today however was as soon as I walked into the gym, I was stopped by the person working because the outfit pictured was

considered inappropriate and violated their dress code. So the staff proceeded to pull out a binder and show me that women were not allowed to wear sports bras alone, open back shirts, and shirts that were cut low on each side even with sports bras underneath. I told her this isn't a sports bra as you couldn't even see my belly button (but even if it was so what!!! I'll get to this later), and they said "okay you're fine for today but in the future even wearing a see through shirt over top would suffice." I must have been staring at her like she was crazy because she replied with "if a man came in here and was wearing a shirt cut so low on the sides you could see his nipples I would tell him the same thing." I went on to do my workout, slightly rattled and pretty angry at the whole situation. As I was leaving, the same person turned to me and said "my coworkers and I discussed what you were wearing and decided it was okay." At this point I was angry and so I asked "what exactly isn't allowed then and why?" She said "sports bras" I asked why, she said "because it shows your abs and cleavage" again I asked "soo why can't women wear them?" To which she said "because we are trying to find a happy medium where girls can still workout with men." So then I asked, daring for her to say it out right, "what do you mean why does that matter?" With her replying "so that [girls] aren't too much, and distracting." As you can guess, I am pretty angry about a lot of things that happened in this event.

1. Why does the gym have a dress code? Are we still in high school? Last time I checked sports bras and leggings are workout gear that athletes everywhere use every. single. day.

2. Why does your dress code regulate women's bodies so much more intensely than men's? The irony of the statement about if a man's nipples were showing the rules also applied to him was lost on the staff as my nipples were certainly not showing let alone cleavage (but that shouldn't even matter!?!?!). If you don't want nipples showing okay that's fine (another convo for another day) but don't regulate other parts of my body if it's not the same for men.

3. HOW DO YOU THINK IT'S OKAY TO DISCUSS MY BODY WITH YOUR COWORKERS WHILE I AM WORKING OUT AND THEN TELL ME YOU WERE DISCUSSING AND ASSESSING ME I AM HERE TO WORKOUT AND RELAX NOT BE SEXUALIZED AND MADE TO FEEL UNCOMFORTABLE. Without the female staff being critical women already face enough misogyny and grossness in the gym. Stop.

4. Abs are not sexual, a back is not sexual, breasts are not sexual unless the woman wants them to be sexual, stop sexualizing women's bodies doing mundane things and let them live their lives in peace

5. Do I really need to comment on the fact the rules are in place so men won't be "distracted" and so "girls (not women !!!!) can still workout," implying if they didn't have a dress code men would be uncontrollable and wouldn't be able to pick up a weight and put it back down because my line of skin is showing around my abdomen, so if there wasn't a dress code then women just wouldn't be allowed to workout? I am so angry that this is something that was implemented just over a year ago. UPEI Athletics & Recreation and the University of Prince Edward Island should be ashamed how they are trying to control and are sexualizing female bodies in such a direct way, how they are making it harder for women to live an active lifestyle (as I wasn't going to be allowed in!!) and the clear double standards set for women. This is not okay.EDIT: for the people who are commenting about how my outfit isn't even "provocative" I know you mean well and are trying to offer support, however there is a problem with this wording. Provocative means "to provoke." So by saying someone is wearing provocative clothing is saying those clothes are provoking something, which in the context of women's clothing means a sexual manner. Therefore, you are saying that those clothes are provoking sexual attention and behaviour from people, which when unwanted, is sexual harassment and assault. This is one of the most implicit ways we victim blame as provocative basically means "asking for it." No matter what anyone's wearing they do not ask for sexual violence. When you say my clothes are not provocative

you are saying someone else's are if they are wearing "more provocative clothing" (whatever that means because it literally means whatever you are trying to sexualize) so they would deserve that unwanted attention. Do not say this. But thanks for all the support everyone!!!"

It was not long after posting this that I was contacted by the UPEI athletic directors asking to meet with me to discuss the matter. I mentioned earlier that whenever you fight against the status quo, you are going to face backlash. Well, this is especially true when it involves calling out sexist, misogynistic products of rape culture that many people have internalized as normal and reasonable, like dress codes. From this post I had people online attacking my character (all of whom had never met me), sexualizing me, harassing me about how I should stop complaining on Facebook and care about "actual sexism" (whatever that is, as their arguments in that regard were racist, Islamophobic, and xenophobic in nature), and finally, that I was an attention seeker just looking for my fifteen minutes of fame. Therefore, my third piece of advice is this: if you ever experience this type of media attention, just turn the comments off and stop reading the replies on news articles. You will not be able to reply to every comment so focus on what you can change; your mental health will be better for it.

Despite all the negative interactions, I also had many great ones. People I did not know began reaching out to me, offering support and sharing their own stories, and classmates who I were not close with began fighting the trolls for me in the comments. I even had two students, Kari Kruse and Chelsea Perry, from the UPEI diversity and social justice program, offer to attend the meeting with me to offset some of the intimidation I was likely to face. We also created an online form where students and community members could submit the experiences they had at the UPEI gym regarding the dress code. In the end, it was not just my one experience and issue with the dress code that we brought forward, but more than forty. I appreciated Kari and Chelsea working with me on this more than they know, as there was a clear power imbalance between me, a new student at UPEI, and the two long-term athletic directors we met with.

The meeting itself was discouraging, as it involved a lot of respectability politics, defensiveness, and excuses made to distance themselves from blame. Although the directors apologized for the comment made by the staff, they continued to advocate that the guidelines were needed due to community members' complaints on what was "respectful attire." Thus, despite the apology, the UPEI gym was still implying that women could not workout wearing a crop top or sports bra due to men's behaviour, as these community members did not see women wearing these items as worthy of respect.

How many times have you heard someone ask, "What was she wearing," or say, "She was asking for it" to try and justify sexual assault? They try to determine whether someone is worthy of respect based on their clothes, with respect being the determining factor of who can be assaulted free of consequence. Respect is equivalent to who you humanize and credit as a person. If you do not respect someone, justifying and excusing violence against them is easier. This concept is fundamental in upholding rape culture, as it is a form of victim blaming that is used to excuse sexualized violence, which then allows rape to become normalized. Another justification for the dress code that we encountered was for the gym to be inclusive to "multicultural" and "bigger" individuals. We had to explain to grown adults that dress codes were arbitrary rules and that the concepts of professionalism and respect are rooted in sexism, misogyny, rape culture, racism, homophobia, fat phobia, and transphobia. It was difficult to explain that while we personally did not agree with having any dress code, if a dress code is found to be absolutely needed, it must be applied equally; yet, this would be virtually impossible to implement due to people's inherent biases. Further, we had to explain that the rule of "not having your ribcage exposed" unequally targeted women's common workout apparel, and that if these guidelines were applied subjectively, fat women, BIPOC women, and trans women would be targeted more due to these biases.

Before entering the meeting, I believed our stance was firm and clear. We went in with a plan of attack and were prepared. However, upon listening to the meeting (which we thankfully recorded) after the fact, we were not adamant or harsh enough. While I did talk about the definition of respect, I did not utter the words rape culture. I said that the rules in place targeted women unfairly but did not call it what it was to their faces: sexism and misogyny.

My fourth piece of advice is simple: stay true to your convictions and say them confidently and loudly. Authority will try to treat you like a wide-eyed, naïve little girl to make you go away and shut up. Do not let them walk all over you. I am not sure if I was just exhausted from talking in circles, cautious of pushing too hard with an already defensive party who felt they were "on trial," inexperienced at dealing with derailing tactics, or hopeful the wording we suggested to change the guidelines would be enough. What I know now is that I unfortunately did not get a firm enough commitment on the changes the UPEI gym was going to make. The meeting ended with a promise to reconsider the "guidelines," a reassurance that our thoughts had been heard, and a backhanded compliment about passionate young women.

I thought I had made real change and went on with my schooling, although I did take some time off from going to the gym due to anxiety at being recognized or harassed because of the whole ordeal. I didn't hear anything more about the gym dress code for about a year. At least, not until a woman named Ray Noftall, a year below me at Atlantic Veterinary College, reached out detailing how she was dress coded by the same UPEI gym for wearing almost the exact same outfit. I was furious and tired—furious that someone else had to go through the embarrassment, harassment, and intimidation that I had, but also that I had been deceived. I was led to believe changes would be made, and the UPEI gym thought that I would go away quietly. Despite the very public backlash the UPEI gym experienced due to my post, they continued to implement a sexist and misogynistic dress code that was created in the name of rape culture. This is my fifth piece of advice: get it in writing and with witnesses. So instead of just making it public, I made it personal. With Ray's permission, I cc'd every UPEI organization, professor, or personnel I could think of who might care about a misogynistic dress code, for a total of twenty contacts, on the following email addressed to the UPEI gym directors:

To whom it may concern,

It was brought to my attention that on September 3rd, 2019 around 5pm, one of the UPEI fitness centre staff approached a female student, Ray Noftall, who was in the middle of her workout asking if she could "put a shirt on" and told that the top she had on "violated the dress code." The student replied that she was already wearing a top, which led to the staff asking if she had a sweater she could put on. Once again, the student replied no, and was told to wear a shirt next time she came to workout. This event

*was so unsettling and uncomfortable, Noftall reached out to me and gave
permission to address this issue with the UPEI fitness centre.*

*This action taken by the UPEI staff member is inappropriate on several
fronts. To start, it is publicly humiliating, disruptive, and uncomfortable
to have someone approach you saying your apparel is not appropriate during your workout. It is even more concerning as we believed this issue had
already been resolved following a similar incident last year where I was
asked to cover up while wearing a similar outfit. The reasons given then
were the same as those used in this case, namely that the apparel was inappropriate and violated the dress code. We believed this issue had already
been dealt with by the administration, and it is incredibly disappointing
to have to revisit it now after assurances were made that the university would
fix their outdated and sexist rules policing what women can and cannot
wear while exercising. ...*

*To recap, this interaction was angering, disturbing, and uncomfortable.
The comments made by staff during this interaction, such as "we are trying
to find a happy medium where girls can still workout with men, so that
[girls] aren't too much, and distracting," highlight the underlying issues of
sexism, discrimination, misogyny and the unequal treatment and policing
of women's bodies that are enshrined in this dress code. Because of the disturbing nature of this event, it quickly went viral online, getting thousands
of likes and shares, as well as being picked up by news outlets across the
world. The immense backlash that the UPEI fitness centre received from
this encounter threatened the reputation of the university itself. This led
to a meeting with the director of the fitness centre, [redacted], the director,
[redacted], the manager, myself, and two other students to discuss this issue.*

*In this meeting, I learned that this "dress code" was implemented only
a year earlier and was based on policies implemented at other schools.
The position of the students was clear: the implementation of a similar*

policy at another institution does not automatically make it legitimate or acceptable when implemented at this institution. It was put in place due to complaints received from a select group of community members on what (mostly) women were wearing at the gym, specifically that the apparel was "not respectable" and "distracting." We obviously took issue with this language as the respect that women deserve is not tied to the amount of skin they choose to show, and we felt strongly that the basis of this dress code was rooted in misogyny. This explanation was unfortunately met with resistance from the UPEI fitness centre representatives. We explained why the current code was discriminatory, misogynistic, and predatory, and how it discouraged and intimidated women from returning to the fitness centre in the future. The director clarified for us that this dress code was not an official policy, and therefore could be changed without the board of governors being involved. After some debate, a compromise was reached with the understanding that if a dress code is necessary, its language must be changed to be gender-neutral and non-discriminatory. We even offered a solution to change the wording of the dress code to "must have some type of top on the torso." The meeting concluded with the director and manager apologizing for the incident and implying that changes would be made, including speaking with staff, and assured us that nothing like this would happen again.

Therefore, you can imagine my surprise and disappointment to hear this has once again, almost a year later, happened to another female student. The purpose of the gym is to feel good about one's self and to promote health and well-being, not to be judged for one's appearance or apparel. Many people, particularly women, already feel uncomfortable and intimidated at the fitness centre, and the dress code reinforces outdated stereotypes of how women "should" act while in a public space. The current dress code is not only confusing but is discriminatory in its nature as it seems to only be applied to certain people and certain body types. The dress code was implemented to prevent women from wearing a sports bra or cropped shirt while working out, due to the exposed skin being "distracting" and "not respectable." This language implies that women are to be held accountable for the predatory behaviour of men and tells women that their [men's] opinion matters more than women's rights – in this case, the right to workout in a safe, comfortable environment. Until the dress code is changed, and staff are retrained, the UPEI fitness centre is supporting misogynistic, discriminatory and predatory behaviour towards women. We suggest that the UPEI fitness centre grants students the ability to opt out of the gym membership that is automatically included into their tuition, or else accept that we are living in a progressive era where everyone deserves equal rights, and adjust accordingly.

Please note: this is only being shared to the UPEI community currently, but we will be taking our story to news outlets if we do not see evidence of concrete steps being taken to handle this issue.

What resulted from this was a short, public email exchange between the director and me. They tried saying the changes had been made, staff were trained, and that they were surprised it had happened again. However, they also publicly stated that the same guidelines they previously promised to revisit after our initial meeting were still being used. I was also informed that they were trying to meet one-on-one with Ray, and specifically did not want my presence at this meeting. I feared they were trying to smooth things over just to quiet us, not to mitigate the situation, but I was not going to let that happen again. Therefore, having learned from my mistakes the first time, I was adamant that until the dress code was changed or removed altogether, more women would be targeted and intimidated from working out in the future, which was not only misogynistic in nature, but at this point, also discriminatory. I demanded public commitment from UPEI athletics to make these changes, and to address their toxic and misogynistic culture. Finally, I received an email from the director that satisfied these demands:

"Effective immediately, we have removed the existing "Clothing Guidelines" from the sports centre. The signs are down and we are working on our digital images now. In the event that we decide to create a new version, I would greatly appreciate it if you could send me the wording you deem to be appropriate for clothing guidelines in a sports centre so respect, hygiene and safety are priorities of all of our fitness centre users."

Upon succeeding in finally having the dress code removed, I could only think of it as bittersweet. I was disappointed in myself for not following up with the gym after our meeting the first time, and I felt personally responsible for what happened to Ray. The first meeting was more about insincerely appeasing me, which itself felt misogynistic. They thought what I had to say the first time did not matter and that I could easily be taken care of without changing a thing. It wasn't lost on me that similar tactics of deception and appeasement were used by serial rapists Harvey Weinstein, Bill Cosby, Larry Nassar, and R. Kelly, who were exposed during the #MeToo movement. Sexualized violence is about power imbalances. Rapists and sexual predators, through their own actions and the inaction of bystanders, maintain a culture where survivors are shunned, ignored, intimated, harassed, forgotten, mistreated, and marginalized, until victims are silenced, and then the cycle continues.

While a gym dress code is not the same level of violence and magnitude as sexual assault, it is nevertheless a part of rape culture. It is the steppingstone that allows sexualized violence to be pervasive and normalized in society, as both circumstances use the same tactics to excuse men's predatory behaviour, blame women for it, and silence them. If certain men say they cannot respect women working out in a crop top, they do not respect women at all. And if men cannot respect women, those women are vulnerable to harassment or worse. The UPEI gym recognized this vulnerability, either consciously or unconsciously, when they made their dress code limiting women's apparel. They limited what women could wear, so that they could be seen as "respectable" by men and therefore decrease the amount of conflict in their gym. However, they decided that instead of holding men accountable for their predatory behaviours and opinions, they would put the burden and blame on women: victim blaming. Let me be crystal clear, your worth and right to have your wishes and bodily autonomy respected will never be defined by how you look or how much skin you show. Being human is what makes you worthy of respect, nothing else.

The message I received from the UPEI gym, in not taking my concerns seriously the first time, was that *I* was not worthy of respect. They did not consider my safety and wellness as a woman important enough to make a change, and my rights and that other women were definitely not important enough to disrupt the predatory behaviours and entitlement of men ... until they were forced to. And that is where my final piece of advice comes in: never stop speaking up, never stop fighting for change. Because when you stop, they win. We have come too far to be silenced again; we are never going back. If I had not kept fighting, if Ray did not speak up when she did, other women would have been intimidated and embarrassed. Events like what Ray and I experienced are enough to deter women from working out in the future. Luckily, we were both experienced at the gym and knew these rules were unfair. But we did not want other women to suffer like we did, so we spoke our truths loudly.

In one of my poems (which you read earlier in this anthology), "#MeToo," I say "*We are tired of shrinking ourselves just for you to be comfortable,*" and I think about this line frequently. We are tired of people telling us what clothing is professional and worthy of respect, what gym attire is not "distracting." We are tired of being cat-called on the street for simply existing, we are tired of being afraid to go for a run after dark, or walk home alone from the library. We are tired of guarding our drinks, throwing elbows at the bar when dancing, and tired of learning our friends and loved ones were assaulted or harassed. We are tired of holding our pain, our truth, our experiences inside until they crush us, and we are tired of seeing others be crushed by these truths. We whisper around the dinner table and try to laugh about unfunny experiences to survive. This is why we speak up and stand together, as there is power in numbers. We do this so, eventually, we can all be free from the burdens, expectations, fears, and restrictions that make up rape culture, and that is why we need you to stand up too. We need women, especially BIPOC, disabled women, trans women, gay women, and femme-presenting individuals to feel empowered and supported to speak their truths, so we can work to make these spaces better for everyone.

As I alluded to earlier, my involvement in activism was not a slow build. Since its beginning, I have often been asked why I didn't go into sociology or gender studies, as it seemed to make sense given how passionate I am about these subjects. My answer was always that I never thought to, and at times, I regretted not entering this field as I genuinely believed that was how you made change. However, I have come to peace with choosing the field of veterinary medicine, as all aspects of our professional world need revamping. They are all a part of not only the rape culture that we live in, but are also built on sexism, misogyny, racism, transphobia, homophobia, and classism, and only cater to able bodies and neurotypical brains. If people like me (and you!) do not speak up, no one else will, and therefore nothing will change. So, if you are reading this and doubting your career path, just know there is often more work that needs to be done in the hard sciences, business, law etc., that does not directly involve sociology or diversity and gender studies. It is important to have advocates and people who are passionate about change in these spaces, so one day we will no longer have to shrink ourselves just so that they can feel comfortable.

1989

Penelope Hutchison and Julie Glaser

Content Warning: Mention of suicide, murder, gender-based gun violence; moderate description of sexualized violence and harassment
To skip to the next story, turn to page 110.

Six of us sat in my student house, huddled in my 6' x 8' living room, transfixed by the TV screen. It was December 6, 1989. Marc Lepine had only hours ago walked into an engineering classroom at the École Polytechnique. He ordered the men to leave and then shouted, "You're all a bunch of feminists, and I hate feminists," and opened fire.[1] Lepine began to roam the corridors shouting, "I want women." Fourteen women lost their lives, and four men and ten women were injured before Lepine turned the gun on himself.

---

1. Bindel, J. "The Montreal Massacre: Canada's Feminists Remember," *The Guardian*, December 3, 2012.

99

A three-page suicide note was found in Lepine's jacket pocket. "The feminists always have a talent to enrage me. They want to take the advantages of women while trying to grab those of men."[2]

There was a collective outpouring of grief, rage, and bafflement as we struggled to come to terms with the shooting of fourteen innocent women. Many called it the act of a "mad man." But to "a group of concerned women" at Queen's University, Lepine's act was intimately connected to a battle we had been waging throughout our time there. A battle which had culminated that fall of 1989 with a showdown between us, a group of young men, and the Queen's administration.

It started during Orientation Week. As members of the Queen's Gender Issues Committee, we helped launch a "No Means No" campaign to increase students' awareness about date rape and consent. The campaign was one of the first in North America to tackle the socialization process that bred the belief that women do not mean it when they refuse sex. An awakening was happening at Queen's that year and at campuses across Canada, a heightened awareness about the need to reset the sexual ground rules between men and women.[3] We were leading the charge for change at Queen's.

The "we" was a group of young, politicized, female students who regularly gathered at the Queen's Women's Centre, a house amongst the residences that we shared with International and 2SLGBTQ+ students. We had been trying to put an end to the chauvinistic practices and male bonding rituals that occurred on campus with what appeared to be the

---

2. MacDonald, N. and P. Mansbridge, "Montreal Massacre murderer's suicide note released," *The National*, CBC, November 28, 1990.

3. Dickie, A. "The Art of Intimidation: Sexism and Destiny at Queen's," *This Magazine*, March 1990.

quiet, implicit consent of the university's administration. Our activities were starting to shake up the institution, but not necessarily as we envisioned; the house was frequently targeted with eggs or threatening phone calls to the shared line. Once, we even had a bomb threat.

We called ourselves ROFF—Radically Obnoxious Fucking Feminists. Each year, a group of engineering students hung effigies of female nursing students outside Clark Hall to celebrate the last day of exams. A few of the women in ROFF came across one of these effigies, pulled it down, and stuffed it in a trash can. A group of male engineers spotted us walking away and shouted, "There go those radical obnoxious fucking feminists." We took the name as our own. A few months later, a reporter with the *Globe and Mail* would go on to describe us as a "shadowy group called ROFFs (an acronym for something crudely akin to Radically Obnoxious Fuddle-duddling Feminists") and said we were "a rambunctious group that had shaken the serenity of Queen's, a campus renowned as a hotbed of social rest."[4] We wore the name with pride.

We were young women, many of us in our last year of undergraduate degrees. We were filled with anger. We had arrived on campus as first-year students thinking we were equals to male students only to be shocked with the time-honoured sexist rituals of Frosh Week. We faced a male-dominated faculty and administration that quietly acquiesced to the sexist antics that were deeply embedded in Orientation Week games. We felt the not-so-subtle pressure to refrain from being aggressive or outspoken as women, to play along with the sexist games in the name of "just having some fun."

It was a wake-up call for many of us. We fought back by immersing ourselves in feminist discourse. We took women's studies classes, held

---

4. French, O. "Sex Wars Still Rage on Campus," *The Globe and Mail*, November 11, 1989.

discussion groups on bell hooks' theories at the Queen's Women's Centre, started a short-lived feminist newspaper—*The Queen's Rag*. We had a mission: attack the archaic, chauvinistic bonding rituals and acts that occurred every year on campus. We believed we could change Queen's.

Our first prominent act was Valentine's Day, 1989. ROFF painted ten Stop signs and placed them at sites across campus where sexual assaults were purported to have occurred, places like Alfie's pub, Victoria Hall student residence, MacIntosh-Corry Hall, and in parking lots. The signs stated in large blue letters "a woman was sexually assaulted here." Our impetus had come a few days before, when we learned a first-year female student was attacked in a campus parking lot. She was forced to walk with her assailant for several blocks while he threatened her, then he hit her over the head with a beer bottle before running off. Many of us had been sexually harassed and a few sexually assaulted. Queen's felt far from a safe place to be a woman.

ROFF put out a press release with our Valentine's Day sign act. The release deploring the "victim-blaming and the lack of effective action which has typified the treatment of sexual assault in the Queen's community. Those guilty of perpetuating a policy of silence include the Queen's University administration, the campus media and the Alma Mater Society." As we planted our sign in front of Douglas Library, a librarian came out and told us we had no proof a woman had ever been sexually assaulted in or around the library. She called campus security. By the end of the day, security had removed the signs around campus, and many had already been vandalized by other students.

We were not deterred. In September 1989, we targeted the Golden Tit. This was an infamous Queen's speed bump that the engineering students annually painted with a white circle for a nipple. First-year engineering students were required to lie down and kiss the "Golden

Tit." In the early morning light, more than a dozen women painted over the speed bump in bright yellow and scrawled our signature in large black spray-painted letters, "ROFF."

Then came the "No Means No" Campaign.

As members of the Gender Issues Committee, we talked with students in the various residences about consent. The backlash was swift. A group of first-year male students in Gordon House took offence to the campaign. They taped signs in their dorm room windows. "No means harder." "No means kick her in the teeth." "No means more beer." "No means tie her up." "No means dyke." "No means now." "No means down on your knees bitch."

Those first-year male students were not the only ones who responded to the campaign. A few young women expanded on the 'joke' and taped up their own window signs. "Yes means Yes." "Yes means it's too small." Several female students turned up at a campus football game with "lick it, slap it, suck it" and "slip inside and ride" written across the bottoms of their overalls.

We, ROFF, were angry. We took our anger up with the Gordon House Residence dons but got nowhere. We spoke with the Queen's Dean of Women, Dr. Elsbeth Baugh. She ordered the signs taken down. They were still up a week later. A Queen's Council, set up by the Dean of Women, was trying to decide what, if any penalty, would be imposed on the students involved in the sign displays. The Council lacked any authority to act. It was up to the senior Queen's administration to impose sanctions, but there was silence. Not a single statement or action by Principal David Smith or the Queen's Senate. A single, untenured professor, Christine Overall, was the only faculty to speak out on our behalf, condemning the actions of the male students.

The lack of action was no surprise. The Queen's administration had been turning a blind eye to campus sexism and misogyny for decades. It was all just a bit of fun being had by a group of harmless boys. The campus newspaper, the *Queen's Journal*, interviewed the Gordon House students, all of whom gave their name as "Dave." They said the signs were intended as a joke. "We did it just for fun. We kept on making slogans until we ran out of tape."[5]

We were fed up with the inaction. It was time to take measures into our own hands. We researched the names and contact details of the Gordon House students who had posted the signs. ROFF made harassing phone calls to them, warning them to take the signs down. We wrote letters home to their parents, telling them what their son had done, that he was part of a group of young men who, by posting the sign in his window, was suggesting he wouldn't take 'no' for an answer from a woman. We signed the letters "A Group of Concerned Women."[6]

There was still no response from the Queen's administration. In mid-October, in the middle of the night, a few of us spray painted "ROFF's watching" and "No means No" on the pavement outside the Gordon House residence. We sent letters to residents through the campus mail, two photocopied sheets of paper with letters cut out from magazines that read "You fuckers. ROFF," and "What part of NO is it that you don't understand? ROFF." We were not interested in taking the proverbial high road. We were angry and we were vengeful.

The *Toronto Star* broke the story of the Gordon House boys' signs and ROFF's anger on Page One on November 2, 1989. Within two days,

5. Torrens, J. and J. Zima, "Residents try to 'lighten up' campaign." The Queen's Journal, October 13, 1989.

6. Tyler, T. "Why Campus Pranks Turning Nasty," *The Sunday Star*, November 5, 1989.

Queen's was making national headlines in newspapers and on newscasts across the country. Global TV filmed "sport-humping" during Orientation Week, a misogynistic game where a woman is told to lie on her back on the ground while a man does pushups on top of her before taking a coin from her mouth with his teeth.

Queen's was not alone in being singled out for sexism on campus. The news articles reported on panty raids at Wilfred Laurier, where male students splashed ketchup on women's underwear and hung them out for display. At Carleton University, blind-folded and bikini-clad mannequins were lynched on campus. A fresh debate was on in the media on just how effective the sexual revolution had been in changing attitudes and behaviours towards women.[7] Prominent feminist columnist Michelle Landsberg received "letters of blazing indignation" after condemning the sexist antics occurring on Canadian campuses. "Dozens of students and even male graduates wrote me in angry bewilderment. 'Why would "feminists" complain about such trivia?' they asked. Panty raids are 'just good clean fun.'"[8]

Faced with media attention, the Gordon House students began apologizing for their actions. "Our humour was in bad taste," they said. Some male students did not take responsibility for their actions, and instead blamed their response on ROFF. In an article in the *Toronto Star*, one of the young men states, "As for the feminists, I find it a little disheartening to realize that a small vocal minority can twist things and

---

7. Dickie, A. "The Art of Intimidation: Sexism and Destiny at Queen's," *This Magazine*, March 1990.

8. Landsberg, M. "Students Learn Sexist Lesson at Universities," *The Toronto Star*, November 11, 1989.

make something very minor, taken lightly by most, into international news."[9]

ROFF had managed to tarnish Queen's reputation. The media attention resulted in donors calling the administration and threatening to pull their funds. One donor said he was removing Queen's as a beneficiary of his will. Another vowed never to let any more of his children attend the university.[10]

The Queen's administration continued to refuse to act. No penalty was meted out to the male students posting the signs. As women, ROFF felt unheard. Silenced. Belittled. We wanted justice. We wanted an end to the complicit silence of the Queen's administration for the years of misogynistic acts that were perpetrated on female students by males, with no recourse or retribution.

On November 9, 1989, at 9 a.m., a group of more than thirty women, clad in scarves over our nose and mouths to protect our identity, marched into Queen's Principal, David Smith's, office. We handed Principal Smith a list of seven demands and told him we were not leaving until those demands were met.

We demanded the Main Campus Residence council be stripped of all autonomy regarding the residence system due to their lack of action regarding the signs. Smith said he did not have the power to override the Council and it was up to them to take action.

---

9. Editorial, "Send in the clowns...," *Queen's Journal*, November 7, 1989.

10. "Queen's students apologize for crude signs," *The Ottawa Citizen*, November 3, 1989.

We called for him to make a public statement denouncing the actions of the Gordon House students. Smith said he had written a letter to the *Queen's Journal* more than a month after he had been told about the signs. Again, he said the judicial process in place at the school made it impossible for him to take further action beyond his own personal statement.

We demanded a complete review of Orientation Week, Homecoming, and other Queen's traditions, such as the Golden Tit and the nursing effigies. Smith said Orientation Week was the purview of the Alma Mater Society and Homecoming the Alumni Association. Again, out of his control. As for the Golden Tit, those were the pranks put on by a group of students, not a practice condoned by the university.

Smith responded to every demand as if he was powerless. After more than an hour of discussion, Smith left his office. We stayed.

To keep the media attention on Queen's, we sent out a press release.

We, a group of concerned women at Queen's, strongly believe that this university plays host to many activities, rituals and traditions that serve to alienate, degrade, silence and encourage violence against women. The administration's lack of appropriate action in responding to the misogynist signs displayed in campus residences ("No means kick her in the teeth", etc.) has forced us to bring our concerns about sexism at Queen's to the public's attention. This sit-in is designed to non-violently express our outrage with the administration's refusal to acknowledge sexism at Queen's. Today, November 9, 1989, we will occupy Principal David C. Smith's office with a list of demands for action.

We continued to occupy the principal's office all that day and throughout the night. We put up "No means No" signs in the principal's office windows. We hung a red banner out the window that said, "End misogyny now." A dozen male students camped out overnight on the front steps of the principal's office [in solidarity?]. Other students came by to show their support. Inside the office, it was a different story. Late into the evening, we began to turn on each other. We argued about strategy and tactics. How long were we going to stay? What if only a few of our demands were met? What then? What if Smith refused to meet any of our demands? By midnight, we had split into two factions. One group wanted more press, more action, and to keep the sit-in going until all seven demands were agreed to. Another group felt our agenda had been met. We had made our point. A core group of ROFF left the protest.

The sit-in lasted about twenty-four hours. It was successful on several fronts. We got the Queen's Board of Trustees to give ten-thousand dollars to the Kingston Sexual Assault Centre. The position of the Dean of Women was reaffirmed. The media attention and loss of donors meant the administration was keen to be seen as actively supporting women's safety and rights on campus.

ROFF's successes came at a personal cost. We did not feel safe anymore on campus. We were afraid of retaliation by the Gordon House students and by other men on campus who had had enough of us "ruining their university year" by tarnishing Queen's' name. Many ROFF members received harassing phone calls. We were followed as we walked home through the student housing. The vitriol came from other female students too, angry women telling us our actions and protests were only making it harder for female students on campus and would cause male students to be more violent.

And then came the Montreal Massacre less than four weeks after our sit-in. It was everything we had feared. It was what we had feared as we sat in class and walked the hallways of Queen's in those early weeks after our protest. We felt targeted, that we were going to be made to pay for speaking up and speaking out against the actions of the Gordon House students.

As we watched the news footage December 6, 1989, we saw our own lives in the lives of the young women being wheeled out on stretchers. Our expressions were reflected in the faces of the frantic parents on the streets outside the Ecole Polytechnique crying out their daughters' names. The misogyny we had been battling that fall had become deadly.

It is a remarkable thing to find your power, your voice, and to demand justice and make the wheels of equality turn, if only a tiny inch, towards progress. To be 'woke,' as the terminology is now, is the lifting of a veil that shrouded you in acquiescence. You never imagine that such attempts at betterment could be deadly, that fighting back against being a target—for racism, for sexism, homophobia, ableism—might beat you right back.

Theorizing Lepine's deadly targeting of women as more than a "madman's" actions is not a popular point of view. But as ROFF sat together in the aftershock, we saw the attack as a continuum of what we were experiencing at Queen's just down the highway from Montreal. And it set us back, ripped holes in our hearts, and messed with our heads. Some of us were angrier, others depressed, and it was a struggle for many of us to continue to focus on the end goal of graduating from university.

Yet what came from ROFF's actions was something unexpected: our unabashed feminism and radical actions sparked a minor revolution in the hallowed halls of Queen's, as they did on university campuses across Canada. Younger women were marching, speaking out, organizing, fighting for their rights. They would seek us out and tell us that we inspired them. They explained that they were woke because of ROFF, and there was no turning back. They held out their newly ignited feminist flames to our shielded hearts, ready for the next chapter of the feminist uprising.[11]

---

11. Please note that elements of this story were previously published in *Briarpatch* and the *Queen's Journal*.

violence against women is a men's issue

KYLEE GRAHAM

This poem was first published online in The Sanctuary Magazine.

How many layers
do we need to pull back
to reach the root / bone / foundation
of this epidemic
how many men have spilt their guts
by accident
charmed by the warm aroma of
male dominated spaces
aftershave and entitlement
more scared of what they admitted than committed
will hitch a ride
on someone else's shoes
anticipate when its spores germinate
hit the open air
[when we can breathe deeply again]
after suffocating on the musk of cologne

for so long
they try to laugh it off
before it consolidates in the room
the air being pushed from their mouths
demanding it to dissipate
without sticking to their clothes
try and wash it away
prevent it
from oozing out of your pores
[it doesn't work well at all]
[we know]
they don't want to be exposed
no more than the women
whose names
are only punch lines in jokes
who gag on that sharp smell of
aftershave and cologne
every time
they try to date again
who were left to figure out
it wasn't them at fault
but the silence
perpetuated in these spaces
by men who were not
"man enough"
to stand up
from their leather backed chairs
too comfortable
with scotch in hand

to spray some soft vanilla scent instead
a more welcoming smell
might ensure it doesn't happen again
but the worst part is
these men leave
knowing no one will tell

Echoic Memories

Micah Kalisch

The poem was written in response to the University of Toronto's Sexual Violence Prevention and Support Centre advertising their phone number but not having anyone there to answer it.

―――――

I remember my assault in sounds
a car door locks
a heart   maybe mine
screaming loud in my chest
a grunt
a groan
a breath
the sound of me holding my breath
the heavy silence in between
the soft sound of the moon hitting the sunroof
a distant shout
a cry   maybe mine
but one sound I didn't expect to remember so vividly

was the sound of the
voicemail machine
from the
university sexual assault helpline
echoing off my stale dorm room carpets
telling me
they couldn't take my call.

Futures

Emma Kuzmyk

The following speech was written for and performed at an annual International Women's Week march and rally, hosted by St. Francis Xavier University and the Antigonish Women's Resource Centre and Sexual Assault Services Association, in March 2020.

———

In one of my classes we've been talking about the future, and the way the future's being imagined.

We talked about how in the past there's been a pretty clear narrative that we strived for, which would lead us to flying cars, metallic clothes, hoverboards and holograms—but when you notice that the future part of *Back to the Future* takes place in 2015, it becomes pretty clear that this isn't the way we think of the future today.

So, my class was asked how our generation is imagining the world, in, say, fifty years.

And after a heavy silence the answers were pretty bleak.

We're imagining fires, floods, hurricanes that wipe out cities, food shortages, water shortages, and war.

Many of my friends don't want to have children because they feel it's unfair to bring them into a dying world.

We don't know what a hopeful future looks like, or how we'll ever be able to get there, when the people who control our society seem to have no intention of planning for it.

And I think that one of the most disgusting things I've ever learned is that there are enough resources in this world to solve all of it.

Scientists know how to stabilize the climate crisis, and we're not doing it.

The United Nations knows how to solve world hunger, and we're not doing it.

We know that in the year 2020 something like equality is still just a hope for the future and not a reality of the present, and what are the people in charge *doing* about it?

We can say that the system is broken but it isn't. It's working exactly how it was supposed to work.

It's protecting who it was built to protect and it's failing those who it was built to fail.

It's a system that established "property" laws on the stolen land of Indigenous peoples.

It's a system that is more likely to protect a rapist than a survivor.

It's a system that has created, allowed, and perpetuated genocide.

It's a system that has built a home for racism, homophobia, ableism, sexism, hatred, and violence.

So, I suppose it's no wonder that now we don't have a clear view of an optimistic future.

In this system, it isn't possible to create one.

The first women's march was 107 years ago. And today, we're still marching.

We're still fighting. And what is happening in our country, in our world, is still not right.

And there have always been strong women.

There have always been strong voices, strong messages.

Women have held positions of power, won legal battles, become judges, and women have been changing the world.

The problem is not that we aren't strong enough, it's not that we aren't fighting hard enough, it's not that we aren't loud enough.

We are.

But we are fighting in a system that was built against us.

And on days like today, and every day for that matter, I want you to look around and think about who's fighting with you, and who is not.

If you've been to one of these marches before, you may have noticed that there are certain voices missing.

If you've been engaging in this work, if you've been part of an activist community, if you've been to any open forum that has anything to do with sexualized violence or gender inequality or any other issue that happens to disproportionately affect women, you may have noticed that there are certain voices missing.

Think about why they aren't here, what they aren't doing, and what they could be doing.

If we want to have an optimistic future, if we want to imagine a world where our children are able to live and thrive, then we have to break this system and create a new one which allows for it, but we can't do that if the people of privilege, the people in power, and the people who this system protects, continue to be silent.

Not Our Policy: A Story of Policy and Resistance at Carleton University

Caitlin Salvino

My journey combatting campus sexual violence began on October 6, 2016, when—while studying on a fellowship in Washington D.C.—I received an email requesting feedback on Carleton University's draft Sexual Violence Policy. I often regard this moment as a crossroads in my life. Had I decided to delete the email, as one often does during a busy term, my life would be vastly different than it is today. The email I received was a standard-form email, sent out to the whole student body at Carleton. It included a link to the draft Sexual Violence Policy and requested general feedback through a response form. The draft was already in the final stages of review. The email set out that the draft policy would be considered at a Board of Governors meeting on December 1, 2016, and had to be passed before the beginning of 2017.

Although I wasn't aware at the time, I now know that Carleton's Sexual Violence Policy was drafted in response to provincial legislation. Bill 132, *The Sexual Violence and Harassment Action Plan Act (Supporting Survivors and Challenging Sexual Violence and Harassment)*, passed on March 8, 2016, required all post-secondary institutions to pass sexual violence policies by January 1, 2017.[1] The legislative requirements in Bill 132 were minimal. In essence, the sole requirements set out were:

1. create a sexual violence policy;

2. ensure an undefined standard of student input is considered in the creation of said policy;

3. review the policy every three years;

4. provide statistical information to the overseeing Minister.[2]

Despite being away from my campus at the time, I was drawn to this consultation email. I printed off the twenty-two-page policy and began to read through it. Even without the background knowledge of the controversy surrounding its development, there were clauses within the draft that were evidently inappropriate. They included barring a "complainant" from being informed of sanctions determined in their own complaint, a President's exception clause, and very strict limitations on a complainant's speech.[3] The feedback was required by October 28, 2016, leaving only twenty-three days in the middle of the midterm exam season for students to analyse and respond to the complex policy document.

---

1. Sexual Violence and Harassment Action Plan Act (Supporting Survivors and Challenging Sexual Violence and Harassment), RRO 1990, Reg 132.

2. Ibid at schedule 3, sections 1-7.

3. Carleton University, *Carleton University Draft Sexual Violence Policy,* (Vice-President Students and Enrolment, October 2016).

Concerned with the disconnect between the claims to survivor-centrism from university officials[4] and the actual text of the policy, I checked-in with the leaders of the Carleton Human Rights Society (CUHRS). CUHRS was a club I co-founded in 2015, which was dedicated to bringing together Human Rights students at Carleton to apply our academic studies to systemic injustices in our communities. The 2016 CUHRS Co-Presidents were equally concerned with the Sexual Violence Policy draft. Upon reaching out to other student representative groups (including the undergraduate student union) and learning that they had no intention of seeking reforms to the draft Sexual Violence Policy, we decided to take action. We set out to mobilise the student community to advocate for reforms before the December 1, 2016, Board of Governors meeting.

Our strategy was two-fold. First, we would research and draft a comprehensive open letter requesting a set of reforms. Then, following the completion of this letter, we would seek out signatories from campus clubs and individual students. This grassroots collective response would hopefully gain enough support that it could be seriously considered by the University administration before the draft was finalised.

The letter we co-drafted was comprehensive. It totalled nine pages and included five key recommendations. Each of the recommendations included an analysis of the existing clauses and suggested reforms:

1. *That the Sexual Violence Review Committee be made up of a diverse group of neutral third-party experts, independent from the Carleton administration.*

2. *Expand and strengthen the use of the terms "rape culture" and*

---

4. In the email inviting feedback, the University administrator referred to the term survivor-centrism multiple times while discussing the draft policy.

"intersectionality" in the Policy beyond the Purpose of the Policy section and the Definitions section.

3. *Strengthen Carleton's commitment to providing a complaint process that is*

"survivor-centred" by:
1. *Removing the prohibition on Complainants' making public statements*

before, during, and after the complaint process;
1. *Amending the policy to allow the Sexual Violence Review Committee to inform the complainant of the disciplinary action ordered against the defendant;*

2. *Removing the clause that enables the President of the University to create exceptions to any and all parts of the Policy.*

survivors of sexual violence.
1. *Expand the definition of the "Carleton Community" and address the loophole that enables Respondents to suspend the complaint process by ending their relationship with the University.*[5]

We published the open letter on October 19, 2016, and paired it with an op-ed in the student newspaper.[6] The opinion piece sought to direct student groups to the open letter and highlight the five reforms

5. Salvino, Caitlin, Jodi Miles, & Sally Johnson, "Open Letter to the Carleton Community and Administration on the Draft Sexual Violence Policy," Carleton Human Rights Society, October 28, 2016.

6. Salvino, Caitlin. "Opinion: Students can't afford to ignore call for feedback," *The Charlatan,* October 19, 2016.

we were asking for. This piece, combined with student networks we had developed in past CUHRS projects and the drafting stages of the letters, allowed us to gain support beyond what we could have imagined.

The open letter received unprecedented support from members of the Carleton community—it was signed by 281 individual students and staff, 35 clubs, 6 service centres,[7] and all levels of student government (CUSA, GSA, RRRA and CASG).[8] We could not believe the amount of support we received from students. In that short period, we also witnessed a major shift in the community's culture. Sexual violence, a topic rarely acknowledged or discussed in the pre-#MeToo era, became a unifying force on our campus.

We submitted the open letter through the official channels by the deadline of October 28, 2016. This letter represented thousands of Carleton students expressing serious concern with the Draft Sexual Violence Policy. Shortly thereafter, the Carleton University Vice-President (Students and Enrolment) responded with a twelve-page community update. The update, titled: "In Response to Sexual Violence Policy Feedback, Carleton Makes Changes to the Sexual Violence Policy Draft and Commits to an Additional Resource for Survivors," shared that a series of changes had been made to the draft policy. Many of those changes were in direct response to the concerns raised in our letter, including:

1. *Modified the definition of "University Community" to elimi-*

---

7. The Womyn's Centre (now called the Womxn's Learning, Advocacy, and Support Centre); the Gender and Sexuality Resource Centre CUSA Service Centre; Carleton Disability Awareness CUSA Service Centre; Race, Ethnicity and Culture Hall CUSA Service Centre; International Students' Centre; and the Mawandoseg Centre.

8. The Students' Unions were Carleton University Undergraduate Union, Carleton Graduate Student Association, Rideau River Residence Association and Carleton Academic Student Government.

nate the possibility that Respondents could suspend the complaint process by ending their relationship with the University.

2. *Reworded the policy to ensure a survivor-centric approach to support services, by making it clear that Equity Services/Sexual Assault Support Services continues their traditional role of supporting and advising survivors of sexual violence.*

3. *Removed the clause that enabled the President to make exceptions.*

4. *Defined what is meant by "public statements," clarifying that those who have experienced sexual violence can still seek counselling and other support services, and speak to their friends and family.*[9]

The community update was designed as a series of questions and answers, where the administration had drafted specific responses to concerns raised in the feedback. In these series of answers, the Carleton administration made clear that many of the more substantive recommendations made in the open letter would not be adopted. A new draft of the Carleton Sexual Violence Policy was released November 25, 2016, five days before the Board of Governors meeting where its implementation would be voted on.

Although we achieved some "wins" by way of reforms to the draft policy, our group was disappointed. The final draft of the policy retained a series of clauses that would harm survivors. We knew that individuals who would seek recourse through the policy would face significant challenges and were at risk of experiencing re-traumatisation by way of the

---

9. Carleton University, Community Update: Sexual Violence Policy, Vice-President Students and Enrolment, October 2016.

administrative processes. As such, in the final days before the Board of
Governors meeting, we signed onto a joint statement drafted and signed
by CUASA, CUPE 4600, CUPE 2424, the Graduate Student's Association (GSA), and the Carleton Human Rights Society, encouraging the
university administration to commit to more reforms before the policy
was passed.[10] Despite our efforts to encourage the administration to
include more comprehensive changes to the draft policy, it was made
clear to us through informal channels that no further changes would
be made. On December 1, 2016, the unchanged Sexual Violence Policy
was passed by the Board of Governors in a twenty-eight to three vote
while student protesters gathered outside. The only three votes against
the passing of the policy were from the student representatives.[11]

The passing of the policy, however, was not the end of our story at
Carleton. Determined to continue to advocate, the CUHRS decided to
draft a second open letter. By this point I had returned to campus, having
completed my exchange in the fall semester, and was ready to work in
person with the CUHRS and the other allies we had made.

The basis of our second letter was a single off-hand comment made
by the Carleton University Vice-President (Students and Enrolment) in
their community update:

*It is important to see the policy in action for a significant period before it
is reviewed. The policy will be reviewed on the 3-year timeline required by
the Ontario government. This said, there is no provision that prevents the
University from reviewing the policy sooner if it is determined that there*

10. Graduate Student Association, "Statement from GSA Board of Governors Representative
re: Sexual Violence Policy," December 1, 2016.

11. Salvino, Caitlin and Jade Joy Cooligan Pang, edited by Jodi Miles, Sally Johnson and
Fa'Ttima Omran, "Open Letter to Reform Carleton's Sexual Violence Policy," Carleton
Human Rights Society, February 10, 2017.

are clauses that need to be amended. All feedback sent to [email redacted for this piece] will be valued and considered as they are shared.[12]

Although not a commitment to reform the policy before the required three-year review, this statement offered us a glimmer of hope. We believed there was a chance, albeit small, that if we garnered enough support, the Board of Governors would pass amendments on the Sexual Violence Policy. In hindsight, the belief that administration would listen and respond to a mass mobilization of student voices was extremely optimistic.

Our second open letter was published on February 10, 2017. It was co-written by five students and re-affirmed some of the initial recommendations from our first open letter, in addition to a series of new recommendations:

> 1. *Amending the definition of "University Community" to include alumni and visitors on the Carleton campus.*
>
> 2. *Strengthen Carleton's commitment to providing a complaint process that is "survivor-centred" by [the]:*
>
>> a. *Addition of a clause that facilitates a complaint process that does not require the Complainant and Respondent to face each other in a formal hearing;*

---

12. Carleton University, *Community Update: Sexual Violence Policy*, Vice-President Students and Enrolment, October 2016. http://carleton.ca/studentsupport/wp-content/uploads/Sexual-Violence-Policy-Draft-Feedback-Summary.pdf.

b. *Addition of a specific immunity clause that protects a Complainant from punishment for violations relating to alcohol or drug use;*

3. *Amending the policy to allow the Sexual Violence Review Committee to inform the complainant of the disciplinary action ordered against the defendant and establish clear enforcement mechanisms to ensure that the ruling of the committee is being adhered to.*

4. *Creation of a new position entitled Sexual Violence Survivor Advocate that would encompass the Sexual Assault Services Coordinator while providing more support to the Complainant.*[13]

Since the publishing of the first open letter in October 2016, we had had several months to meet with allies and conduct consultations in partnership with student centres. This time allowed us to better understand the needs of our survivor community and amplify the voices of students through our collective efforts. As a result, we developed additional recommendations that were not included in the first open letter.

Our second open letter had one more key distinction from the first: our comparative research. In this letter, we had significantly more time to research other campus sexual violence policies. Bill 132 required every post-secondary institution in Ontario to pass a sexual violence policy by January 1, 2017. This development provided us with dozens of new policies that we could analyse and compare with the Carleton policy. We

---

13. Salvino, Caitlin and Jade Joy Cooligan Pang, edited by Jodi Miles, Sally Johnson and Fa'Ttima Omran, "Open Letter to Reform Carleton's Sexual Violence Policy," Carleton Human Rights Society, February 10, 2017.

decided to engage in comparative research in part due to the administration's responses to our initial letter. In the community update response, the Carleton University Vice-President (Students and Enrolment) rejected a large portion the feedback we provided, saying that it wasn't possible because of a range of constraints placed on post-secondary institutions, including legal requirements.

We decided to challenge what we perceived to be inappropriate claims to abstract legal limitations by demonstrating that other policies had been passed in the same jurisdiction and included the same clauses that we were advocating for. For example, we included an example from the York University Sexual Violence Policy to demonstrate that it was possible to include an immunity clause[14] in a policy, something that the Carleton administration had rejected in their initial response to our feedback.[15] In our second open letter we drew on examples from multiple post-secondary institutions in Ontario, including York University, Queen's University, and the University of Ottawa.[16] We found that a comparative approach had the most traction in our discussions with university officials, a development that would later influence our approach to national work.

---

14. In our open letter we argued for a "specific immunity clause" from existing drug and alcohol policies within the student code of conduct. It was recommended that the Carleton University Sexual Violence Policy specifically indicate to survivors that they will not be prosecuted if they were in violation of alcohol or drug use policies at the time of the incident.

15. Salvino, Caitlin and Jade Joy Cooligan Pang, edited by Jodi Miles, Sally Johnson and Fa'Ttima Omran, "Open Letter to Reform Carleton's Sexual Violence Policy," Carleton Human Rights Society, February 10, 2017.

16. It is important to note that our reference to other campus sexual violence policies were in no way an endorsement of the policies. Rather, we recognised that the existing policies were deeply flawed but sought to identify singular best practices to use in our comparative analysis and advocacy.

Surprisingly, our second open letter received even more support than the first. It was signed by 413 individual students and staff, 51 clubs, 10 service centres,[17] and all levels of student government (CUSA, GSA, RRRA and CASG). We worked behind the scenes to arrange meetings with university officials to discuss the letter and hopefully secure a re-opening of the policy for amendments.

Before getting to the outcomes of these discussions with Carleton University officials, it is important to highlight that our efforts at Carleton were not limited to policy reform. Although this has been the focus of what I have written about here, we as a collective initiated and led a multitude of efforts to respond to sexual violence on our campus. In a period of six months, we ran a student-led Campus Sexual Violence Survey that was completed by six-hundred students, secured bystander intervention training for all varsity athletes, created a consent team to be present at high-risk events (such as Frosh Week and sporting events), hosted open Survivor Speaks events, and developed a mandatory peer-to-peer anti-sexual violence training program for clubs that has since trained thousands of students.

Additionally, I would be remiss not to mention the banner drop campaign that was initiated by an anonymous group of students. Every day, students would trek through the heavy snow with a hand-painted twenty-foot banner and affix it to the Carleton University sign. This sign was at the entrance of the Carleton campus and was visible from the main road. The banners had a range of slogans, including "Not Our

---

17. The Womyn's Centre (now called the Womxn's Learning, Advocacy, and Support Centre); Mawandoseg CUSA Service Centre; GSRC (Gender and Sexuality Resource Centre); CDAC (Carleton Disability Awareness Centre); International Students' Centre; REC Hall (Race, Ethnicity and Culture Hall); Health and Wellness Resource Centre; HATCH (CUSA Service Centre); Foot Patrol and The Food Centre.

Policy" and "Stop Sexual Violence." The banners were taken down by campus security within minutes. However, anonymous photos taken of the banners were shared heavily online. These photos were a central part of the success of the second open letter.

Following that success, we were cautiously optimistic. We arranged a series of meetings with members of the Carleton administration who were leading the implementation of the sexual violence policy. We truly believed that we could get at least one or two reforms, particularly around extending the policy to apply to visitors and to add in a specific immunity clause.

To say the least, this optimism was immediately shut down at our first and only meeting with the Director of Student Affairs. At this spring 2017 meeting, there was no discussion. Although our letter, comparative research, and specific points were acknowledged, it was of no consequence. We were told: "at this time, there is no appetite among administration to reform the policy." This statement, from the Director of Student Affairs, marked the end of five months of student-led efforts to reform the Carleton Sexual Violence Policy. We had hit a wall; working within institutional channels to address campus sexual violence was no longer a viable option. This, however, was not the end of our efforts. We were determined to continue advocating for reforms to Carleton's Sexual Violence Policy. In the end, we were successful, but only after we elevated our movement to the national level.

This Will Not Blow Over

Connor Spencer

The following speech was written for and given as the opening for a rally held at McGill University's Community Square on April 11, 2018, protesting inaction on sexualized violence perpetuated by faculty at McGill and Concordia and calling for a response to the demands in an open letter published by the Students' Society of McGill University. The demands included:

1. That an external investigation be launched into the handling of sexual violence complaints against professors in the faculty of arts from the past five years,

2. that the McGill Sexual Violence Policy be made stand alone, and

3. that there be a shift in the culture on campus that included making student activists and survivors proper stakeholders in any anti-sexualized violence work done on campus.

The letter was signed by 102 student organizations, 2,413 students, and publicly supported by 148 professors across campus. Close to 1,000 people walked out of class and gathered in Community Square despite the cold and the fact that it was exam season. The title of this piece comes from a chant led by Sophia Sahrane.

Thank you, folks, so much for being here. I want to do a quick little check in—could any undergraduates who are here today cheer? [loud cheer] Graduate students? [slightly smaller cheer] Professors and academic staff? [small but mighty cheer, and the entire crowd erupts at their solidarity]

Amazing! Thank you all so much for being here today! It's truly overwhelming to see this many people. I don't think we've had this many people in Community Square since 2012 or 2013, so that's really, really exciting.

Before we begin, I want to acknowledge that we are on the unceded territory of the Kaniekehaka, who are members of the Haudenosaunee Confederacy. This is incredibly important—most of us here today have not been invited to be here, and colonial and sexualized violence are incredibly linked. The continued colonial violence that is perpetuated on this territory is part of what we are talking about today, and we cannot commit to addressing one form of violence without committing to address—and destroy—them all. It is important to remember throughout this rally and mobilization on campus that Indigenous women are three times more likely to experience violence than non-Indigenous women, and it's important to remember that our country is currently in the middle of the Missing and Murdered Indigenous Women and Girls investigation. Sexualized violence and colonial violence are linked within our neoliberal colonial country and government.

I also want to take a moment to clarify what we mean when we say sexualized violence, as often when one hears the term "violence," one's head jumps to "assault." Sexualized violence refers to the myriad actions and behaviours that occur either in person or online that target a person's sexual and/or gender identity and includes, but is not limited to, sexual assault, sexual harassment, stalking, voyeurism, and sexual exploitation.

Today, we will be hearing from folks who have been working in various capacities to address campus sexualized violence in various forms, often for many, many years. I do want to take this time right now to address the fact that I have been occupying a lot of public media space around this topic, but I am definitely not the leader of this movement. I am occupying this space as a white woman because I am given more privilege, but the movement, especially on McGill's campus, to end not just sexualized violence but other forms of violence on campus, has always been and will continue to be led by women and non-binary folks of colour. Actually—could we just give a round of applause to those folks, some of whom will be speaking today, but many, many of whom are not, for the work they do that is so invisible on this campus. [large applause]

The first students to speak up about this on campus and who began to pressure administration were women of colour. They were, are, and will continue to be the ones in the rooms, writing the petitions, advocating for and supporting survivors ... It is truly incredible, and I am in awe every day of every single one of them who I have had the pleasure to work with, and whose labour I actively benefit from.

The SSMU and CSU have organized this rally today to address the lack of institutional response to violence perpetuated by academic staff on both of our campuses. We wish to show that this is not one individual or even one group of individuals who are calling for acknowledgement of a problem. Instead, it is a call to action from students across departments, across faculties, and across university campuses. Although each of our campuses' stories have made it into the media, we know many more at other universities that have not. Today, we also show up for them and for students on campuses across the country doing the invisible work of addressing campus violence that their university will not. This is work that will never go on resumes, work that is incredibly exhausting and emotionally draining, work that often puts their academic careers in jeopardy, and work that is incredibly vital to the survival of many students on this and other campuses.

So why now? Why are we here, right now? Well, in the McGill context, on Wednesday morning of last week, the SSMU sent an open letter to members of McGill administration demanding that an external investigation be launched into the office of the Dean of Arts' handling of complaints against faculty members. This letter was spurred by the frustration of working with administration on this issue, where we felt we had been given excuses and had deadlines pushed off further and further. A few weeks ago, we brought to the attention of the administration our concerns over the safety and well-being of a student who was being targeted by a professor who thought they were behind a campaign calling them out for violence. We presented a dossier of evidence, and no action was taken. [crowd: "SHAME!"]

As student representatives, we have a duty to protect our members. As students on this campus, we have a duty to protect our friends, to protect each other. That is why we at SSMU are no longer accepting that the reason for the administration's inaction in addressing problems they are aware of stems from students' inability to file formal or detailed-enough complaints to warrant investigation. Instead, we wish to focus on the complaint system itself as the problem, as contributing to a culture of students not wanting to come forward or file complaints, fearing legal action being taken against them, risk to their academic careers, and above all that the university would do nothing with their complaint.

When I first came to McGill at seventeen years old from a little bumpkin town in Ontario, within three weeks I had been sat down by a group of fourth year women and given a list of professors and TAs whose classes and office hours I should avoid to keep myself safe. And I know I'm not the only one who had that talk. Could everyone here who has been warned about a professor during their time here raise their hand? [almost everyone in the crowd raises their hand]

That. That is why we are here today. Thank you.

———

A few days following this rally, SSMU reported McGill to be in violation of Chapter four, sections fourteen and fifteen[1] of Bill 151, Quebec's provincial campus sexual violence legislation. The Minister of Higher Education dismissed the complaint, saying she trusted McGill to do the right thing. Three years later, none of the demands from students have been met, and student survivors and activists continue to push to hold administration accountable.

---

1. In these sections the Minister has given themselves the authority to impose oversight and monitoring measures to any institution that is failing to implement the Bill. The minister and their delegates may also step in to perform the duties the institution is failing, and the institution is obliged to work with them. However, we have yet to see these sections be used.

They Watched Me Burn

ANONYMOUS

Content Warning: Moderate discussion of suicide, sexual assault, homophobia
To skip to the next story, turn to page 171.

To skip to the next story, turn to page 171.

Please note: all identifying names, locations, and details have been changed to protect both the innocent and the guilty—because no one deserves to live through the toxicity and abuse that I'm going to tell you about.

I kept everything. All the papers stayed squarely and silently stacked, sitting in a closet until I needed them again. I knew I would need them again, someday. Each page was flat and flawless. Scanner's glass or journalist's hands—those printed words would look lovely anywhere with their crisp text and unfaded ink. I kept everything loose-leaf in a small green binder. It is unornamented, except for a concise and imprecise label that reads: "Book of Bullshit."

At first, my involvement with sexualized violence policy (SVP) was strictly professional. I was a student executive in my university's (referred to henceforth as "The University") Students' Union in the late 2010s. My portfolio should have dictated my focus. I was supposed to be looking inwards at the union, its policies and finances; that's what I wanted to do. I cared about student groups accessing funding, about the sustainability of the food bank, about better communication with the student body. I was naïve. Those things mattered, and they still matter—but, as a jaded veteran of student politics, I would later reflect that those "early days" issues were trite and tired compared to my work with SVP.

In that regard, I was supposed to be an assistant. Other people would attend meetings and do the work; I would take notes and offer information. It would have been an elegant solution. I could remain within the constraints of my portfolio but still provide meaningful support to my peers. I could "stay in my lane," synthesizing new ideas from familiar data, providing malleable numbers and rules, working within the union to affect change—but at the same time, I could assist other people in the execution of meaningful work, work that was *owed*. All student leaders have a responsibility to their constituents that increases proportionally with the importance of matters such as sexualized violence. I believed that sentiment with unwavering faith.

Other people, however, *did not* do the work. I provided a summarized reading list of every sexualized violence policy and procedure. They told me that they were too hard to read. They were busy with conferences, classes, courtship. So, I read it all for them. I annotated everything and pressed pristine PDFs into inboxes. The response? It was too hard to understand, even with the annotations. I swallowed my annoyance and provided paper copies, as requested, carefully outlined in a neon palette. "I still don't understand," they said, while I quietly wondered: had they even bothered to try? "There's just so much. It's overwhelming," they complained. I bit my tongue and pushed down my frustration. I'd tutored students before, patiently rotating through explanations and experimenting with new tactics until something clicked. So be it. I became an unenthusiastic teacher with an unfamiliar curriculum, fumbling to disseminate my limited understanding. We had meetings. They marvelled at how much simpler it all seemed after I explained things, despite the fact that my "explaining" was just reading the highlighted sections out loud.

For the record, The University's SVP was only six pages long. There were other important documents, but they made up fewer than thirty pages in total. I didn't understand these people. They were busy with their own lives, sure, but they said that SVP mattered to them, that they were passionate about doing the work. So why couldn't I see them doing it? Why did these abdicated responsibilities end up on my plate when I was already overburdened? Despite being salaried for thirty hours per week, I often worked more than forty just to address the work under my portfolio. Any work on SVP was not only unpaid—it came at the direct expense of time for my studies or rest. I had to rationalize the sacrifices I was making, thinking to myself, *I don't know enough about SVP work. Considering the severity of sexualized violence, it might be the most important issue for Students' Unions. I want to help, but I feel weak and ineffectual. I'm already tired from school and work. I'm a scientist—maybe a bureaucrat, now—but not an activist or politician by trade. I don't know how to advocate, I don't know how to organize, and I don't have time to learn ... But I suppose, even so ... I'll have to try.*

So I tried. Each week, when I wasn't responding to student emails or pouring over documents, I was engaged in backroom conversations with administrators, hoping that we could collaborate quietly to effect change. My mentor cautioned against using an openly aggressive approach when critiquing The University. Instead, he said, we should open with tact and discretion. I liked that idea. We both thought that The University would accept respectful and persuasive suggestions with open arms. We would have rules of engagement. We would give the institution an opportunity to pre-empt problems and avoid embarrassment behind closed doors. If that didn't work, well, we could always escalate matters. As it turns out, escalation and conflict were inevitable. We frequently screenshotted professors or low-level administrators chatting shit about us on Facebook. If I had a quarter for every time I saw those people being unprofessional on social media, I'd have had enough money to go to a better university.

Let me begin this story by telling you how university structures generally don't work and how universities are often dishonest in their rhetoric. On a cloudy day in March, The University's Office of Enrolment (OE) published their response (hereafter, "The Response") to the Students' Union's strategic plan for orientation, addressed to The University's Senate. It's a fun little read that:

1. Excludes my name, but thoughtfully remembers to name the men working at the executive level in the Students' Union, despite the fact that I was an equal contributor;

2. Has unique section headers that showcase the OE's patent derision for the validity of our work while

3. Whinging about how we didn't consult them as stakeholders.

We, the Students' Union, made a request to the Senate: we wanted one or two non-instructional days to host an orientation for new students without university interference. Why a separate orientation from The University and why non-instructional days, you ask? Separation from The University was necessitated by the toxic ways that they tried to exclude student voices. They would exclude the Students' Union from holding membership on committees, refuse to add our items to agendas, speak over us, and outright ignore what we had to say. They didn't want us in their spaces. We were barely allowed to attend, let alone participate. We couldn't do anything at *their* orientation. I won't even go into how The University and other stakeholders have a demonstrated interest in downplaying and trivializing "controversial" topics, rendering their orientations devoid of information that addresses the practical realities of sexualized violence. If student government didn't get a chance to speak, there would be no honest conversation about sexualized violence on campus.

Why did we want non-instructional days allotted for our orientation? We wanted students to attend without having to miss class. I'm fairly certain that most, if not all, Students' Union orientations had been held at the same time as regular classes. Do I need to spell out why it would be bad for students to potentially miss their only *real* introduction to sexualized violence on campus? We were basically being told that orientation from the Students' Union was, at best, an afterthought. We could have our little half-day affairs, rattle off our opinions at lightning speed in between explanations of our services, but we would neither be equal partners in running their orientation nor would we be given the time to run our own adequately. The Registrar said it was too hard to add non-instructional days to the schedule; the academic calendar was too tightly packed with learning! There were policies to observe, and it couldn't be done! Pearls were clutched and bureaucratic panic set in. I guess The University, unlike their national peers, couldn't match the quality of planning required to host a welcome week in collaboration with student government. That "we can't find enough time because scheduling is too hard" was one of the predominant arguments is embarrassing. I should have bought The University a calendar and stapled our list of seven example schedules to the front. It could have served as a cheeky reminder that their limp protests were seen for what they were, that we witnessed The University's willingness to proudly parade their asses in a series of extracurricular humiliations and declare incompetence as a defence for their practices. Class scheduling was, in their eyes, evidently far more important than a minor concern like sexualized violence prevention.

———

Now that we've examined the uselessness of collaborating with The University via its committees and structures, let's talk about weak arguments and intellectually dishonest rhetoric. In our proposal for non-instructional days, we argued that first-year students are a uniquely vulnerable, high-risk demographic for experiencing sexualized violence and that they should be the focus of our orientation. OE argued that targeting first-year students as a primary audience would be exclusionary to a majority of incoming students, noting that "traditional entry" students made up only 35% of any incoming cohort at The University. That's a fairly weak argument. I guess providing any specialized programming for minorities or vulnerable populations—y'know, anything that isn't targeted towards the majority—is too exclusionary to run. I can practically hear The University now: "Sorry, 'the Gays' and anyone with a skin tone darker than 'peach,' your tuition money spends the same as anyone else, but we can't run any programming for you because it excludes the white heteronormative majority!"

We also claimed that, based on research we reviewed, upper-level students were more likely to be perpetrators of sexualized violence than first-year students during the first six weeks of the fall semester. For your potential edification, dear reader—those first six weeks, sometimes cited to contain around 50% of the sexual assaults that will occur over the year, are referred to as "The Red Zone." To put this another way, we cited an uncontroversial statistic, then made a slightly bolder assertion about the demographics behind it. The University countered that there was "little research to support the claim." I suppose the validity of these opposing claims would depend on the quality and quantity of evidence for each side. Now that I'm out of the post-secondary environment, I don't have access to research tools—funny how The University gets access to academic databases, while I, an activist, cannot afford to read or cite literature behind a paywall and therefore can't support my claims with research—so in the year 2021, as I write this, I might have to pencil this in as a tie. Though we thoroughly consulted academic resources to compile our proposal, the bibliography did not make its way into the agenda package, and I cannot prove the completeness of our research using archived content.

Returning to the OE's response document—they decried our lack of sources and said that our proposal was scientifically unsupported. In contrast, "The Response" cited only one book (*Blurred Lines: Rethinking Sex, Power, and Consent on Campus*), a 2012 document titled "CAS professional standards for higher education," the University of Western Ontario's orientation plan from 2016, The University's own damn website, and the two documents that we, the Students' Union, had already put forward. I had hoped that the Senate would see the smack of hypocrisy—after all, OE was calling us out for not being scientifically valid, but their "academic" sources included a single book and a six-year-old standards document from which they'd pulled massively misappropriated quotes—alas, no one commented on the painfully obvious double standard. Even if we generously categorize the book and the standards document as "academic," how were those quotes used? What ideological or argumentative function did those cited documents accomplish? OE held up the book to say that hypersexualized activities tend to happen at student-run orientations and that first-year students are most often victimized by other first-year students. These two arguments

1) imply that, *actually*, student-run orientations are more sexualized and, therefore, more dangerous compared to university-run orientations, and

2) state that the Students' Union was wrong in its statement about the demographics of perpetrators.

Fine, fair enough. I hadn't read *Blurred Lines: Rethinking Sex, Power, and Consent on Campus*, so I'd accepted that someone might have said something factual. Immediately after that quote was used, however, OE synthesized the new idea that separating first-year students from upper-level students may cause first-years to become more vulnerable to sexualized violence via a siloing effect. *What?* Shouldn't there have been a citation there to support this new idea that—in contrast to the book's plain statement that they aren't primary perpetrators—upper-level students are actively *protective* against sexualized violence? There was a pretty big logical leap being made there, but no one seemed to notice.

OE also quoted the Council for the Advancement of Standards in Higher Education (CAS), another institutional power. They used definitional quotes to argue that orientations should integrate new students into the university environment and be sensitive to "intellectual, cultural, and social" contexts at each institution. Effectively, OE merely quoted a dictionary and hoped no one would notice. Our proposal *did* include those "intellectual, cultural, and social" contexts. Our proposal *did* take a tailored approach towards students and accessibility. In contrast, OE quoted some definitions, completely ignored or misunderstood what we had written, and in doing so, pretended to an unearned level of scientific validity in refuting our ideas. As many of my colleagues in SVP activism have pointed out, however, scientific validity is just another fog machine in a university's fetishistic collection of smoke and mirrors. It wouldn't have mattered if we had all the research on our side anyway. They wouldn't have goddamn read it. One of their core arguments was that The University hadn't formally documented a case of sexualized violence during the Red Zone in the last five years. I find their reliance on that fact chilling and disturbing. This fact—from the idea that *reported* sexualized violence is an adequate measure of *actual* sexualized violence, to the idea that no sexualized violence occurred during five years' worth of Red Zones—has disgusting implications, and I hope that it lives on in infamy for the callous disregard it represents.

"Not here," they said. But they lied.

———

I don't know if I can call myself a "survivor," at least in the context of my experiences at The University. Imposter syndrome won't let me. My cloudy little tessera is just part of a bigger mosaic, meant to be viewed holistically within the context of the many people who have told their stories before mine. But just for a moment, please, join me in revisiting my revulsive memories. They're greasy flumes that pump maggoty lies into your mouth until your throat is retched and scorched, your heart is pulped, and your lungs burn with bile. My story is slimy, vomited trash laid at your feet, for your consideration, in a crush of crumpled hopes and unswallowed bitterness.

A small group of people, almost exclusively women, spread rumours about my personal and professional conduct, likely with the intent to cause harm in my personal life and loss of political power in my professional life. In fewer words: some girls decided to cancel me by fabricating an adulterous sex life and Machiavellian persona for me. Enough time has passed. I can spitefully laugh about it now. I invite you to chuckle with me. You've got to laugh to keep from crying, and I certainly did a lot of both.

Many of the people who harassed me proudly proclaimed that they were "feminists." They wrote condescending rebukes and reprimanded people for nebulous wrongdoings. They'd publicly post ambiguous, passive-aggressive rants on Facebook—obviously targeted at a specific person—then wait for the sympathy comments to roll in as they sighed heavily at "some people." The imperious, self-righteous pageantry left a sour taste in my mouth. They were armchair activists who arrogantly purported to have moral superiority over the uneducated masses while taking no action to support marginalized peoples. They derided the "likes and prayers" crowd, blissfully unaware of their hypocrisy. I remembered thinking, *Somehow, I don't think these people are feminists. Call it 'no true Scotsman,' tell me that I've made a critical miscalculation in my estimation of their politics, but I don't think that feminism is supposed to be* anything *like this.* My criticisms are harsh, but I think they're fair under the heuristics I've chosen. A pattern emerged that allowed for a simple, if coarse, separation between feminists and "feminists" in my personal life. Let us briefly examine these thumby rules, acknowledging that I am white-passing, my abusers were overwhelmingly white-passing, and marginalized peoples, particularly people with disabilities and BIPOC, are often engaged in activism by different means, exempting them from categorization under this particular exercise:

1. Feminists know talking points and can often articulate a deeper understanding of *why* certain issues are important; "feminists" gesticulate weakly to trends.

2. Feminists are orchestrators and organizers of social change who actively participate in collective action; "feminists" don't do the work.

3. Feminists seek ways to leverage their knowledge of intersectionality and synthesize new understanding; "feminists" are barely able to define intersectionality.

4. Feminists are introspective about how their internalized misogyny, colonialism, and racism affects others; "feminists" struggle to define the terms, which may render them incapable of assessing their own problematic behaviours.

5. Feminists wield criticism and empowerment alike to punch up at authority and uplift marginalized voices; "feminists" punch down and speak over their peers.

I'm sure those heuristics have limited generalisability, but in my case, *if the shoe fits* ...

Rumours swirled around me at any given moment, the most common strain focusing on my alleged sexual indiscretions. In theory, I had slept with a then-friend of mine, thereby cheating on my then-fiancée,

Isabelle. In practice, the instigators of the rumours knew that these claims were untrue. I had neither slept with that friend nor any of the myriad other men I had supposedly seduced in subsequent rumour-mill retellings. I'm sure it would have been an indictment on my personal character if I actually *had* cheated on Isabelle and broken her trust. Of course, the "cheating" element was almost an afterthought. The "feminists" really showed their hand in *how* they told their rumours. The narrative was always that I was having sex with some guy. Isabelle was forgotten at first, then added to later retellings for dramatic effect. She became a prop—not even a side character—in the stories told about me. I find it intriguing, maybe even telling, that no one bothered to inform her about my chronic "cheating," despite the fact that she was also a student at The University. There I was, a virgin slayer, sleeping with every man in a ten-kilometre radius—and no one was going to alert the poor dear to my steadily climbing body count? Isabelle wasn't a public figure, but we had some overlap in our digital presence and contacting her would have been easy enough. I find it *really weird* that no one thought to. If the rumour mill was so certain that I was a cheating bastard, wouldn't they have said something? And if the rumour mill *wasn't* certain that I was a cheating bastard, wouldn't they hesitate before trying to ruin my life? In either event, those "feminist storytelling techniques" were entirely insensitive to the other woman in the picture. She was collateral damage, with nary a thought spared to her well-being.

Let me return again to the central premise lurking behind all of those sexual rumours: *"She's a slut. She slept with _____. Isn't that awful?"* The misogyny is on full display. It wasn't about cheating or infidelity—I was very private, and most people weren't sure that I was partnered, let alone engaged—it was about me sleeping with men. If I was having sex with a bunch of guys, well, that was bad enough! Case closed! As we all know, the correct response to female promiscuity is a gauntlet of punitive measures, social ex-communication, and slut shaming. Again, may I direct your attention to how weird it was that these rumours were both created and perpetuated by "feminists"? It seemed bizarre and hypocritical that these women felt fully comfortable in their moral position while they passed judgment on the bodily autonomy of another woman. And the verdict was in: my supposed pursuit of consensual pleasure was "no bueno," in the parlance of today's youth. Note also the Crouching Misogyny, Hidden Homophobia: despite having been outed some years prior as bisexual (or pansexual, if you like), these stories always portrayed me misleading menfolk to the exclusion of women or enby folx.

The "feminist" bourgeoisie, as proprietors of the rumour mill, were also frequently members of the Pride organization at The University. In my opinion, the group had a troubled history and suffered from growing pains shared by most small social movements. Meeting minutes published by the organization in 2016—bravely—entered unredacted complaints about exclusion into the public record, since some attendees had reported feeling unsafe or unheard in the organization's spaces. There was some acknowledgement that, at times, The University's Pride organization was not inclusive. This is an *exceedingly* diplomatic reading of the history I knew. Many of the queer folx spearheading the movement had been drastically mistreated in many areas of their lives, and positive models of queerness were substantively lacking in the conservative communities around The University. Religious fundamentalism in the region naturally and inexorably clashed with queerness in a tale as old as time. I'm empathetic to stories that arise from that context. In fact, two former members of that Pride organization served as positive and inspirational models for my blend of feminism.

However, the other Gays outed me among themselves. Twice. The first time, they outed me as a bisexual/pansexual woman. The second time, well, I don't really want to talk about what it was. (It's a type of Gay that I like to keep to myself, you know? I kind of enjoy reclaiming my identity in this intimate space.) Now, I'll say it again, but louder for the people in the back: the "feminists" and Gays outed my queerness, dragging me forth from my wee little closet. I didn't like that very much, especially because of my second Gaymer Tag: to be outed as that *particular* type of Gay had negative implications within that same Pride organization, let alone in the wider world of stigma. That "secret Gayness" that I keep talking about? I was actually introduced to the very concept of it when a member of the Pride organization outed *another* member with that identity to me. In other words, the inciting incident for my second Foray Into Gay was the outing and subsequent harm of another queer person. This was merely one entry in a lengthy list of toxic behaviours that paradoxically rose from purportedly "inclusive" queer spaces where "The Gays" outed "The Other Gays," among other things. In my case, outing caused a lot of personal harm. I think it could, or even still might, cause harm in my professional life. It's hard to tell because so much of the rumour mill operated in cliquey whispers and noxious group chats. Who knows if I'll miss a job opportunity someday because of the stigma that surrounds my identity? There's one thing I know for sure: tort law is *whack*, and I certainly didn't have the requisite levels of privilege to defend myself with a lawyer.

I want to end this gay section with a shout into the void. The "feminists" and The Gays that abused me also outed Isabelle. Remember how she was used as a prop in those earlier rumours? In the past, with Isabelle's explicit consent and blessing, I had spoken to someone else, Flare, about Isabelle's identity as a trans woman. I lamented the way things had changed in my relationship with Isabelle, even though she was much happier, that driving her to biweekly appointments in the city was essential but also time-consuming and expensive. I was supporting a transitioning woman to the best of my ability, and I wanted a confidante to affirm the growing pains associated with that process. I made it explicitly clear that Isabelle was in the closet and struggling with mental illness, and the highest confidentiality was requested. Absolutely no one else was to know of her identity or my burdensome feelings. Flare agreed and a promise was struck.

Some months later, Flare approached me with what they said was "a very difficult problem." That amorphous descriptor was all I was given, but I resolved to be thoughtful and kind. I agreed to listen to their problem and help out however possible. Flare *immediately* outed a mutual acquaintance, Lauren, as trans. Lauren was in the early stages of their transition and had requested information, so Flare came to me as a subject expert on "helping trans people." I was horrified. I didn't want to know. I didn't *choose* to know. More importantly, the disclosure was invasive and unnecessary relative to the treatment, which was the simple provision of information. I said, "You didn't have to tell me who they were. I would have told you anything, no questions asked." I recall Flare saying something along the lines of, "Oh, I didn't think about that." Apparently not. Nonetheless, I promised secrecy to both Flare and Lauren.

Some months after that, I crossed paths with Teresa, a work contact. We exchanged pleasantries. I mentioned that I had been having an emotionally tough time. They paused. Their lips pursed. *They knew something.* My heart dropped to the centre of the earth when they told me: Flare had outed Isabelle (and I) to strangers. Teresa happened to attend a social event where my promise was flagrantly discarded, where

Isabelle's identity (and mine) were distributed cheaply like party favours. I was disgusted, furious, and worried. But even after that admission, their lips remained pursed.

Haltingly, unwillingly, they added, "There was someone else too." We looked at each other, uncomfortable and uncertain. At that moment, I was trying to triage the level of harm being caused by my ex-confidante. I thought to myself, *How many people have been outed and harmed by Flare? How much should I worry about Isabelle's exposure? Can I even tell Isabelle about this without causing her to spiral? Are there more people that I now need to protect from Flare's toxic behaviours?* Teresa and I stared at each other sadly. Neither of us wanted to participate in this guilty game. Three questions asked, three answers received: "What is their hair like? Any political beliefs? Do we both know them?" No name was said, but we both knew. It was the same person who had been outed to me months earlier. It was Lauren. Flare had repeatedly dispensed the most intimate secrets of at least three people. And now, I had used Lauren's secret as an investigatory tool to prevent further harm. I asked Teresa to avoid speaking to anyone else, and I resolved to take action. That's when I started proceedings against Flare.

Though at one point, Flare and I had been friends, I discovered over time that they had been spreading malicious lies about me. They fabricated events and twisted facts. Grains of truth passed through the rumour mill, and the grist's gist was that I was a horrible person. Through oversimplification, a presumption of guilt, and abstraction, claims about my sex life, general conduct, or political activities became absolute statements on my character. The following model of abstraction is drawn directly from YouTuber ContraPoint's 2020 video essay, *Canceling*.[1]

---

1. N. Wynn, *Canceling*, ContraPoint, January 2, 2020.

Many initial claims against me mutated memetically and lost so much of their context as to become unrecognizable via this mechanism:

1. Flare knows about my difficult relationship with a trans woman.
   - Oversimplification

2. Flare accuses me of abusing trans people.
   - Presumption of guilt

3. Everyone thinks I abuse trans people
   - Abstraction

4. Everyone thinks I'm an abusive transphobe.

Historically, I took few actions to protect my reputation and resigned myself to demonisation in public discourse. I hated looking at Facebook comment sections, where I'd find explicit public comments from Flare and Lauren about how stupid, toxic, and incompetent I was, and how little pushback they received for their invectives. The University is not a big university. Everyone knew everyone, at least within the "feminist" and Pride student circles. People who knew me, who had reason to dissent and defend me—were silent. It was Flare who had repeatedly broken trust, but I was seen as the outing transphobe. It was Flare who had knowingly and spuriously concocted a false narrative about my sexuality, but I was seen as the misogynist. It was Flare who harmed me—but instead, they perverted the narrative to claim full victimisation at my hands and paint me as a villain. The well was poisoned. Calling me a stupid slut or incompetent whore was *in vogue*. It didn't matter what I had to say: I was presumed guilty. So, I didn't lift a finger in retaliation. I didn't comment on the toxic and abusive ways in which my character was attacked. I only did what I believed was necessary to stop Flare from hurting other people. There were many people on the periphery who stood silent and apathetic despite knowing what was being said about me, and there were many more people who were oblivious to the whole context. Fair enough. But to those who participated in the abuse, to those apologists who stood by my abusers—and there are many—shame on you. Flare set the kindling, but *all of you* threw the torch.

Eventually, I tried to fight back, sitting down at my computer to begin my personal journey in SVP. At The University in 2018—as it remains *now* when I write in 2021—policies for student conduct were drowned in a cacophonous sea of documentation. Sure, once you picked out what was important, the reading was fairly short—but you had to read *everything* first to know what mattered. I trawled all of the pages and downloaded all of the policies. I found three major policies of interest (titles edited): "Safe Academic Environment," "Sexual Violence," and "Discrimination, Bullying, and Harassment." I felt that I had the strongest case under the latter, as the sexual rumours spread about me didn't count as a form of sexualized violence under The University's policy and were, therefore, "bullying" by default. As a fun aside about The University's policies—every type of student conduct is handled through "Safe Academic Environment," so you could theoretically undergo the same process for "misplacing library equipment" as for "sexual exploitation."

I started filling in the report form. I had two witnesses, Teresa and another acquaintance, who were willing to attest to the outing and sexual comments made about me. Teresa labelled Flare's patterns of behaviour as character assassination, which was affirming. At that time, I felt like I could trust Teresa as an ally, but they eventually broke their confidence, called out Flare for their actions, and threw me under the bus. *That* argument inevitably made its way to the rumour mill and infinitely exacerbated negative opinions toward me, but I resolved to press forward. My report was well-written, and my supporting documentation was organized. Its submission began a conduct investigation against Flare. The process was retraumatizing. Though Flare was aware of the allegations against them, including my witness statements, I couldn't say the same. Whereas my witnesses had degrees of separation from me, Flare called in direct personal contacts—their roommate and Lauren—as counter-witnesses. I was never told about the counter-allegations made against me in their testimonies. Well, that is, I was never made aware by The University. Flare's witnesses broke confidentiality and oozed more septic sludge about me into the rumour mill, which is how I heard about the general tone of their testimonies. It was something that one might expect from the deepest recesses of the internet. In essence, my abuser received more information during the process than I did.

Now, one might say that a discerning and impartial intellectual should take the time to illustrate the motivations of each party; the grains of truth in their testimonies; the nuance and criticisms against me that *were* fully valid—but my discernment is not impartial, and many of the arguments brought against me were so far removed from the truth as to be outright lies. I will *not* be a false centrist in my own story. Instead, I will momentarily stop and affirm to you that I am not perfect. If I don't explicitly mention my own fallibility, I may well be accused of *bias* in my personal narrative. I was flawed in my approaches at times and there are things that I would change about my behaviour back then, if I could. However, these failures were not for lack of trying. I made genuine, compassionate, and radical efforts to treat everyone well, even when they were viciously attacking me. I explicitly anonymized Lauren during the investigation process and did not provide their name, gender identity, or even pronouns; they were just "a person outed by Flare" in my testimony. Aside from (A) that one exchange with Teresa and (B) the reiteration of that conversation during proceedings against Flare, I never spoke to a soul—not even to Isabelle, my fiancée—regarding Lauren's trans identity. I learned better methods for apology. I stopped saying, "Well, actually ..." and instead took the high road in all of my dealings. This detail will be lost forever if I don't say it, because the narratives of my abusers caricatured me into an avant-garde Hitler. I played the games run by The University and my abusers on hard mode because my morals demanded it. I did *everything I could* to be kind. I understand the deep traumas that motivated Flare, Lauren, and Teresa. They deserve compassion for the abuses they lived through, and I hope that they acknowledge that their actions were genuinely harmful, *regardless* of their intentions or personal circumstances. I hope that they make progress in their journeys toward healing, and *if* they manage to get that far, I hope they forgive themselves for the hurt they caused in my life.

Many days after submitting my report, I received a decision letter. Eighty calendar days, or fifty-four working days, or 88% of an academic semester, had elapsed since I submitted the initial report. The letter was also retraumatizing and the decision included several "problematic" ideas both implicitly and explicitly:

- Isabelle's experiences and perspectives were considered irrelevant. For any of her experiences to matter, she would have to start her own complaint. Anything explicitly regarding Isabelle was thrown out before investigations even started. To that end, she is unmentioned throughout the entire decision letter.

- Because I worked at the Students' Union during the abuse, the letter abdicated responsibility for much of it and said, "Hey, not our fault that Students' Unions suck!"

- Pre-report, both of my witnesses agreed that Flare was spreading sexual rumours with malice; contrastingly, the decision letter said that my witnesses believed Flare was *without* malice. Their opinions served as "mitigating factors" that supported my abuser.

- Teresa couldn't remember specific dates for conversations held over the two years that had passed. Forgetting those dates represented "mitigating factors" in support of my abuser. Their testimony might have mattered more *if I could have just given them the fucking dates,* but I wasn't allowed to speak with my witnesses during the investigation. Flare didn't follow that rule.

The decision letter closes with some mildly Insulting statements and some real zingers. We'll build up to those spicy meatballs with some appetizers. The man behind the decision letter proposed a sit-down mediation: just me, the person who had abused me for over two years, and himself, the middle-aged white man I regularly had to work *against.* *Sounds great, dawg!* I exclaimed to myself, thinking back to all the times I'd butted heads with him *during* the investigation process as part of my Students' Union work. Oh, how I longed for arm's-length distance with my adjudicator! How my heart did trill at the very *idea* of impartial investigation! I think each participant would have preferred re-enacting *The Human Centipede.* In the words of Ariana Grande: "Thank u, next." There's a sweet bit of background information in the decision letter as well. He wrote one line stating that (paraphrased) "gossip has negative impacts on interpersonal relationships and can sometimes result in harassment allegations."

Thanks, Fuckface. I'm glad you thought my two years of hell could be distilled into its most essential form: gossip. I already had to file my experiences under "bullying" because my circumstances didn't count as sexualized violence under the policy; the semantics just served to further trivialize and infantilize my abuse to playground antics. How consistent of you to equate my abuser's actions with that of an ill-mannered and angry child. Truly, I now understand that gossip is counter-productive! What a *novel* piece of information! Fuckface basically said that my abuser didn't do any of it on purpose (paraphrased): "It seems plausible that a reasonable person would have understood [Flare's] comments to be injurious, but given the evidence presented, I do not believe that Flare spoke with any harmful intent."

Yeah, fucking right. As I alluded to earlier, both of my witnesses said they would explain Flare's long history of rumourmongering and character assassination—but apparently Fuckface didn't receive any information to indicate that they harmed me deliberately. Incredible. I thought that "the balance of probabilities" served as the evidentiary standard during the proceedings, but apparently, I needed to prove Flare's *mens rea* "beyond a reasonable doubt." Flare told people that the way I was treating Isabelle, my fiancée, was causing her to be depressed and suicidal. They told other people that I was a domestic abuser and that I would cruelly lambast people to instigate panic attacks. In Flare's subtler retaliations after receiving the decision letter, the stories about me must have spun beyond the realm of plausibility, for vilification had hit critical mass. Racist, homophobe, transphobe, bitch, slut, whore, abuser—apparently, you can affix those labels and their intrinsic meanings to anyone without "malice or intent to cause harm." Now, let us arrive at the final course. Dessert is at hand, children. Get your forks out. To top it all off, Fuckface decided to give *me* a little smack on the wrist in the decision letter. After trivializing my abuse as "gossip" and drooling about "why you shouldn't be a meanie with words," he included one last-minute jab, writing (paraphrased), "I hope that this process will be educational for both parties."

Eat shit, Fuckface. Though, I suppose it was a learning opportunity. I learned about the most vile, apathetic, and mindless traits of public discourse. I learned about how corrupt systems prey on their weakest members. Thanks for telling me to learn and grow from my abuse, you evil little imp of a man. Flare was to avoid referencing me online. They were also supposed to avoid personal or electronic contact. Both "sanctions" were equally applied to me.

There was an appeal available—I took it. I went straight to the university executive who was responsible for appeals, and I'm sure the fact that we had to publicly brawl over student affairs had no bearing on their impartiality at all. Surely. My notes were so specific, so beautifully detailed. I felt like it was my magnum opus. Every problem I had with the system was laid out in a numbered list with dates and times and supporting documentation. It was sent in an email, but I decided to be *extra*—there were bolded headers and concisely-worded critiques, and the whole email was easily digestible. If anyone actually wanted to improve SVP, my email would have been a great template for change.

I received a meeting time with the university executive. They admitted that they hadn't read my notes or email in their entirety due to their busy schedule and vacation. I said fine, no problem. I had paper copies, highlights, and an elevator pitch prepared. They nodded solemnly as I listed my issues. I took it on good faith that they were listening and that they would at least consider *some* of the changes that I recommended.

For example, I pointed out that the SVP listed a review date that was five years after the policy was introduced, contradicting a straightforward legal mandate in BC's *Sexual Violence and Misconduct Policy Act*, which stated that the SVP had to be reviewed at least every three years. The Vice President of Students assured me that it must have been a typo; *of course* they were going to comply with the required dates. This could have been a token change to increase faith in the system, to show some intent to meet their legal obligations, let alone enact more complicated or useful policy changes. It was a simple litmus test. I waited and watched while the legally required review date streamed past with no alterations to the documentation. The "typo" was not fixed. The policy was not changed. As of writing this, it's been three years since my meeting with the university executive. I was willing, tentatively, to give them the benefit of the doubt. Now I can clearly see that their promises and assurances meant nothing.

———————

Flare retaliated after the investigation. The abuse got sneakier and continued via word of mouth. "Feminist oral traditions," as a storytelling technique, do not leave incriminating paper trails. I once confided in Flare regarding my other harassers at The University, people who had seriously traumatized and threatened me: Flare sought them out deliberately and weaponized communal knowledge of my greatest weaknesses. Things got worse, but by then, I didn't have witnesses, friends, or peers for collaboration or protection. I was completely isolated. To this point, my story has been loosely chronological. Here, I'm going to take a different approach. These events occurred before, during, and after the investigation—while the severity of the claims made against me rose dramatically *after*, there was still abuse and harassment throughout.

Twice, my car was keyed in the Students' Union parking lot. Noting my ongoing harassment, my mentor voiced concerns over my safety and suggested that I get escorts to my car. It had been a week since an unknown student had told me to kill myself. I didn't know who they were and had no faith in The University's processes anymore. "Just another day on the job, right?" I joked weakly, looking down at my painfully interlocked hands and gritting my teeth against unshed tears. My mentor was concerned but didn't press the issue. The "safe walk" program was underpromoted—possibly discontinued or picked up by The University's security, which meant delays—not to mention, even if it were running as advertised, all of the student volunteers would have been drawn from a pool of people that hated me. That would have been *more* traumatizing than "assisted *seppuku*"[2] in the parking lot, so I declined. Instead, I went to The University security, hoping to catch the keying culprits. It turned out that my usual parking spot, and indeed, seemingly most of the parking lot, was not equipped with cameras. The security officers had patiently scrolled through footage of a few days, looking for my white car in its usual parking space—and found that it was never in frame. Even if there had been footage, proving the identity of the vandals would have been onerous.

Incidentally, once my term finished at the Students' Union, I let one of the new executives know that most of the parking lot—including the "safe" women's stalls—was not covered by the camera angles. I don't

---

2. Seppuku is a form of ritual suicide originating from Japan; historically, the person dying by suicide used a knife to cut their abdomen. The practice evolved to include an assistant or "second" that limited suffering by landing a clean killing blow on behalf of the dying person.

think they ever did anything about it. After the keying incident, I made small changes to protect myself. I stopped staying late at the Students' Union building so I wouldn't get isolated or cornered at night. I never wore headphones while walking so I could hear people approaching, and I always kept my hands free so I could defend myself. I was perpetually alert and vigilant. "At least if someone stabs me and I wind up in the hospital, someone might actually feel bad for me. Maybe they'd stop ... Or, hopefully, they'd stop. You can dream. It's okay to dream," I whisper-laugh-sobbed to myself.

It was hard to deal with the personal attacks too. Like many base-ment-dwelling troglodytes fascinated by video games and computerized pursuits, I had bad posture. I played far too much Minecraft one sum-mer, had a kinesiology professor remind me about the importance of posture the next, and resolved to become healthier by improving the set of my shoulders and neck. I never wore ballet flats prior to my job at the Students' Union, and I liked the way that it felt to glide smoothly and stride confidently with my head held high. I felt *nouveau riche*. I thought that's what people wanted out of politicians: confidence and poise. When the rumour mill told me that I "walked around like I owned the place" and that I was "full of myself," I stopped feeling good. An employee of the student-run coffee shop told me to "strut it, princess," and my posture fully deflated. I used to go to the coffee shop for tea or hot water, sometimes twice a day. When I started to hear "bitch" or "fuck *her*" whispered angrily behind the counter, or more frequently, when those same baristas would be on-campus and indiscreet about their conversations, I realized that I needed to start getting my hot water elsewhere. Otherwise, someone was going to *literally* spill the tea (on me). I had to pass directly in front of the coffee shop every time I went into the office. Simply coming into work started to become traumatizing.

This next example will seem like a minor event compared to keyed cars and misogynistic slurs, but it was honestly the moment that left me the most ... hollowed. There was a barbecue for students in my program. A few professors and students stood on the green, maybe twenty-five to thirty-five people in total, some chatting politely and others familiarly. It was a quaint little scene. I had been in my program for five years and knew the names of almost every attendant professor and student. There were people from the student newspaper there too, who wholly despised me. I gave them a wide berth. There were also a few executives from my program's student association; like most student groups, they were unfond of me due to changes I'd made to their funding process. My political efforts put me at odds with many of the more vocal or involved students on campus, and I had long since accepted that my quest for fiscal accountability would make me unpopular with groups that chafed under the additional oversight. It was unsurprising that none of them wanted to speak to me.

The professors were a slightly different story. For two years, I poured my entire life into the Students' Union, and for two years, my grades commensurately suffered. I wasn't a terrible student, but I wasn't great either. I wanted to do graduate studies of some kind, but I knew that I needed academic references to get in. As a quiet, unmemorable person in some classes and the Asker of Dumb Questions in others, I didn't think my odds were good. I also didn't participate in social climbing. The University had a culture that promoted schmoozing with professors and I didn't want to play that game. As a person in the outgroup, I quietly ruminated on the professionalism and long-term ramifications of a system that many larger universities had long since discouraged. Plus, I didn't think most "in the know" professors liked me after my speeches at the The University Senate. Politics had taken a toll there too.

I saw a professor whom I'd taken a class with more recently—he'd been remarkably supportive of my mental health—and he made a point to smile at me from among the gaggle of students that surrounded him. I smiled back and nodded congenially.

I had no connection with the other professors since more than three years had elapsed since my last class with them. There was no point in speaking with them; I wasn't in the honours track, didn't get A's, didn't have scholarships, couldn't do research, and maybe that meant there was no point in them speaking with me either. I tried smiling at a few of them I liked, anyways—just to see what five years in my program might net me. Eye contact, no smile. *Well, that's okay. I'm not entitled to their time,* I thought. That was the first moment I really believed I might be well and truly boned for getting into graduate school. My extracurricular activities were "straight fire," as the youths say—and my Students' Union work was fairly impressive—but the faculty of science, unlike the faculty of arts, was at *best* neutral about social justice initiatives. If I had been in the humanities, maybe a professor could have pitied me or appreciated the thousands of hours I'd put into activism and centred their reference around that. But I wasn't in the humanities.

The realization continued to dawn on me with a slow-burn revelatory dread: my five-year candle, both ends burnt at terrible cost, hadn't been enough. I wasn't going to get into graduate school. I could feel low-grade panic flickering in my rib cage and told myself to make one last-ditch effort. I tried to put on a radiant smile—a warm disposition, an unthreatening posture, every trick I'd ever read about being charismatic—and offered my cordial salutations to a group of unaffiliated students I'd spoken to at various points over the last five years. I received only a few strained smiles in return. *Alright, I'll try something a bit more ... restrained. Deferential. They'll like me more if I'm a bit muted.* I tried a polite smile and minuscule head nod at the remaining parties when they happened to glance my way. No eye contact, no smile. I would have sworn that some of those looks were of disdain. They spoke more quietly after. No one would talk to me. I grabbed a ginger ale, hoping I could pass off my excursion as a simple food run. Turning away quickly, I prayed that no one would see the tears spilling onto my cheeks as I hurried back to the Students' Union building. I called a suicide hotline that night.

I could tell you about the truly dark places my mind receded to over those two years. I could tell you about crying on the bus, about search histories plastered with hotlines and anti-suicide campaigns, about my twisted pride in knowing the best way to end my life. After all—some people had suicide attempts, but I, a scientist, would only have suicide *success*. I did learn something from those physics and chemistry classes, after all. I'll spare you the incredibly considerate, detailed, and morbid plans that would have neatly ended my life and tidily resolved every contingency. *That* would go a bit too far into macabre, irresponsible, or outright dangerous territory, I think. I was so deeply embittered and troubled by the abuse. I also *hated* that some people would take perverse pleasure in my death, so even that wouldn't be an escape. I thought about incriminating notes and firmly-worded manifestos, but I was dissatisfied by that, too, since it had limited potential for helping future victims. Even the best-written suicide note could only do so much, and it's not like notes deliver measurables for the dead. "No," I insisted while I wept, "I'll keep going for a bit more. Maybe I'll take a short break, maybe a month, once I'm finished my term. After all, if life can end at any time, why don't you at least try to enjoy the fruits of your labour, just for a bit? Death is a patient partner. He'll wait for you at the dance."

I had one final general meeting to close out my student government career. We expected about one-hundred students. The student newspaper readied video cameras for live streaming. They didn't notify us that they were planning on bringing in video equipment, so it was a mild surprise. Given their embarrassingly childish understandings of, well, *anything*, I had expected this issue to crop up someday. We politely asked them not to go forward with the recording, but my boss feebly capitulated. It was a tough situation, to be fair—you don't want to restrict *students* from watching a livestream—but I had reservations about those meetings being made public on Facebook, since anyone could view the proceedings. The practice of making the general meeting public did not track with my personal opinions on the role of student government and the importance of privacy in students managing their own affairs. Apparently, I was the only one who cared about how The University could use those public records against the Students' Union. God damn me and my desire to "act with principles." Oh well—maybe this time, the newspaper would finally capture the "corruption" and "house of cards" they'd always threatened and intimated about. After all, forcing people to be on camera without warning is *precisely* how to get quality content.

I saw Flare, my abuser, milling around the entrance for the general meeting. I asked them, politely, but firmly, for a private chat. They nervously peered around at their partner. Flare asked if they could bring a friend, clearly hoping for a legally protective witness as a second. I said, "No. It's a private discussion," and repressed a sour, tooth-cracking smile. Flare had obviously broken confidentiality with everyone in the posse to remind them that I was *literally Satan*, but they couldn't break their confidentiality directly in front of me. Flare couldn't just say, "I need someone to come with me because, otherwise, I'll be alone with this heinous, vicious, infamous, torturous abuser ... that I've been telling you so much about." They looked shifty. Pissed off. The two of us stepped aside. It was less than an hour before the meeting was meant to start. I said that they weren't supposed to have contact with me and therefore shouldn't be at the meeting. Flare said that they had a right to be there. I privately thought that their democratic right to be in physical attendance *should* be suspended in light of their abuses, if not their right to vote, but there wasn't an easy bureaucratic solution that preserved Flare's democratic rights as well as my right to relative safety or comfort. Damn my willingness to be fair. There was also very little to support me if I outright barred Flare from entry, and the newspaper would certainly invent outrageous scandal if I turned a student away. I conceded that they could come inside if they had permission from Fuckface.

Despite Fuckface never responding quickly to detailed inquiries, despite taking eighty days to resolve my complaint, despite being told that my investigation was put on hold during convocation ceremonies because the investigators were all *so* busy, it took less than twenty minutes for Flare to wrangle a response via email. *Good thing my abuser got faster service than I ever did,* I snarked inwardly. I took a minute to steel myself against the nausea and heart palpitations. I knew without opening it.

"... In regard to the restrictions on personal contact—you are both prohibited from communicating online or in person. There are no specific limitations on space or distance. Therefore, you are both entitled to attend this meeting, so long as you avoid interacting with each other directly. Please don't hesitate to reach out if you have any questions. Sincerely, Fuckface McGee."

I'm positive that Fuckface was gleeful over how much I would stumble and fall, having to sit in front of my abuser and defend the union. I'm sure he cackled and wrung his hands in exuberant anticipation or whatever the hell he normally did to celebrate the destruction of students. I confirmed with Flare that they were allowed entry.

There were four student executives to run the meeting, but I was practically the only one that spoke. Even when I saw my abusers whispering among themselves, even when I heard Flare's voice puppeteered through their lackeys, even when I felt nearly one hundred students glare at me and me alone, *the abusive son of a bitch they'd been warned about*, I stayed strong. It wasn't perfect, of course. *You* try running a meeting for one hundred people who think you're a subhuman monster. I did my best, with cameras pointed in my face, with multiple abusers sitting in the ranks, with no friends, no colleagues, no support of any kind but for the small and silent handful of people that knew and believed in me. I planned and executed. I narrowly dodged most of the moronic bylaw additions and skillfully outmaneuvered my less eloquent opponents. I tempered my rage and kept my face neutral. They recorded it. *That's* what it looks like when the system fails you, over and over again. *That's* what it looks like when you have an expressly pro-university student paper that sides with the university and not survivors. *That's* what it looks like when no one hears your story or gives a *fuck* about your struggle ... but you have to show up anyway.

———

After my term ended, I kept in touch with a small set of people and cut contact with everyone else. I blocked people on Facebook until I felt safe using it again. I changed my phone number after receiving some disturbing anonymous phone calls; I didn't know that they'd let you change it for free, if the change was for privacy or safety reasons. That's a fun fact, right? When a student followed me off the bus and watched me enter my house, I shrugged. I couldn't win in a "bureaucratic, administrative process" with "the balance of probabilities," so why would the police help me deal with creepy people? Maybe that passerby was just intrigued by the exotic lifestyle of someone entering a basement suite. Probably not. If I voiced my concerns to anyone about safety, it was likely to be viewed as paranoia. After all, my abusers had (rarely) touched me inappropriately. If my body was safe, then, supposedly, my mind was too. I wonder how many other women heard that bone-chilling thesis when accessing services and support groups.

My sense of self was substantively damaged by the abuse. Friends, lovers, and even some hotline operators took pains to soothe me. They reminded me that I was kind. That I was a good person and a hard worker. That I didn't deserve to die. The last one took a lot of convincing. My entire identity, my guiding principle—everything had always centred around "kindness"—but somehow, through abstraction and abuse, my peers at The University had twisted me into a modern monster. There are people that believe factually untrue but devastatingly malicious things about me. Someday, I will have to interact with some of those people again. The city The University is based in isn't *that* large. It was painful to see my true self—a (sexually reserved), kind, and competent woman who wanted to make things better—distorted and hideously misrepresented. At the end of it all, there was no debate regarding my ideas or critique of my politics. I was the Antichrist and there was nothing more to say.

Except for those few people I cherished from The University, I never want to speak to anyone else from there ever again. Some were wholly innocent in the affair, but *so many people* were willing to sit on the fence and watch me take blows that nearly ended my life or otherwise contribute passively to the immoral and infernal machinations of the rumour mill. Some detested me for political reasons and some abhorred me for sexual reasons, but I suppose I should remain grateful that the silent majority knew nothing of me at all. I'll close this section with one final anecdote.

At The University, Fuckface McGee got to decide if a given complaint counted as sexualized violence. Then, if he decided that it *was* sexualized violence, was it "violence" violence or just harassment? From there, if it was "violence" violence, he could then decide if the investigation merited an external (and actually impartial) investigator. That option was available if, and only if, Fuckface felt that the severity of the situation justified the cost of that third-party investigation. You can see why The University's sexual violence policy received the lowest known score on its OurTurn scorecard,[3] and why it was rightfully (though quietly) deemed "the worst policy in Canada" as a mark of infamy.

During my time as an executive on the the University's Students' Union, an external and impartial investigator was invoked at least once. I had been informally notified. Whoever that student was, whatever circumstances brought them into that investigation, it must have been unbelievably harrowing and damaging. I remember thinking about how broken the system was, about how I wanted to help, about how I—along with every complicit incompetent and obstinate dissident—had failed them. My heart shattered for that unknown student. No changes had been made to the policy or procedure. Nothing had been done. If anything, my conversations with The University's executives and the rapidly deteriorating political climate suggested that things would only get

---

3. Salvino, Caitlin, Kelsey Gilchrist, and Jade Cooligan Pang, "OurTurn: A National Action Plan to End Campus Sexual Violence," Montreal, QC: Student's Society of McGill University, October 2017.

worse. When I left the Students' Union, I was sure that the last true bastion of SVP activism at The University was lost with me. There was no successor to continue the work, no place to leave a repository of what I'd learned. I had walked the solitary road to hell, through fire and flame, on a path paved with good intentions, and still—I wasn't able to save myself. I wasn't able to save that student. I failed ... but I promised to try again. I carry their story as a reminder: I fight for those who come after me.

This story picks back up on page 272.

Revolutions

ADDY STRICKLAND

You ask me what a revolution looks like, and laugh when I tilt back my head and scream just for the sake of it—just for the sake of hearing my own voice louder than yesterday—"See? It's still here"—and we listen to the echoes. You ask me what a revolution looks like, and I take your hand in mine and refuse to let go (even though our palms are sweaty), and together we trace the canyons carved into our cheeks by tears. I think they've gotten deeper. You don't disagree. And together we tilt back our heads and scream just for the sake of it—just for the sake of hearing our voices dance along the canyon walls, and we dance with them—hand in hand, and listen to the echoes.[1]

---

1. This poem was first published online in *The Elevation Review.*

What We Built

The projects, policies, and organizations that emerged in the aftermath of protest or unrest.

The StFX Peer Support Program

Addy Strickland

The idea for a Peer Support Program on our campus began, for those involved, with an email from a member of the school's administration. The email stated that the sender had given an interview earlier in the day, talking about an alleged sexual assault, and that they expected it to air that evening. The following few sentences reassured students that all appropriate procedures had been initiated in accordance with the sexual violence policy, which was linked below, and then ... well, that was it.

I was with friends when the email notification popped up on my phone. We were all shocked that news of a sexual assault on campus was being delivered like this—with no context, and no resources. The next email, this time with resources, came three days later—on a Friday evening, when all of those resources were closed.

This was the first of many times that my peers and I became aware of the gaps in our campus mental health and sexual violence support services, and as it didn't seem like the university was planning to address the issue, we decided to do something about it ourselves. We recognized that many of the existing support services available to us were either insufficient or inaccessible, and that students were most likely to turn to their peers or to a trusted friend before they started the journey of seeking professional support. We also recognized that seeking support for the first time (or even for the thousandth time), could be an intimidating process, and that just the idea of picking up the phone to make an appointment was enough to push people into suffering in silence. Someone floated the idea of a peer-led mental health and sexual violence support service in our class group chat—somewhere students could go without having to make an appointment, where they could vent to a trained volunteer who knew what it was like to be in their shoes, and where they could learn about accessing professional supports in a relaxing, informal environment. A few months later in April 2018, a small group of us came together to further develop the idea, setting in motion plans for what would later become the StFX Peer Support Program (PSP).

The group shrank as some of us transferred schools or got pulled into other projects, but Emma and I pushed ahead with the task of bringing the PSP into existence. By the end of September, we had hired volunteers, registered as a society with our Students' Union, convinced the student newspaper to lend us an office space, secured funding through the support of the We Stand Together campaign, built a network of faculty and community supports, planned an intensive program of volunteer training, written an impressive mission statement, and were excited to start welcoming students into our space. There were only a few details left to figure out, including submitting a key request to the school so that Emma and I could stop passing the one key for the space back and forth. What we didn't expect was for that key request form to set us back more than a year.

Instead of a key, we got invited to a meeting with the Society Review Committee. No one had bothered to check whether we were eligible for society status when we registered the program, and we slipped past the radar. Given the nature of the PSP, there were worries about whether we'd be covered by the Students' Union insurance policy, or if the work we were doing was too much of a liability risk. Ultimately, what came out of that meeting was the decision that we didn't fit the criteria to be considered a student society, and that the PSP wasn't a service the Students' Union could maintain or oversee. In order to operate on campus, we needed an overriding body that could be responsible for the program's quality and sustainability—but it seemed like no one at the university was eager to tie themselves to our project. So instead of launching the PSP like we'd planned, we launched into a year-long battle to prove the worth of peer support on our campus.

It came as a shock to us and to our team of faculty and community supports that there were so many concerns about the risks of a peer support program. In setting up the PSP, we had researched dozens of similar programs at universities across Canada—many of which had been operating successfully for more than a decade. This wasn't a new, scary idea—it was a concept that had been proven to work time and time again. And yet, every time we stepped into a room with admin, we were met with a barrage of concerns—many of which we'd already addressed through our research prior to our intended launch. Some were reasonable: avoiding boundary issues while supporting others, handling the limits of confidentiality, a high prevalence of dual relationships on a tiny campus, screening volunteers, ensuring the program's sustainability ... To these, we had answers: volunteer training, ample opportunity to debrief, confidentiality agreements, volunteers working in pairs, vulnerable sector checks, grade and conduct screening through the Student Life office, extensive documentation, community partnerships, and months and months of research.

Other concerns, it became evident, had no basis, and were simply attempts to deter us from making the program a reality. Among the more memorable, "What if someone leaves your office, upset, and gets hit by a car? Who do you think their parents will sue?" We might have laughed, despite the gruesome scenario, had we not been so completely shocked by the fact that this was even a question.

In other meetings, we had to answer the same concerns over and over again, even after we'd presented the research and gone over our policies what seemed like a thousand times. As the only students in the room, it wasn't like we had a lot of power to call out the adults (and supposed "experts") for what they were doing. Thankfully, however, we'd planned for that too. In the earliest stages of the PSP, we built a network of supports made up of our favourite professors, as well as representatives from the Antigonish Women's Resource Centre and StFX's own Diversity Engagement Centre. We never showed up to a meeting alone, and the people on our team were rockstars at calling out admin when we felt that we couldn't. I remember one meeting in particular when we were being asked, once again, to repeat information we'd given dozens of times, and one of our faculty supports got so frustrated that they actually started yelling—saying exactly what Emma and I were feeling, which is certainly something the two of us would have gotten in trouble for. Another faculty support, sitting next to them, had to swat their arm and remind them to lower their voice.

The team we built was also a vital part of maintaining our own mental health and sanity throughout the process. Frequently, we'd leave those meetings with admin and barricade ourselves in the office of whoever worked closest—venting and ranting about whatever foolish things had been said and sharing all the sarcastic things we wished we could have said in response. We'd host "pre-meeting meetings" to troubleshoot and prepare, and then schedule follow ups for a few days later. I can't tell you how grateful we were to have people in our corner willing to dedicate so much time and energy to a project that faced obstacle after obstacle. With the support of this network, we showed up to every meeting—over-prepared and over-researched—for months, and we never showed up alone. Ultimately, I believe that those are the two biggest reasons behind our eventual success.

In March 2019, after months of these meetings with admin, it was decided that maybe the PSP would fit best under the Students' Union after all—but we'd have to get the service approved by Council. It took until July 21 to get an audience, and Emma and I spent hours sitting at my kitchen table preparing our presentation. Just in case, we also scoured my front lawn for four-leaf clovers—we were well prepared, but, given our history, we wanted as much luck as we could get. You can probably guess what happened next. We pitched the program to Council and were yet again slammed with a wall of concerns we'd already worked to address. The motion to launch the Peer Support Program failed 1-4-2 because the councillors didn't think we had enough information (yes, you can read that with an eye roll).

We were upset, of course, but you've probably figured out by now that we aren't the kind of people who give up easily. Emma had just started a term as Vice President Academic of the Students' Union—a full-time commitment—so we brought in our friend Riley to help us carry on the fight. For the next month, the three of us compiled every piece of research we'd done, all our documentation, our training outlines, our resource lists, and the letters from our faculty and community supports into an eighty-page council package. We most certainly could have been more concise, but they said they wanted more information—so that's what they got.

Emma and Riley presented at council again on August 25 and succeeded in passing a motion to launch the PSP as a one-year pilot. If after a year we could prove that the program was "successful" (a term we were all hesitant to quantify, given the nature of the work), we could present the results to Council for another vote, and hopefully be incorporated as a permanent service under the Students' Union. It was too late for us to prepare for a September opening, but when classes started a few weeks later, Riley and I jumped headfirst into making sure everything would be ready to launch at the start of the winter semester—hiring, training, and screening volunteers, and setting up our new office space.

When we launched in January, we had a team of thirty highly-trained, committed, and compassionate volunteers. Our office was cozy and welcoming—filled with twinkle-lights, cute pillows, colouring books, and of course a whole wall of resources from local and on-campus support services. What was most exciting was that people were finally *using* the space. Students were coming in to check out the office and to chat with our volunteers about school stress, relationship issues, and how to seek professional support. There wasn't a lineup to access our services, but as a new organization, that isn't what we expected. Success, for us, would have meant that one person came in and found the resources they needed. To have a dozen people walk through the door each month was huge. The question we had tried to answer with research at the beginning of the process, "Will students use this service?" was being proven in practice.

Our pilot came to an abrupt end in March 2020 with the start of the COVID-19 pandemic. Not knowing when we'd have another chance to do so, we opted to present our pilot findings to Council as soon as we could, on March 22. Campus had shut down a week earlier, so we presented virtually—detailing what our two-and-a-half month pilot had looked like, going through all our safety and confidentiality procedures one more time, offering an idea of what the future of the program might look like, and asking both for a permanent place with the Students' Union as well as a small amount of funding to help make the program sustainable. I think we all held our breath as the vote was called and councilors started to chime in; the relief that came when we hit quorum was monumental—almost two years of work, we finally had confirmation that we wouldn't have to fight for the PSP any longer, that we had, at long last, a permanent place on the StFX campus. The motion passed 8-0-0.

With too many residual nerves to sit through the rest of Council, Riley and I met outside my apartment to debrief, and to walk off our abundance of energy (Emma, sadly, as Vice President Academic, had to stay for the rest of the meeting). The majority of the student body had already left to go home after the university shut down, and it was late enough in the evening that the streets were empty. We power-walked down Main Street and the length of the Antigonish Landing, shouting with excitement and listening to our relief as it echoed back to us. FINALLY! WE DID IT!!

Throughout the 2020-2021 school year, the PSP was a safe space that students could go to learn about the resources available to them and to talk to trained student volunteers who knew what it was like to be in their shoes. I took on the role of coordinator alongside another student we hired over the summer and was so excited to see things finally going smoothly. We had even more visitors than in our pilot months and received nothing but positive feedback about their experiences accessing the service. Our volunteers, too, shared how grateful they were to have gone through our training process, often expressing how useful the skills and knowledge they gained were in supporting their friends and family outside of the PSP, and in understanding and managing their own mental health. This is something we prioritized from the very beginning, because even if the program had failed, having thirty individuals on campus able to support their own mental health and that of those around them would always be beneficial.

In May 2021, I passed the baton to our incoming team of program coordinators, and I couldn't have been more proud of where the program ended up. Back in 2017, when that initial email about a sexual assault case popped into our inboxes I know so many people who would have benefitted from having peer support as an option. Knowing that it will be for every StFX student moving forward means the world.

The StFX Peer Support Program: A Second Perspective

RILEY WOLFE

My role as co-coordinator of the StFX Peer Support Program (PSP) came about in a roundabout way. It was initially in the class group chat when someone floated the idea of a peer support program, but, at the time, I was working through my own trauma related to sexualized violence, and I didn't have the energy to be involved. Instead, I watched from the sidelines, cheering Addy and Emma on as they pulled the PSP together and experienced various bureaucratic frustrations. Addy and I used to meet before class, and it seemed like every week she had a new story about endless meetings with admin, ridiculous questions she'd received, and new roadblocks. She was constantly researching peer support and emailing contacts across Canada. For the first ten months, I was a spectator, but my involvement in the PSP changed with the Students' Union election in 2019.

Emma ran for Vice President Academic and won. This meant she could no longer be a PSP co-coordinator, not only because it would be against the Students' Union rules, but because she would have a ton on her plate. I was talking to Addy about the future of the PSP shortly after the admin decided that it would work better as a Students' Union service. Addy asked what I thought about coming on board as the new co-coordinator.

Initially, I thought I would be too busy in the last year of my undergrad to help run a brand-new program. I went home to think about it. I thought about how personal the PSP was to me. After I was sexually assaulted in the first weeks of my undergrad, I felt completely alone. As an out-of-province student, I had no support system in Nova Scotia, and looking for professional support felt like an insurmountable task when there were days that I struggled to get out of bed. But if there had been a group of students who I could have talked to about getting help on campus in a building I had to visit regularly anyway? That would have been doable. The feeling of isolation that comes with mental health struggles was something I was very familiar with. I knew I wasn't the only one to feel that way, and that the PSP could be the intermediary between students and the supports that were so needed. When I eventually sought professional help, through therapy, I also realized that participating in sexualized violence prevention activism was an empowering way for me to deal with my trauma. I went to protests and town halls and sometimes I spoke, but I also felt that these protests were not enough if nothing came out of them, and here was an opportunity to do something concrete. I had been speaking with Addy about the future of PSP, and she asked me to consider becoming a PSP co-coordinator. To me, it was an opportunity to channel all my passion for sexualized violence prevention into something tangible, and so, I accepted.

The first of my responsibilities was to help prepare for the second presentation to the Students' Union to convince them to accept PSP as a service under their umbrella. I had attended the first presentation to support Addy and Emma, and sitting quietly on the sidelines was torture as I listened to councilors question their knowledge and preparedness. As we prepared for the second presentation, we decided to overload them with information. If they questioned the dedication of our community and faculty supports? We'd show them our collected signed letters of intent. If they questioned the usefulness and viability of a PSP program? We'd compile even more research on similar programs in Canada. If they were worried about the liability of the program? We'd further highlight that the university administration, Students' Union lawyers, and insurance company had all given us the green light.

Addy was away on the day of the presentation, so Emma and I presented for the second time and proposed a pilot year for the PSP. Staying calm during the presentation and question period was difficult. It felt like we couldn't get some of the councilors to believe in the program, even with all the evidence we came with. It was so ridiculously difficult to get them to even give us a chance. When they finally voted to give us a pilot year, it was with the understanding that we would technically be a service under the Students' Union, but that we would have to fund our own operating budget and basically run the program autonomously.

Presenting in late August, we didn't have much time to shift into high gear to get the program ready to interview and train volunteers in September. Out of everything I was involved with in the year I was a co-coordinator, hosting the training with the volunteers was the best part. After selecting our volunteers, we set up over thirty-five hours of training over the course of the fall term. Since Addy had done most of the training the year before, I was the one who attended all the training sessions this time around. After facing so much opposition from the councilors on the Students' Union, it felt so good to be around more than twenty people who cared enough about the PSP to commit so much of their free time to it. As we got to know each other better, I learned about the many personal reasons volunteers felt passionate about the PSP, from personal mental health struggles, to experiences with friends and family, to their desire to support others.

Reflecting on the training now, I realize how important that time with the other volunteers was for keeping up my energy and motivation to continue pushing for the PSP. Being around other people who cared as much as I did about the mental health of students and supporting survivors made all the struggles behind making the PSP a reality worth it. For me, the power in the PSP lay in bringing a group of people together to focus our energy and passion into a program that had so much potential to help students. Having a space to share that energy and passion and create something with it was the most rewarding thing I did as an undergraduate student.

One of the most powerful moments was when we asked volunteers to reflect on the training after we had completed it. We asked which of the many activities had been their favorite. Every single one of the volunteers listed an activity where we explored our boundaries and talked about how to set them. Volunteers spoke about how this activity made them feel more confident about working for the PSP and how they intended to bring what they learned into their personal lives. The PSP training was not only essential for the success of the program, but it had become personally valuable for our volunteers. The time we had spent together made me feel hopeful.

After we launched the PSP in January 2020, we received positive feedback from volunteers, people who accessed the program, and people who dropped by just to visit. Although it was difficult to launch in the middle of the year, and we knew it took time to build trust in a new program, we were pleased with the results. The COVID-19 pandemic threw a wrench in our plans to end the year on a high note, but we still had to present our pilot year to the Students' Union for full approval. Throughout the year, we spoke with councilors about the PSP and worked to get them to see its potential. We felt more confident, but still nervous, going into this virtual presentation. After we talked about what we had done in the pilot year, from interviewing prospective volunteers, to training, to launching, to closing unexpectedly, we were once again asked questions about liability and our qualifications. Councilors who had previously expressed their support were suddenly opposed to our existence.

Luckily, after the resistance we faced in the past summer, we had anticipated that we needed an airtight presentation and strong justifications as to why the program needed to continue. We gathered quotes from our volunteers and supporters and emphasized our successes. We also reinforced that supporting the program would be a way for the Students' Union to fulfill their promise to prioritize student mental health. Addy and I had worked throughout the year to build relationships with councilors and it seemed we finally may have done enough.

My heart pounded as the vote was called. Finally, after a year of uncertainty and answering the same set of questions yet again, our motion to become a permanent service passed! Addy and I immediately met to go for a walk and debrief about the presentation. Even though we had won, I still felt so angry. It was as if all the emotions about how difficult it was to get support for the PSP emerged all at once. We walked for kilometers down an eerily deserted main street and then on a walking path in the woods, both celebrating our success and raging about all the people who opposed us. It felt like instead of working with us to make the PSP a success and helping us find solutions to their concerns, the university admin and Students' Union had looked for reasons to prevent the program from happening. Poor mental health and sexualized violence are two of the most common issues for university students, so you would think that there would be support for initiatives to address them.

After I graduated in May 2020, I left the PSP in the capable hands of Addy and a new co-coordinator. I watched as the PSP grew over the course of the 2020-2021 academic year, even in the middle of COVID-19. When I think about my time as a PSP co-coordinator, my mind often lingers on the opposition we faced, and it still makes me mad. Then I think that for all the people who opposed us, there were so many who supported us: our faculty advisors listened to us rant and helped us talk through our plans; our volunteers invested their time in the program and dedicated themselves to its success and the people who visited the PSP and found a service that helped them. Addy and I supported each other throughout that pilot year, and there is no way I could have joined the PSP or made it through the year without her. The hoops we had to jump through were high, but we were able to bring together a wide range of individuals to support a common cause.

Sometimes I can't believe we persevered to make the PSP a reality, but I'm so glad we did. For me, helping build a program that would have helped me when I was struggling was a healing experience, and seeing it continue to grow and succeed from a distance reminds me of two things. First, that sexualized violence prevention work is almost always harder than it should be, and second, that there are so many people out there who care about and are committed to making change. When we come together, we make room for so many new possibilities.

Teal Ribbon Campaign

Shelby Miller

My name is Shelby Miller, and alongside my friend Kyra Brett, I somewhat unintentionally started an almost-national teal ribbon campaign. It all started very small, with a Facebook group known as X-Resist. Following a great injustice that happened on the StFX campus, uproar from students resulted in the group's creation as a space for students to organize and show  the university that this was a serious issue and that they had royally messed up, to put it lightly. The group also wanted to show support to a survivor whose case was so greatly mishandled by the university. A young female student had been sexually assaulted, action had been taken, and her perpetrator had been suspended from campus for the following academic year. When the woman showed up on campus in the fall, her perpetrator was there, and the university had failed to communicate that they had changed their decision. As previous StFX students who had many friends participating in the X-Resist movement, Kyra and I wanted to participate but felt somewhat powerless being at two different universities in different parts of the province. We learned that X-Resist members found out that teal was the colour in support of sexual assault awareness and began making ribbons to hand out on campus. This was how Kyra and I could help: we could make ribbons on our campuses and hand them out. While the sexual assault in question did not happen at Dalhousie or Mount Saint Vincent, other sexual assaults had, and students were upset about those too. This was not just a StFX issue, it was, and still is, a *university* issue. Some students from each school would likely want to show their support.

I reached out to the members of X-Resist and asked if they were okay with the idea of me making another Facebook group as a way to get students from other campuses involved. The members agreed this would be fantastic, and I created the group "I'm With Her." I made an initial post explaining the situation that happened at StFX, and that we would like to make and wear teal ribbons in solidarity with the students there and the survivor. The group started in mid-October 2018 with thirty-three members. When Kyra and I woke up the next morning, there were thirteen hundred, and the number continued to grow. Within a week, we had over two-thousand. We had told the initial thirty-three members to add their friends, and the group took off. This showed me just how important of an issue this was, as so many students from so many different schools wanted to participate and show their support.

Many people who were not in the Facebook group also participated, whether by wearing a ribbon, donating money, or simply asking about a ribbon that someone else was wearing. The word continued to spread. At one point, a junior-high teacher from Newfoundland reached out and asked if this was something she could address with her class and have them wear ribbons as well. A professor at the University of Toronto reached out and disclosed that he had been a professor at StFX and wanted to help in any way he could. Of course, these educators were met with enthusiasm as we explained that this was an issue everywhere, and the more people involved, the better. I even had a nurse from Oklahoma reach out to say she had been added to the group and did not have any ribbons but that she and her coworkers were wearing teal scrubs. I couldn't believe how many schools and people this initially small Facebook group had reached in such a short period of time. Every university in Nova Scotia participated, as well as many schools in each of the other Atlantic provinces. Before the day that the ribbons were set to be distributed and worn as a collective, at least one school in Quebec also joined, handing out ribbons in their meal hall. Then, a few different schools in Ontario popped up to participate as well, including Ryerson[1] and multiple University of Toronto campuses. It was honestly very exciting to see this come together in such an organized way. People from each school were using the Facebook group to organize when to make and hand out ribbons at each of their campuses. Individuals who were not students but wanted to show their support reached out to find out where they could get ribbons as well.

We decided that the ribbons would be worn everywhere on October 18, 2018, in solidarity with the survivor who was forced to leave StFX. As exciting and as organized as everything became in such a short amount of time, it was also overwhelming. People began reaching out to me personally to say thank you for doing this, that it needed to be done, that they had a story, and that they were finally feeling heard. Of course, I appreciated hearing this, that what we were doing and working hard at was helping people feel heard and that it was important to them. This was the goal; however, it was hard to hear people's stories of sexual assault over and over. Some people divulged their personal stories in detail, and some just shared that they had a story of their own. I was grateful that

---

1. Now Toronto Metropolitan University.

these individuals felt I was a safe space to share their tale with, because I was. Everyone deserves to have the right to share. However, I wish I had been more prepared to hear these things, to know that there would be so many, and that I would have to bear witness to them all. I'm glad these people shared, and that they felt safe enough to do so. I wouldn't change anything about that, but I wish I had been given a heads-up that this is what would follow my involvement in the campaign. I would have done more self care or made it more evident that the entire group was a safe space and that it wasn't just me they could share with. Eventually, some people did begin to use the group as a safe space to tell their stories and their work surrounding their experiences, and the outpouring of support for these people was another incredible result of the teal ribbon campaign.

Another unexpected outcome was that the campaign started to gain media attention. There were articles in the paper, radio interviews, television spots ... all of which I felt very unprepared to participate in. I felt like I didn't deserve to be on television or the radio just for making some ribbons and starting the group that everyone else was participating in. However, it was Kyra and me in the administrator roles of the Facebook group, so we were the ones they called to speak to. It just so happened that recreational marijuana became legal in Canada the day before we were planning to wear the ribbons, but our story still got airtime on the same day.

The day to wear the ribbons finally came, and the outpouring of support was absolutely amazing across all campuses. People posted pictures of themselves wearing the ribbons, explained where to find them on each campus, and someone posted a thank you on behalf of the survivor whose story sparked the campaign. On my own campus, which is quite small, there were multiple places to pick up ribbons for those that had yet to hear about the campaign. So many people across campus had ribbons on their coats, shirts, hats, backpacks, and anywhere they could stick them. Professors and students were both wearing them, and those who did not have them were asking other students what they were for before getting their own. I don't know what the other campuses were like, but I imagine it was a similar atmosphere to Mount Saint Vincent University, with similar photos coming to the Facebook group from each campus. At the end of the day, Kyra and I asked that people keep their ribbons on their backpacks or their coats to continue to show support for sexual assault awareness and as a symbol that each person with a ribbon is a safe person to reach out to. At MSVU, people took this message seriously, and I saw many backpacks and jackets with ribbons on them throughout the year.

I also attempted to collect resources for students at different universities in Nova Scotia. This proved to be quite difficult, and took a lot of energy out of me due to the fact that, again, many people were contacting me about the resources. I became quite overwhelmed. I have had to take a break from moving forward with this for the time being in the interest of self-care.

Overall, I would not change how the campaign was handled or the outcome, as I believe it helped a lot of people feel heard and supported. People still share articles and news surrounding sexual assault awareness in the Facebook group, nearly three years later. As a result of the teal ribbon campaign and the efforts at StFX, universities across Nova Scotia were asked to revise and revisit their campus sexual assault policies. The perpetrator at StFX was asked to leave campus, and the survivor was able to reach out and share how much this movement meant to her and her family in the difficult time they had to endure. I hope that in the future, universities will continue to adjust their policies around sexual assault and work to make their campuses safer places for students.

OurTurn: A National Action Plan to End Campus Sexual Violence

Caitlin Salvino

Sitting down to write this piece on the OurTurn National Action Plan to End Campus Sexual Violence wasn't easy. I struggled to come up with the words to describe or capture the whirlwind that was OurTurn. The report was produced over the course of six months and has subsequently taken up the past five years of my life. There were countless individuals involved in shaping the action plan, and I would be remiss not to acknowledge the collective effort that went into this project. In this piece, I will provide a snippet of my experiences co-developing OurTurn and reflect on this period that resulted in the creation of a tool that continues to be used across the country five years later.

Returning to where our story left off earlier in this book, our groups of activists at Carleton University had just been told by the Director of Student Affairs that "at this time, there is no appetite among administration to reform the policy." This rejection marked the end of five months of student-led efforts to reform Carleton's Sexual Violence Policy. We had hit a wall. Working within institutional channels to address campus sexual violence was no longer a viable option.

After leaving that meeting, we were in shock. It was almost inconceivable that everything we had done over the past six months could come to such an abrupt end. We had mobilised the student community to demand reforms to a deeply flawed sexual violence policy and felt as if more needed to be done to oppose such a callous dismissal of student voices. We committed to continuing this work, and in March 2017, we started the next phase of our efforts.

It began as a Carleton-specific project. We partnered with Students' Unions and started to design an action plan that students could use to prevent and respond to sexual violence in a holistic manner. The plan would be holistic and encapsulated three branches: prevention, support, and advocacy. In preparing to make this action plan we created task forces, ran a survey, held consultations, and fully committed to creating a step-by-step plan that could be used in the coming years to challenge sexual violence and administrative apathy on our campus.

In June, however, the project began to shift. This was based on two factors. First, we had the idea to create an OurTurn policy scorecard. This was part of our work developing the advocacy branch, a project I was leading at the time. We had been in the process of reading every campus sexual violence policy across Canada to identify best practices to include in our action plan, and as we were examining these policies, we were surprised by the vast differences in procedures and protections for survivors that they included. It was apparent to us that a survivor of sexual violence could seek out processes to report the harm they experienced (formally or informally) and that they would have vastly different experiences based on their campus. This included campuses in the same provinces, falling under the same provincial legal and regulatory regimes.

In light of this concerning discrepancy between the policies and the lack of a clear guidance from the provincial governments as to what should be expected, we decided to design our own set of standards—from the student survivor perspective and based on an intersectional feminist approach.

Over a period of several weeks, we worked to construct a set of standards that student survivors pursuing a complaint process would need. We are often asked how we came up with our forty-five different criteria. The standards were developed through a combination of factors. For some, we examined protections for survivors in the criminal justice system. Even though the existing criminal justice system is documented as an extremely hostile environment for survivors of sexual violence, we found that even the few basic protections for survivors in courts were not being met by these sexual violence policies. This included, for example, protections from face-to-face encounters[1] and "rape-shield" protections regarding inappropriate questioning.[2] For other standards, it was based on extensive consultation with survivors, including those who had undergone or were undergoing complaint processes. For example, our standard regarding "clearly defined timelines" was developed after a survivor shared with us her multi-year ongoing sexual violence complaint process against a professor that extended beyond her graduation date. Our standard that a policy should "not include the ability to suspend a complaint if the complainant also seeks recourse from the criminal justice system" was included after being told by a survivor that they were barred from filing a complaint with the institution because they were also pursuing a criminal complaint. Many of our standards

---

1. Under the criminal law, survivors have access to a screen or CCTV participation in sexual assault trials. See section 486.2 of the Criminal Code.

2. For an critical analysis of the history and existing criminal law framework for "rape shield" protections, see Sheehy, Elizabeth A. *Sexual Assault in Canada: Law, Legal Practice, and Women's Activism.* Open Access E-Books. Ottawa Ont: University of Ottawa Press, 2012.

were also informed by extensive comparative and intersectional feminist research. For example, our inclusion of a requirement that "stealthing"[3] be explicitly mentioned is based on a recently published academic article on the harm-associated with this form of sexual violence that is systemically dismissed.[4] We ended up with a set of forty-five criteria on a hundred-point scale to evaluate whether existing campus sexual violence policies met survivor-centric standards set by students.

Once the action plan had been developed, the project shifted from local to national. This was in part influenced by our connections to other student leaders and student survivors across the country.[5] As we exchanged stories, it was apparent to us that the challenges we were facing at Carleton were not unique. Students on every campus we spoke to shared similar challenges of institutional apathy, dismissal, gaslighting and re-traumatisation in relation to sexual violence. Although each campus had their own unique and context-specific challenges, we all shared a common experience. Connecting with these other students had a profound impact on us. After spending six months at Carleton feeling so extremely isolated, it was incredibly meaningful and powerful to connect with other students and hear their stories. It was these shared experiences and the ensuing feeling of solidarity that inspired our decision to shift the action plan into a national project.

---

3. The term "stealthing" refers to non-consensual condom removal during sexual intercourse. Stealthing "exposes victims to physical risks of pregnancy and disease," and has been described by survivors as a "disempowering [and] demeaning violation of a sexual agreement." Alexandra Brodsky, "Rape-Adjacent: Imagining Legal Responses to Nonconsensual Condom Removal" (2017) 32:2 Columbia J Gender & Law 183 at 183, 185, 186.

4. Brodsky, Alexandra. "'Rape-Adjacent': Imagining Legal Responses to Non-consensual Condom Removal," *Columbia Journal of Gender and Law,* 32, no. 2 (2017).

5. It should be noted that these categories can also intersect.

As a result of this decision, the action plan project moved to McGill University and the Student's Society of McGill University (SSMU). Although the project was not led by the student union and was completely unfunded, the executive members at SSMU offered in-kind graphic design, translation, and web hosting services. In addition to our move to Montreal, we began travelling across the country and setting up impromptu meetings with student groups at various campuses. This included taking weekend road trips across Ontario to Kingston, Toronto, London, and others. As the only unemployed member of the writing team, I travelled outside of Ontario and across the country meeting with even more students' groups. To reiterate, the OurTurn project was completely un-funded, and our work, including travel, was unpaid. I used existing Aeroplan points I had accumulated for a graduation trip to cover a flight to Winnipeg, where in a period of two days I visited three different campuses and held meetings with their Students' Unions. I received a student fellowship award that included a funded trip to speak at a conference in Halifax, and I used this opportunity to continue our work on the action plan as well. I met with five student groups across multiple campuses in Nova Scotia to discuss the OurTurn project. I also spent personal funds to extend this trip to include a flight to Newfoundland and Labrador to meet with student leaders at Memorial University and hear their stories.

This cross-Canada adventure was possible largely because of the kindness of people I met along this journey. In Winnipeg, I slept on my colleague's sister's couch, and in Halifax I stayed in the dorm room of a (now) dear friend at Dalhousie University. These in-person meetings were crucial to the success of OurTurn, as we were able to consider the individual campus contexts and needs as we were drafting the action plan. We were also able to develop personal relationships with students across the country, many of whom we continue to maintain friendships with today.

At this point, the action plan had reached its final form. As such, student groups and Students' Unions were asked to sign on to the action plan and work in collaboration with us to grade their campus sexual violence policies. The process of signing onto the action plan consisted of much more than solely grading the policy and advocating for reforms; however, the policy scorecard and the advocacy piece of the action plan were what I was most heavily involved in, so I will focus my energy here.[6] In terms of policy grading, we ended up partnering with a total of twenty Students' Unions and groups from fourteen post-secondary institutions.[7] These campuses also ranged in jurisdiction, spanning eight provinces.

Working closely with so many people, we decided that we didn't want to grade the policies unilaterally. We wanted the students who studied at any given campus to grade their own sexual violence policies in partnership with us. We wanted them to work with us. This strategy was adopted for a few reasons, including the approach we wanted to take with the action plan in general. We intended for OurTurn to be an adaptable action plan that could be adjusted based on the needs of any specific campus community. It was important that all aspects of the action plan, including the policy grading, was a grassroots method rather than a top-down process. Thus, for OurTurn, we worked alongside stu-

---

6. During this period in addition to leading the advocacy branch, I was co-leading the overall drafting of the action plan.

7. Salvino, Caitlin, Kelsey Gilchrist, and Jade Cooligan Pang, "OurTurn: A National Action Plan to End Campus Sexual Violence," Montreal, QC: Student's Society of McGill University, October 2017

dent groups to grade their own policies, and every grading was approved by the students who were affected by the provisions.

I also want to include a note about adopting an intersectional feminist analysis and approach. With the OurTurn report and the subsequent organization we founded, now known as Students for Consent Culture Canada (SFCC), we are always learning and improving our intersectional practice. It is important to us that we are intentional with our intersectional practice and move beyond statements to specific actions. In the OurTurn One Year Later Report,[8] we outlined a set of examples of how we sought to incorporate an intersectional approach in our work. We also used an intersectional feminist approach throughout the original OurTurn report. In the early stages of reaching out to individuals to be on our research team, this included holding specific consultations in partnership with the Carleton service centres,[9] defining the concept of intersectionality as written by Kimberlé Crenshaw in our report, including a specific analysis of the additional impacts of sexual violence on survivors from marginalised groups, and including an expectation that intersectionality is mentioned in campus sexual violence policies. We always aimed to be open to feedback while drafting the report as well. For example, we were asked by Indigenous women at a consultation to not only mention the higher rates of violence that Indigenous women and Two-Spirit individuals in Canada face, but also to link it to the

8. Salvino, Caitlin and Connor Spencer, "OurTurn: One Year Later Report," Montreal, QC: Concordia Student's Union, April 2019.

9. The Carleton Service Centres were: The Womyn's Centre (now called the Womxn's Learning, Advocacy, and Support Centre); the Gender and Sexuality Resource Centre CUSA Service Centre; Carleton Disability Awareness CUSA Service Centre; Race, Ethnicity and Culture Hall CUSA Service Centre; International Students' Centre; and the Mawandoseg Centre.

ongoing crisis of Missing and Murdered Indigenous Women and Girls. Following the publication of the report, our organization has continued to improve our intersectional practices and centre the voices of the most marginalized survivors.

The OurTurn National Action Plan was officially released on October 17, 2017. The bilingual action plan was signed by twenty Students' Unions across the country and sought to initiate movements by encouraging Students' Unions to create their own taskforces, run surveys, and implement the twenty recommendations at the grassroots level—all with the goal of reducing harm on our campuses. The OurTurn National Action Plan was also the first comprehensive review of over sixty campus sexual violence policies, which was complimented by the sexual violence policy scorecard. Working alongside student union partners, we used the scorecard to evaluate fourteen post-secondary institutions across Canada with a national average grade of C- (61%).[10]

The success and the reach of the action plan was beyond what we could have ever imagined. In the year that followed the publication of the action plan, we reached over forty student groups from across eight provinces, representing 650,000 students who signed and/or used the OurTurn National Action Plan to support their anti-sexual violence work.[11] The action plan was raised on several

---

10. Salvino, Caitlin, Kelsey Gilchrist, and Jade Cooligan Pang, "OurTurn: A National Action Plan to End Campus Sexual Violence," Montreal, QC: Student's Society of McGill University, October 2017, 19-22.

11. For a full list of signatories to the action plan, see Caitlin Salvino, Kelsey Gilchrist, and Jade Cooligan Pang, "OurTurn: A National Action Plan to End Campus Sexual Violence," Montreal, QC: Student's Society of McGill University, October 2017, 14-15.

occasions in the House of Commons, and in 2018,

funding to address campus sexual violence was included in the federal budget.[12] We were invited to consult with five provincial governments on their campus sexual violence legislation.[13] We were covered or invited to comment in over 115 news articles on the subject of campus sexual violence.[14] And perhaps most meaningfully, we connected with hundreds of students and survivors across the country to hear their stories and offer support. It was a whirlwind of a year that I know was both exhausting and deeply inspiring for many of us.

12. Lum, Zi-Ann. "Canadian Universities To Face Funding Cuts If They Fail To Address Campus Sexual Assaults." *Huffington Post,* February 28, 2018.

13. Salvino, Caitlin and Connor Spencer, "OurTurn: One Year Later Report," Montreal, QC: Concordia Student's Union, April 2019, 29.

14. Ibid., 61-72.

Risks of the Research—"A serious lack of judgment on my part"

Vicki Mackintosh

Content Warning: Graphic description of sexual assault
To skip to the next story, turn to page 231.

Not that long ago, I was a bright-eyed graduate student with a passion for knowledge and a desire to change the world. That previous self seems like forever ago. Sure, I had been assaulted before, and while some said this should have "taught" me, I thought that was long behind me, that I had "healed" and learned to trust again.

Traveling for my master's project was exciting. As a new grad student, I didn't quite understand my project or the dynamics, but I was grateful for the opportunity to travel to a country I had never visited before and to try to do something to help.

Before my journey, I had been warned of the dangers of being a student travelling abroad. Id' been warned by flight attendants, friends, travel groups, and training sessions prior to departure— *"be careful, don't go anywhere alone, hide your body and your hair when possible, blend in best you can"*—as if that is even possible with my florescent white skin—and I took this advice. I didn't travel with large amounts of cash, I kept covered, I didn't leave the hotel after dark, and it still happened—sexual assault happens everywhere.

I was travelling with some research students, and the University set us up with in-country support, such as interpreters, a driver, and others working in the in-country office—paid specifically to support us and keep us safe. But who was supposed to keep us safe from them?

I had been in Ethiopia for two weeks, travelling to different areas and universities to provide local farmers with training on the basics of farming poultry. While I spent some of my time with fellow researchers, they were travelling to more remote areas with their driver, so I spent the majority of my time with my university colleagues and the Ethiopian University research staff.

I had been sick in bed for almost two days and beginning to feel better, so I left my bed to head to the café to grab something light to eat and head back to bed. The researchers had just arrived back, and the next day we would be heading back to the capital for a few days before continuing to other areas, and with them came their driver, let's call him D. D was friendly, outgoing, charismatic, charming, and always helpful. We had spent a significant amount of time with him, and he had taken us all over parts of Addis; hiking, to the markets, out to the local dance clubs, and he informed us all about Ethiopian culture. I trusted him to keep us safe, we all did—after all, he was paid to do so.

Once back in my room, I crawled back into bed and fell asleep. While I am not sure how long I had been out, when I awoke it was pitch dark and there was a rapping at my door. Not my door that was inside the hotel, but the door to my patio. I ignored it. My heart raced as I tried to remember whether it had been locked. Again, I heard the rattling as if someone was trying to get inside, then a few taps. I panicked and quickly turned on the light—the noise stopped. I waited for a few minutes to allow my breathing to slow and got up to check the door. It was unlocked, as the lock had malfunctioned, but no one was there—was I imagining this? Was it a dream, or the wind? I convinced myself it was and went back to bed. The next morning when I awoke, I informed the people I was travelling with, and while it was commented on that this is why hotels do not usually put foreigners on the first floor, nothing was discussed further. As the day went on, I tried to forget about it; after all, I would be travelling back to the capital soon, and only had a day left in this part of Ethiopia.

Later that day, my stomach had finally begun to settle and I was eating solid food again, and the whole group went out to a local restaurant to celebrate our last night together. I didn't drink. Not that this matters—it should never matter, but I chose not to. My stomach was still queasy, and I wanted to be alert if someone tried to get in my room again. The driver, D, sat next to me during dinner. He had a great sense of humour and was so chatty and charismatic. We joked around, teasing each other about something or other, but we were laughing along with everyone else. It was meant to be a great night.

Heading back to our hotel, I had not eaten much at dinner as I wanted to be sure my stomach settled before our training session the following day, so D, along with one of the other in-country employees, offered to take me down the road to get bananas for my stomach. I agreed, not thinking much of it, though I had found it strange when they dropped off the others first. But, the banana run went along without a hitch. When we arrived back at the hotel, I asked D if this area was safe for people to walk around alone.

He exclaimed, "No way! Especially not a foreigner, and a female, such as yourself, you must always be accompanied by one of us." I often wonder if I would have been better off going alone, because, honestly,

I never felt unsafe in Ethiopia until that night. "I will take you around town if you would like," he said with a smile.

I agreed, thinking that it would be nice to see the surrounding area with a local and learn more about the culture and experiences of the local people. We went off the resort, arm in arm, which was nothing new to me, as you get used to Ethiopians being very fond of physical touch. Once out of sight of the hotel, he began by asking me if he could share something with me.

"Of course," I said. Over the last two weeks, we had become quite close.

"I am worried about my job—our employer is very strict."

At this point I was definitely confused. "What do you mean?" I was quite curious and naïve as to what he was trying to tell me.

"Please do not tell them," he said under his breath.

"Tell them what? Of course, I won't tell anyone," I said, still completely out of the loop.

"I am so fond of you," he exclaimed.

Not sure what to say, and a little taken aback, I said, "I'm fond of you as well." At that moment, I began to second-guess my decision to leave the hotel.

"No, I mean I am really fond of you, like, I think I am in love with you," he said as he looked me dead in the eyes.

I instantly became uncomfortable. Not only was this man at least double my age, he was married and has several kids. I just stood there in disbelief, not sure what to do or what to say, and feeling incredibly awkward and uncomfortable.

"What do you mean?" I exclaimed. "You just met me two weeks ago."

"Yes, and I love you, I love you so much."

The shock on my face must have been noticeable, and I couldn't even respond. Usually, at this point, I have told the guy I am queer, and while they might mumble something homophobic under their breath, it usually ends with them walking away. This was not an option in Ethiopia, as being queer is punishable by death in some areas—usually by being burned alive on the street. I just stood there staring at him, unsure of what to say to keep myself safe and get me back to the hotel quickly, without much awkwardness.

"Can I kiss you?" he asked.

"No," I said without even considering it.

"Why not, Vicki?" he asked.

"Well, D, you are married, and I am not okay with that." Using this as an excuse.

"That doesn't matter here, Vicki," he responded.

"I am sorry, but it does to me, and in Canada, most people would agree," I said, just trying to say anything to get the point across to him that I was not interested.

"Let me kiss you," he stated again, coming closer to me without my consent. I cringed and recoiled, as I could feel his breath on my face.

"NO," I said with more enthusiasm this time. "No, that is not okay."

He came closer anyway, laughing. "Why do you say no with such authority?" he asked jokingly.

"Because I mean it, D. No means no."

At this time, I was looking around trying to plan an escape, but where am I? Where is the hotel? Am I safer to stay here or risk walking around the streets of Ethiopia after dark by myself? I was weighing my options for safety, and it was looking like a lose-lose situation. What is the safest option? I stayed and repeated myself again, hoping this time he would back down. "NO!"

He laughed again, this time directly in my face. "I'm going to kiss you," he said as he planted his lips on mine.

I stood there stunned, unsure of what to do. While other people might have fought, flown, or frozen at that particular moment, the part of my brain meant to "keep me safe" decided to fawn—performative, surface-level engagement to try and survive or convince the perpetrator not to attack. This is a trait I felt so guilty for. Why didn't I scream, attack him, slap him? I could literally have done any of those things to get him away from me. I never learned about the brain's fawn response to trauma until attending a Pride Symposium a few months later. But my body said to engage, so I did the best I could even though I was utterly repulsed. He began to grope me, putting his hands all over and grabbing me, my breasts, my buttocks, anything he could get his hands on and kissing my neck.

I tried to pull away. "Okay, D, we should head back," wanting to scream at this point, "TAKE ME HOME!!"

"No, we're going to have sex," he said as he pressed his body and hard penis against me.

I shuddered, and this time I couldn't hide it.

"We're going to have sex," he said again, this time with more authority. I wanted to die right then and there; I wanted to scream, to run, to literally do anything to get away from this person.

I frantically looked around and started repeating, "No, no, no, NO, NO! NOO!"

He shushed me and put his hands over my mouth. "Come on, Vicki, we're going somewhere to have sex."

At that point, a light bulb came on in my mind. "Okay, D, let's go back to the hotel," I said, silently hoping he would think we were going back there to have sex and take me.

"Yes, we will go back and have sex," he said, quite proud of himself that he had 'won' me over. On the walk back, he continued to grab at me, and I tolerated it, thankful that we were heading in the right direction, though I had no idea what I was going to do next.

"Please don't tell my supervisor," he whispered in my ear. "We aren't allowed to have sex with the students."

"No problem, I won't," I said, and I meant it. I had no intention of reporting the incident. I was embarrassed that I had fallen for his nice-guy scheme and was blaming myself for being in this situation. I wanted to get away from him, get back to my room, lock the door, and forget what happened.

As we approached the hotel, I fought the urge to run, knowing I wasn't safe until in the presence of one of my colleagues. There they were, standing in the lobby as we got into the hotel: one of the researchers I travelled with. I have never been so relieved in my life, and I let out a breath of air.

"Hi, Vicki! How was your walk?"

Not wanting to raise D's suspicions, I said, "It was great, thanks! I actually have something of yours in my room. Since you're leaving tomorrow, I should get that back to you." I hugged D quickly and wished him safe travels tomorrow. Again, just trying to keep myself safe. You could tell he was completely bewildered, thinking he had gotten me back to the hotel for sex. I rushed back to my room with whom I will now refer to as Researcher One (R1), locking the door several times behind me. I could finally breathe. R1, completely clueless as to what just happened, started chatting, until I turned around.

I'm sure the look on my face said it all—they didn't even have to ask, but they did, "Oh my gosh, are you okay?!"

I couldn't even respond, and the next few minutes were a complete blur. Finally, I said, "Something really fucked up just happened."

"It's okay, you don't have to talk about it."

I was relieved and immediately relaxed, even though my mind was racing. I honestly did not even know the gravity of what had just happened to me. We sat there in silence, and I thought about the attempted intruder the night before, beginning to put the pieces together.

R1 seemed to tell I was uncomfortable. "Do you want me to give you some space; maybe you should give a close friend a call?"

I was so grateful for this response. I thanked them and agreed I should call a friend just to begin to wrap my head around the events of the evening.

"I will come back in a few minutes to check on you," they said, and they left. I locked the door again and crawled onto the floor, positioning myself in the corner furthest from the patio door and called my closest friend at the time; I knew they would know what to say. They didn't answer. I sat there staring at my phone, not knowing who else to call.

Thankfully they immediately called back, likely knowing I wouldn't call if it wasn't important. "Is everything okay?! What's wrong?!"

Then came the tears. I didn't even know why I was crying, but they didn't stop, and I couldn't speak through them, so I just sat there and cried. Through the tears, I started to speak, and I could hear the anger towards the perpetrator in my friend's voice as I explained what had happened. This is one of the many conversations I honestly can't even really recall anymore, but I felt—somewhat—supported.

After I hung up the phone, I thought about the patio door again and went to try and lock it, without success. I left my room and went to my colleague's room next door. They were obviously not expecting me at this hour (though I couldn't tell you what time it was).

"Can you help me figure out how to lock my door? I thought I was okay with it, but I'm not," I said quietly without making eye contact, not wanting them to know anything was wrong, but probably giving it away instantly.

"Of course," they exclaimed as they came right over to sort it out, but again without any success. I sat there on the bed after they left just wondering what the heck to do. *I can't sleep in this room with the unlocked door*, I kept thinking to myself. There was a light knock and R1 was back to check on me. I was so thankful for this as my mind was spinning being alone. I told them about the issue with the unlocking door, and they immediately offered for me to sleep in their room.

"I will sleep on the floor," they gladly offered.

"Oh that's not necessary," I exclaimed, thinking I had already been enough of a burden.

"I will not take no for an answer, we are safer in groups."

I eventually, (and gladly) agreed, and together we decided we should also inform one of the other researchers, for their own safety.

Their first response was, "I'm here for whatever you need, and just so you know, we are here no matter what you decide to do and support any decision you make." I literally could have cried. I was so lucky to be travelling with such supportive and empathetic people. If only everyone had responded this way, I may not have been in for the fight of my life once I got home. We decided that since none of our patio doors locked, we would all share a room for the night, and one that was not mine. One of the researchers was kind enough to sleep on the floor beside the patio door (just in case), and thankfully we were able to settle in and sleep for the night.

The next morning, I was trying to forget it even happened. The driver would be going back to the capital today, and I was staying in my room until they left. As I was getting ready for our training session, I heard a knock at my door and was immediately startled. I quietly crept up to the peephole and, with relief, discovered it was my colleagues. As soon as I opened the door I was met with questions, "What happened last night? Are you Okay? Did someone try to get into your room?" I was confused, as I had not shared this information with anyone else and did not know how to respond. I just wanted to forget it happened.

"Yes I'm okay, no one tried to get into my room." I wasn't ready to talk about it again.

"Okay, well, please let us know if something happened, as a member of the staff back home called and left several messages last night saying something had happened to you." I was shocked. How could someone have known without my consent to share this information, as if my consent hadn't already been breeched.

I was quiet, and they took the hint and left for breakfast. I would be eating in my room that morning. I checked my phone and had received a text message from the friend I had contacted the day before to share my experience. *I'm so sorry, the professor overheard our conversation and called to report the incident.*

I instantly felt sick. Not only had my consent been taken away by the assault, but now knowledge had been shared, and a report had been made, all without me saying yes. This should never happen to any survivor; they should always be able to choose when and where and who to share this information with. For me, this was the beginning of a nightmare.

I took a deep breath and stepped outside. As the driver had officially left with some of the others to head back to the capital, I felt like I could relax a little, though I still felt an unease toward everyone. I was quiet over breakfast but felt I could blame that on the food poisoning I had been suffering from for the last few days. I just kept thinking that in a week I would be on my way home, and I could leave all this nonsense in Ethiopia. Oh, how wrong I was.

When we arrived on Soddo campus, I was fighting tears; being around so many people was a struggle, so when one of my colleagues asked me to go with some of the students (three male students) by myself, I instantly couldn't breathe. I looked at one of the people I was travelling with and whispered, "Do not leave me alone." They looked back at me in shock. Being such a strong and independent person, I am sure this sentence sounded strange coming from me. The tears began to roll, and they grabbed me by the hand and led me back to the car just as I started to hyperventilate.

I sat in the car and cried for a while as they continued to question me. "What happened?! If this was an assault you need to report this! We need to take you to the hospital!" I didn't even have time to answer one question before another one was thrown at me, and all I could hear was "you, you, you. You need to do this, you need to do that," and it made me sick. I didn't want to do anything, I wanted to forget it happened, and even if I did want to do something about it, I sure as heck didn't want to do it alone.

Next came more questions. "Has this happened to you before?"

I'm not sure why this was relevant, but I didn't even have the comprehension to fight it. "Yes, I've been assaulted before, I guess I should have known better."

Looking back now I can't even believe this sentence came out of my mouth—if you have been assaulted, statistics say you are *more* likely to be assaulted again, as much as thirty-five times more likely.[1] This same study suggested that victims are less likely to be believed after being assaulted more than once, which has given me some insight into how this person could have possibly responded this way. What came next made me feel like I had been punched in the gut.

"Tell me what happened," they said with authority and little to no compassion.

I began my story with, "He was taking me to get bananas."

"Well, that was a severe lack of judgment on your part!"

This sentence still echoes in my brain, and I am still unable to comprehend how someone could say that to another who was in pieces in front of them.

I instantly stopped speaking. I wanted to scream, to run, to hide, and I most definitely wanted to go home. I felt as if I had been knocked out; I was so confused as to how or why this person would respond that way, but I knew I no longer trusted them. I sat there for a while longer, just being quiet and trying to hold back the tears. After all, I was there to work, and I needed to get back to it. I was instantly aware that they were no longer holding my hand, and I was wondering when that happened. I felt guilty, I felt disgusting, and I was already blaming myself for what had happened.

Some of the other staff came over to see what was going on, offering to take me to the capital or the hospital if I was sick, as they assumed this had something to do with my food poisoning.

"This is not physical. She's not sick, this is mental; she will be fine," my colleague said.

---

1. Black, M.C. et. al., *The National Intimate Partner and Sexual Violence Survey (NISVS): 2010 Summary Report*, Atlanta, GA: National Center for Injury Prevention and Control, Centers for Disease Control and Prevention, 2011.

I didn't agree with this statement but did not feel I was in the position to say otherwise. When I look back on this encounter today, years later, I truly feel that this conversation was worse than the assault itself. Having someone force you to tell them what happened, second guess you, blame you, and tell you what to do after sharing something so painful really is a perfect example of what not to do.

The rest of the trip was fairly uneventful. The person I was forced to disclose to never checked up or checked in with me as to how I was doing. Thankfully, however, the other researchers did, as well as someone travelling with another organization who was made aware of the situation, as I was concerned for her safety travelling alone. When I informed her of what had happened (without going into detail), she informed me I was not the first person this had happened to, and not just with this particular driver, but with many of the other drivers as well. Assault of female foreigners travelling in Ethiopia happens more often than I originally thought and was never brought up during our preparation or training with the school, which I found strange after the fact. I received a Facebook friend request from this driver and a few "innocent" messages with kissy faces which I chose to ignore. Looking at his face, even on social media, made me sick to my stomach.

A few days before arriving home, I received some emails from the staff on campus asking me to come in and do a debrief—they were eager to get the information from me as soon as possible, but I honestly couldn't even fathom having that conversation. I was mentally and emotionally exhausted from working so hard to keep it together for the remainder of the trip. I needed at least a week of sleep. The emails continued to come in asking me when I could check in and do the debrief with requests for the day I got back or the day after. I politely declined, but they continued to push so I scheduled a meeting for the following week to give me the weekend to relax.

When the time rolled around for me to have the meeting, I tried to pretend I wasn't bothered. I put on my "big girl" panties and strolled over to the office like nothing had happened. Thankfully, it had been a good day so far, and I was feeling strong. When I got into the office, the awkwardness was palpable. The lack of training for staff in these situations was apparent and I could hear the nervousness in their voice when they asked me what had happened. Their anxiety reflected onto me; I brushed it off again—it was no big deal, I don't even think about it, Ethiopia was great, along with all the other lies I was telling myself. I was told that several women from another organization had also reported sexual assault by the same driver. This hit me hard, and I blamed myself for this over and over. If only I had reported it sooner, maybe they would have been kept safe, but I worked hard to pretend this news didn't affect me. I had convinced myself I could get through this meeting without tears and was determined to do so. I was also informed that the driver was on contract, and that his contract was due to expire in the next month; therefore, they would not be renewing it. *Future students would be safe*, I thought. At the end of the meeting, I was offered support and asked if I needed it—I gladly accepted. I have always been an advocate for talk therapy and was looking forward to opening up to someone who understood my lizard brain.[2] They offered to set up a meeting and I was happy about that, as I have never been one to reach out for help unless I absolutely thought I needed it.

---

2. The term "lizard brain" refers to the brain's limbic system, which is extremely prominent in lizards, and which produces fight, flight, and freeze responses.

Following the meeting, I felt like a weight had been lifted, like I could now look forward and move on from what happened without being constantly reminded, but I also felt emotionally drained and exhausted from pretending everything was fine. As soon as I got home there was an email waiting for me. The meeting that was set up with support was not possible as the sexualized violence officer was out on maternity leave. I was given a contact for the Human Rights office and was informed that I could drive to the main campus an hour way for their support or meet with them via phone. I felt defeated. While they did offer to arrange a meeting for me, I was tired and overwhelmed by the thought of reaching out and driving an hour, and, just like that, the support I greatly needed was no longer an option.

A month later, on a regular Tuesday, I had an email come through listed with high importance, titled: *Urgent request re: internship*. I didn't want to open it. I instantly felt sick, and my instinct was right. The email requested copies of the social media messages I received from the driver. Along with the niceties, there was one sentence that will forever stand out. *If we can get copies of these by the end of Wednesday or Thursday morning, then we will have enough evidence to move forward with removing the driver, otherwise they will unfortunately return to work.* All I could read was they would return to work. What do you mean, return to work?! Working for a company whose sole purpose is to keep foreign students safe. That was his role, and despite *causing* harm, he would be carrying on with his position like nothing had happened. Driving students around. Driving staff around. I couldn't and still cannot wrap my head around it.

I screenshotted the messages he had sent to me, hoping that would be the end of it. The response I received contained the phrase *Hopefully this will be enough*. As if my experience wasn't bad enough or relevant.

I know nothing was meant by it, but sexual assault victims pick up on these microaggressions so quickly, and they are forever damaging. The following email was what I had feared. *Unfortunately, we feel like we need more examples of messages and more detailed information to be accepted as evidence.* In that moment, I completely understood why many survivors do not report assault. It is too hard to be told over and over again, "Your experience wasn't valid" or "You weren't assaulted enough" or to feel like no one believes you. While my logical brain knew that this was not the intention, my traumatized brain could not help but feel defensive. The email included a request for a formal statement and a suggestion for me to unblock the perpetrator from social media to see if he had reached out to me again afterwards in order for them to gather more evidence, along with the offer to do it in a safer space with one of their employees. This was not the definition of a safer space for me, so I quickly unblocked him from social media, confirmed there were no new messages, and responded to the email with a brief but formal statement of the facts of my assault.

While I am sure this was a reasonable request, all I could see was, "it wasn't enough, your experience wasn't valid" over and over again in my head. I shut down and I felt detached. I felt as if I was being forced to report these things, even though "it wasn't enough." The response from them was brief, reminding me to block him again and reach out for support if I needed it—but not on our campus (supports were located on main campus, we had no official support on our campus). This was the last I heard from the office, and I honestly just assumed it was over. The driver's contract had been terminated and our students were safe, or at least that is what I was telling myself.

Once school returned in September, I carried on like nothing had happened, though the assault was always in the back of my mind. I hadn't received an update since I submitted my statement, but it seemed as if other folks on campus who had heard my story had a wealth of information to share. Through them, I learned the driver had not only not been fired, but his contract had been renewed, even though it was due to end in August. My heart shattered. Not only had he been allowed to continue in his role, but I also had to find out second-hand, from other staff. Apparently, meetings with the dean had taken place all summer but I had been left out of the process. I was now angry. Angry I had not been properly set up with supports. Angry about the language that was used. Angry that the staff had no idea how to handle this situation, though I knew it wasn't the first time they had dealt with this. Angry that the man who assaulted me was not only free to assault others but was carrying on with his job like nothing happened. I knew something had to be done. No student could go through this like I had. The process needed to be changed, and I knew no one else was going to step up. It had to be me.

A few days later, I saw the researchers in the library and made small talk. They were with another student who had also travelled to Ethiopia, let's call her June. We didn't go into detail, but I could tell the incident was still on her and the researchers' minds. None of us were happy about how the situation turned out. My warped sense of humour was what I had been using to get me through this, joking about how messy my life was to relieve the tension.

As we walked out of the library, June made a comment about how sweet the Ethiopian staff were and I blurted out before even thinking, "Yeah that's what you said about the Driver." I laughed.

She stopped dead in her tracks and looked at me with compassion. "Oh my gosh, I am so sorry."

Once the others left, she approached me again. "I know I am not supposed to know, but I have an idea that something happened to you, and I want to let you know I'm here if you need me."

I was instantly relieved. I didn't care that privilege had been broken. I began talking about what had happened in Ethiopia and the lack of support I encountered when I got home. At the beginning, it was mostly light-hearted jokes, but by the end of the conversation we made the decision to team up and do something. I was so grateful for this support, and I wanted the rest of our students to have it too. It was just the beginning of June and me encouraging each other through this difficult battle we were about to fight.

Our first stop was the Assistant Dean of Students. We pitched the idea of a peer support group to support other students affected by sexualized violence to them via email and they seemed on board and excited. We were feeling optimistic that this was going to take off. The morning of the meeting we were prepared, we had statistics prepped, and had undergone training and research on what changes needed to be implemented and how we could help. We both walked in wearing our most professional outfits. I even wore my lucky glasses—I don't have a prescription, but always struggled with the fact that I look about ten years younger than my age so this was something I had adapted that made me look older, in hopes of being taken more seriously. The meeting went well. They sympathized with us and agreed that more support was needed on campus. They loved our ideas and seemed eager to work with us and introduce more training for students and staff. June and I left the meeting feeling elated, like we had made a positive impact for student life on campus. We continued to say it is up from here! Our follow up email included a presentation we had developed regarding the basics of sexualized violence—consent, how trauma affects the brain, and how to respond to someone who discloses sexualized violence to you, as well as supports for students and staff online, and within the community.

The Assistant Dean responded saying that she appreciated our enthusiasm, but the next step would be to loop in the head nurse in health services. We strongly agreed, as she was often the first point of contact for students, and we wanted her to know about our support group. We also contacted our local Sexual Assault Centre, in hopes to form a future partnership, since we didn't have any trauma supports on our campus for survivors. We patiently waited for things to move along, but it felt like we were in some sort of limbo. Dates were bounced around via email, but nothing concrete was set. A few different times, members had to cancel and eventually the meeting was forgotten about. We pushed with reminders but felt like we had been put on the backburner. Then, one afternoon, we both got a strange email from the Assistant Dean of Students, one that had been sent to all of campus.

Hi, I have been a victim of sexualized violence and so have many of you. The rest of you are affected because you know victims. We all need to learn more. There will be a presentation on Tuesday Oct 29 at 4 p.m. Please come and learn more and show that you care.

While we were a little taken aback at the wording of the email, what shocked us most was that this was our idea, yet here we were hearing about it for the first time with the rest of campus. We swallowed our pride and responded to the email with enthusiasm.

We are so excited this is happening on our campus and really wish we could be a part of it in some way!

The response we received still bothers me to this day:

I think that it is important for you both to talk to the Sexual Assault Centre before you reach out to other students. I understand that you want to help others, but you also need to protect yourselves from possible triggers.

Therefore, I think that you should hold off for now and wait and see what advice you receive from the centre. Perhaps there can be a discussion at the meeting on setting up a support group or other opportunities to provide support.

While we were appreciative of the concern, neither of us had disclosed our history within the meeting, therefore it was being assumed we were both survivors—because only survivors could care about these things? Or had confidentiality been broken at some point? Additionally, it was assumed that we did not know how to protect ourselves, and we felt as though we were being brushed off again. I responded with an update that we were getting registered through the student association, undergoing various types of training, and had reached out to the Sexual Assault Centre with a meeting in the books. No response.

We then heard some of the staff had been speaking negatively about the group and the fact that it was being run by students, and they were not supportive of it continuing, though they had never met either of us face-to-face. Realizing staff were not as supportive as we had hoped, this took us to our next stop, the undergraduate Student Association. The group consisted of student political leaders and was unfortunately another unexpected roadblock. In order to run and advertise a student group or club on campus you need to register through this organization. Registration requires an in-depth discussion of the potential risks of your group, and ours had a big one. Triggers. Many sexual assault victims know this word all too well and unfortunately deal with them daily. We were prepared for this, as we had taken several courses on how best to support victims of sexualized violence, as well as ourselves, and knew the campus and community supports inside and out. We pushed that we knew we were not therapists or counsellors, but we are here to listen and to direct students to the appropriate supports. This is exactly what our campus desperately needed. We registered our group at the end of September, filed the appropriate paperwork with the Student Association, and waited with excitement for our approval, which never came. Radio silence. While we did not hesitate to continue reaching out, the Student Association continued with their radio silence until we finally elicited a response at the end of November, apologizing for the delay and stating the words we would come to know (and hate) all too well:

Now, the thing that has held up the start of this club, which I'm sure you guys know, is that this is a sensitive subject. I want to make sure this club would be okay with the university. We have contacted the Assistant Dean of Students for approval.

Our hearts instantly sank, knowing full well they were gathering on the other side of our fence, but we were prepared for this response, and had our reply:

Thank you for the information. We understand your apprehension when it comes to this topic, however we feel that this is the reason this group is so important. Due to the sensitivity of the subject, there is no place students can feel safe to reach out and the matter of how to deal with it is not discussed. This leaves our school vulnerable to ignorance on the topic. A dialogue needs to be started with subjects that may have been taboo in the past in order to let others know there is no shame from being a victim of sexualized violence, or to ask how to best support someone they care about. We have no support on this campus for sexual violence or abuse and this is something that most university campuses have.

We have both began the government training on "Supporting Victims of Sexualized Violence" and have also reached out to main campus to take the training they offer for student peer supports, as they have a similar club on campus run by students. As mentioned, this is something offered on most campuses across Canada and is something our campus has been sorely lacking for a long time. The purpose of the group is to help people find the avenues for the support they need - and is in NO way a counselling service. People may not realize this club is needed until it is available for students and staff. We want to promote gender equity and safety on our campus.

The way I look at it is that at one point I'm sure someone said our 2SLGBTQIA+ support club was a sensitive topic, but it is now an integral part of our on-campus support for the student body.

I hope you consider this plea for help in bringing something as important to our campus. We will be consulting main campus for support and would love to have the Student Association be a part of the movement.

If you would like to have a meeting with us, please feel free to reach out, we would love to sit down and have an in-person discussion on this topic we are so passionate about.

Thank you for your support.

We attempted to schedule follow up meetings, which, in the recurring theme, also got pushed back, rescheduled, and eventually cancelled. We were starting to feel defeated. We had reached out to several people with no support, and we were not sure how to continue.

Next, we decided to go back to the faculty. While sharing my concerns with a friend, I was advised to contact the Student Services Coordinator, who has a reputation for being an empathetic student advocate. We were excited at the thought of finally getting some staff on our side and reached out via email to request a meeting. The response was that they would sit down with some members of the team, including the school nurse, and get back to us. Radio silence, of course, so we followed up again and said we were coming in for a meeting. We were no longer suggesting it.

During the meeting, we shared our concerns, and while empathy was apparent, it was clear that their hands were tied and nothing was going to be done.

Later, while attending a Pride Symposium for my other volunteer role as president of the campus 2SLQBTQIA+ peer support group for students, I attended a wonderful discussion on trauma, where I learned the term "Fawn." This session was hosted by a previous University employee. The talk was so enlightening that my body shook through the whole thing. Following the meeting, I knew I had to approach the speaker, and I verbally vomited all over them, just thankful someone was finally listening. They expressed their deepest empathy and gave me some direct contacts at the main campus. When I brought this information back to June, we discussed our options. While we were really hoping we could resolve this on our campus, we were already angry and frustrated at the lack of support we were getting and agreed that our next step was likely main campus. We drafted an email and sent it out to the Sexual and Gender Resource Centre as well as the Human Rights Services.

This time we received responses from both offices quickly, with apologies for the lack of resources and a promise to follow up with a meeting. We felt like we were finally moving forward. We were quick to offer to make the hour drive to main campus as we wanted to meet people face-to-face, and we felt it would be more difficult for them to brush us off that way.

Our first meeting was at our Sexual and Gender Resource Centre. You could tell as soon as you walked in that it was a place of student advocacy, and I felt at home. They listened to our story, gave some amazing advice, and offered to help in any way they could. We felt great when we left. The following day we received our second reply from Human Rights Services sexualized violence advisor, saying she had been updated by the

Gender Resource Centre and was inviting us to attend a training session, which we gladly agreed to. She also booked a discussion to tackle the issue of support. We were then informed that the position of Student Sexualized Violence Liaison had been introduced to our campus. We were shocked to hear this news, as we had never seen a posting, and in all our discussions with campus, it was never mentioned. This was what we had been waiting for, and after meeting the student that was selected, we couldn't have asked for a better Sexualized Violence Liaison, and we were elated when Erika joined our team.

Then, one day on a field trip with the Grad Student association, I began chatting with our president of the Association for Graduate Students, and shared my concerns and the issues we were having with the group. I had done this several times before with others and I often received, "Oh gosh, that is horrible," before they quickly moved to change the subject; every time this occurred, it added to my feelings of defeat. Thankfully, this time was different. It was the first time I had heard, "Oh gosh, that's horrible, did you want me to help you do something about it?" I'm sure the shock radiated on my face. I was instantly taken aback by her strong plan of action. Our dynamic duo-turned-trio, was now a group of four, and I couldn't have been more thankful. This really made me wonder why students were so quick to jump into action and staff were not—our group was not getting paid, we were doing the work on our own time, with no budget, while the folks being paid to support us were wavering. I also found when sharing my story that the students responded with more compassion and empathy and a better overall trauma-informed approach than staff, which was really telling for why we needed to do this work.

Now that there were four of us, it really felt like we had some momentum. We had weekly meetings and voted on a name change: SAGE

(Sexual Assault Group Empowerment). We knew the herb sage was often used by our Indigenous community for cleansing and to promote healing and wisdom, and this was a great analogy for what we were all about. We created a logo using an international symbol for sexualized violence and combined it with a sage leaf. Sometimes our meetings were valuable and other times we would just talk about life and the struggle of being an activist, but we were so glad to have each other.

While we had come a long way, we still had a long road ahead. With the help of Ashley, we decided this time to start at the top, with our faculty dean and representatives from other main campus offices such as Human Rights Services and Student Affairs. The meeting was awkward—we quoted statistics, they asked for specific numbers regarding our students that we couldn't really answer (after all, we weren't a registered group). But once it was said and done, we felt they took our concerns seriously and vowed to not only allow our group to proceed, but to do their best to support us in the future, with a promise of a social worker position on our campus. This social worker position would be a huge win for us, as it would give us faculty support on campus and would allow us to really support students.

With their approval, the next step was registering our group, as without formal registration, we still could not advertise our services on campus. So, we were back to our student association. Thankfully, with the backing from Ashley, our group was able to make an appearance at the Student Council meeting and make a short presentation. With some encouragement, the vote was a resounding yes, and the group was officially registered—which also meant funding!

With the help of Human Rights Services and our Sexualized Violence Student Liaison, Erika, we began to advertise. We sat in the library to talk to students, telling them about our group, debunking common myths that surround sexualized violence, included games and pamphlets and even had a chance to win tickets to *The Vagina Monologues*. We did everything we could to get the word out, and students were receptive. We hosted events with our local Sexual Assault Centre and made it a house challenge to encourage attendance. We also hosted training sessions for folks who were interested in being student leaders in sexualized violence prevention. Now, we had to ensure we were strong in our training going forward, so we immersed ourselves in as much training as we could find and set a date for our first official support group. With the help of Human Rights Services, we collaborated with their support group. This group is a discussion facilitation program that covers different areas of sexualized violence each week, such as the effects of sexual assault, healthy coping and self-care, self-esteem, and loads more. It was a wonderful program for survivors, and we were able to adapt it to our campus. We went through more training, we supplied colouring books, snacks, and things for folks to fidget with, we practised and prepared and advertised, and were ready for our first session. Although the first session was a bit shaky, we were excited to have people interested in the group and willing to participate. And just like that, with our blood, sweat, and tears, SAGE was introduced to the our Campus. I think my biggest hope and motivation for all of this is that students who come after us will not have to fight like we did to have our voices heard.

Reflecting back on this whole process, I am beyond thankful. While I recognize my privilege at having the strength and support to fight these battles following a traumatic assault, I could not have done it without those who supported the idea. Therefore, I would like to dedicate this story to the three lovely ladies who helped form SAGE and never gave up. My co-founder—"June," you saw this idea right from the beginning and brought as much passion (or more) than I did. This would still be an idea without you. Our wonderful sexual violence student liaison—Erika Inglis—you had no idea what you were signing up for when you started this role. Your passion for inclusivity made SAGE even better than we could have imagined. Our President Boss—Ashley MacDonald—I truly believe I would still be fighting this losing battle without you. Your amazing leadership abilities and your unwillingness to take no for an answer made this group into what it was. Though half of us have moved on, SAGE will live on thanks to this wonderful group of people.

The PEARS Project

MICAH KALISH

I started my undergraduate education at the University of Toronto in 2019. I was a student at Trinity College and fairly outspoken about what was viewed as "radical" feminism and survivor's rights, so I wasn't surprised when within my first month, a group of students approached me and told me about an incident of sexual harassment that occurred during Orientation Week. With their consent, I brought the incident forward to the registrar's office, where they thanked me for the information but never took any steps to follow up. I spent the next few days attempting to contact someone from the office again before organizing a group of almost one hundred students to send a mass email requesting they respond. As we prepared to meet with members of the registrar, we put together a document that outlined the next steps we encouraged them to take, issues we'd noticed within the system, and even a template for an email they could send out with resources.

They never sent the email.

Eventually, a member of the administration told me about an organization within Trinity College: Trinity Against Sexual Assault and Harassment (TASAH). I got in touch with the single remaining member of TASAH shortly after. That last member was about to graduate, and therefore the club hadn't been very active. I worked with her to restart the club and recruit a small team. This was not widely accepted by the college, or perhaps simply not acknowledged, and essentially all the applicants consisted of my friends and people within shared circles. Despite this, we were able to pull together a small team of people. Working with a number of external organizations, including the Dandelion Initiative, we were able to receive trauma-informed, survivor-centric peer support training and participate in various bystander intervention and consent-based events and workshops, all while providing peer support and referrals to various resources to help survivors of sexualized or gender-based violence. In doing this work, I began receiving disclosures from people outside of Trinity College and across all three of the University of Toronto's campuses. It became abundantly clear that the resources the university was providing for survivors of sexualized violence were not adequate and that more student-led and survivor-led initiatives were needed.

One of the most eye-opening experiences for me, which I have been permitted to share anonymously, was my interaction with one student who decided she wanted to call the university's Sexual Violence Prevention and Support Centre to report an instance of sexual assault. We sat together and wrote out what she was going to say. She spent so much time and energy preparing to disclose her story—only for the phone to ring several times and then take her to voicemail. I began calling the centre on a daily basis, and each time, the phone number they advertised would go to voicemail. When I finally approached the centre about this, they explained to me that they didn't have anyone to answer their phone. When I asked why they would advertise a phone number that no one answered, they said they would work on hiring someone. It's been almost two years since that conversation, and the only change they've made is that they have now put a note next to their phone number letting people know that it'll take them to voicemail, where they should leave a message. As a Survivor myself, I recognize how harmful providing resources that don't exist can be, and how re-traumatizing it is to have someone offer help and then not be there to pick up the phone.

Seeing that this was a university-wide issue, I founded the PEARS Project with the goal of creating TASAH-like equivalents across the university. PEARS stands for Prevention, Empowerment, Advocacy, Response, for Survivors. The PEARS Project is a grassroots, trauma-informed coalition that provides support and resources to survivors of sexualized violence across the University of Toronto, founded and led by survivors through survivor-centred principles such as autonomy, consent, equity, mutual aid, support, and care. PEARS recognizes survivors as leaders and as the voices which need to be heard to implement policy change. To date, the tri-campus initiative has formed nine teams of peer supporters—one at each St. George campus college, one at each satellite campus, and one within the Faculty of Engineering. By formalizing a community and resource network that is by and for survivors, we can better support one another and increase access to legal, mental health, and capacity-building supports. Furthermore, by integrating PEARS 'nodes' or teams into authentic, pre-existing communities, PEARS will be better able to create mutual relationships with broader student communities and help promote the work of other divisional stakeholders. This work is necessary as a result of institutional failure. Survivors deserve better. Unfortunately, the job of this organization has now fallen onto the student body—survivors in particular—who are attempting to navigate support while also navigating the convoluted and often contradictory policies put in place by the university.

PEARS comes after years of struggle, resistance, and activism within the University of Toronto's community by survivors and allies. I use the term "founder" very loosely when referring to myself, as I recognize that it would not have been possible to start this coalition without the incredible survivors and activists who came before me and who surround me now. Despite years of activism experience, starting PEARS has been hard. As a woman and survivor, I have had to constantly prove myself. I have been told that I am too emotional, too close, or too traumatized to do this work, sometimes even by those who call themselves allies. Providing peer support has brought up so many emotions and revealed so much about this institution. Sometimes I sit down and add up the hours I attend at U of T and the dollars I pay them, and then think about how much I am contributing to a place that actively harms survivors. However, with this, I think about the power and privilege that I and so many other activists hold in these spaces, and the necessity of our resistance and collective knowledge and power against these institutions. While it can be challenging to contemplate your complicity in harmful systems, it is necessary in order to enact meaningful change and dismantle structures of harm.

That is why I started PEARS. For the woman sitting on my floor crying and having no one answer the phone. After seeing NDAs and watching students' rapists teach classes on politics. I have put hours, days, weeks, and months into making this project happen. It was not easy, and initially, there was very little support. Some people who said it was great, including Students' Unions and university faculty—who had the power to compensate me, support me, or get involved—simply went no further. It took relentless reminders, follow-ups, and emails to receive any funding or club recognition. In my time doing this work, I have seen pasta clubs have an easier time being recognized and getting budgets approved at the college level.

While PEARS only just launched, there is already a lot on the go. We are starting a policy analysis to review the Governing Council's policy on sexualized violence and harassment. We are collaborating with Students for Consent Culture Canada (SFCC) to conduct research within the university. We want to hear from those who have accessed the centre to better understand the space needed for improvement, the ways it is supporting the community, and to enact the PEARS mandate. This will be done in the form of an anonymous survey, which will be shared with community stakeholders whose experiences will be the basis of proposed recommendations. The goal is to collect accurate data to gain a realistic, statistical picture of how sexual misconduct is handled by the SVPSC at the University of Toronto and the university's inaction to support and protect victims, and penalize perpetrators. We have compiled a document of over one hundred resources for survivors, from legal to psychological, housing, financial, medical, and more. All of our PEARS members are undergoing survivor-centric, peer support training. In addition, we have managed to get a number of Students' Unions to attend training and are working with the TA union to have TA's receive similar training. We are also in the process of developing a curriculum with Stella's Place, an organization in the Greater Toronto Area which provides a variety of mental health services to young adults. Throughout all of this, of course, we continue to provide peer support.

It is so devastating and invalidating to attend an academic institution that not only cares so little about survivor rights but that actively harms survivors through their "support systems." This is what I have seen time and time again within the University of Toronto, and it is about time that changes. This is why I started PEARS—because every survivor deserves better. Despite all the challenges, backlash, and evident unwillingness on the university's part to support survivors, we did it. As a survivor myself, it is hard to explain the feeling of being surrounded and uplifted by a community of survivors. I have never felt more like a survivor and less like a victim than I have since starting and engaging in PEARS. I have never marvelled at the way my body and mind have worked so tirelessly to keep me alive and to survive until seeing it within others through PEARS. We are forming a truly radical space for survivors to uplift one another in ways I didn't think we had the power to do. By creating this collective, we are able to support students without compromising survivor-centric principles, to self-regulate and hold one another accountable, and to provide a network of students who can support each other when triggers or re-traumatizations occur. While I recognize that survivors are by no means a homogenized group and should not be treated as such, we are still able to unite through a common thread and find meaning, build resilience, and hold space for one another.

I truly believe it is only through this type of work, rooted in intersectional feminist knowledges, community-oriented, and survivor led that we can create meaningful change, and that if the systems in question are not there to uplift and support survivors then they are in the way. There is so much resilience and strength in a group of people who believe in one another and recognize that they deserve better.

Progressing Policies

Cameron Smith

Content Warning: Mild descriptions of sexual assault and harassment
To skip to the next story, turn to page 251.

On my third day at Acadia University, I was sexually assaulted. Specifically, I was groped. It happened at a T-shirt signing party. I was approached by a man on the football team who had ripped his shirt open and asked me to sign his bare chest. I signed the one remaining sleeve, the best signal I could think of at the time that I wasn't interested. When he asked to sign my shirt, I held out the bottom and pointed to a clear spot. Instead, he grabbed my chest. Hard. He stared me in the eye as he took his time signing his name on my breast. I didn't say a word, just held my breath and gave him a hard stare. I don't remember which one of us walked away first. Shortly after, I left the party early.

This was in September 2017, and at the time, it never occurred to me to report it. I knew it would go nowhere, that I would be told it was something minor and that I was wasting people's time. This man quickly gained a reputation for this sort of behaviour and was followed by vague rumours of incidents that I never listened closely to. I didn't have to. I already knew what kind of person he was. I don't know if any of those occurrences were ever reported, but it became an open secret among students. This seemed to be how most stories of sexual assault on our campus went. Something happened, someone told someone else about it, and suddenly we all heard, "Hey, I think that guy assaulted someone; stay away from him." Yet, all of these men had large groups of friends, they were at the campus bar every week, and they were in classes during the day. If you didn't want to see them, you had to leave. Not the other way around.

As the #MeToo movement began, people finally realized it was time for change. Conversations surrounding sexualized violence on campuses started happening, and people began to wonder what steps we could take and how we could organize. Acadia had never had any Take Back the Night rallies or petitions for action, and I was a first-year student who didn't have the confidence or know-how to lead these initiatives myself. I knew I wanted to be involved in bettering our campus somehow, so I joined the Acadia Mental Health Initiative (AMHI) as mental health advocacy was something I'd been engaged in since high school. I worked as the Vice President of Events for this group in my first and second years of university, from September 2017 to May 2019. I then took over as the coordinator of the group until May 2021. Through this position, my advocacy work against sexualized violence on campus began.

In 2015, all Nova Scotia universities were told to complete a stand-alone sexual violence policy in accordance with a Memorandum of Understanding (MOU) set out by the province of Nova Scotia's Sexual Violence Prevention Committee. The MOU had a 2019 deadline, giving the universities four years to create effective policies to protect their students. The Acadia policy was started in 2018, less than twelve months before the *four-year* deadline. As a result, the policy Acadia produced was clearly written to meet the deadline and not the needs of students impacted by sexualized violence.

PROGRESSING POLICIES   237

The initial draft of Acadia's Sexual Violence policy was only eight pages long—for anyone not familiar with policy, eight pages is a shockingly short policy document. Yet somehow it was still unnecessarily confusing. The language of the policy was aspirational instead of committal, with sentences such as, "Acadia University *will* create an environment ..." or "All efforts *will be made* to follow the wishes of the individuals(s) who have experienced sexual violence ..." An effective legal document would say "Acadia University *is* an environment ..." and "We *will* follow the wishes of the individual(s) who have experienced sexual violence ..." The policy did not include any noticeable changes in procedure, offering the same non-academic judicial process that had been failing survivors for years. It offered no support from the university for off-campus events, suggesting that anyone who was assaulted or harassed off campus could file a criminal report or see a Sexual Assault Nurse Examiner instead—redirecting students to a different, equally painful, and flawed system instead of to supports or assistance. The most hurtful part of this nonsensical policy was that nowhere in the document did it state that Acadia did not tolerate sexualized violence. In short, it was useless. If any student were to try to proceed with a complaint under such a policy, a lawyer would have been able to pick it apart in minutes. Reading it as a student and as a survivor, *the policy felt like a slap in the face.*

Needless to say, Acadia's policy did not meet the required standards of the MOU. An outside review of the policy by the *Antigonish Women's Resource Centre & Sexual Assault Services Association* (an excellent resource worth checking out, by the way) graded the document with a well-deserved F. The MOU stated that any universities who failed to meet the requirements would lose funding; however, this was not enforced. Lack of enforcement was something Acadia seemed to count on, as it allowed them to coast through with a policy that was such only in name. There were no new or effective structures put in place. Thankfully, there were students, faculty, and outside advocates who were willing to push for something better. Because of the outcry from those activists, a new committee was formed to rewrite the policy into something that would effectively protect and benefit students. The committee was expanded significantly from the initial group right off the bat, which was where I came in. The expansion of the group was, seemingly, an effort to take into consideration all the absent voices which should have been included from the beginning.

The new committee was labelled the "Sexual Violence Policy Working Group." At its peak, the group contained somewhere around thirty members. While it may sound great to have this many people involved, all it really did was create a breakdown in communication. We were trying to coordinate so many schedules that our first meeting did not happen until December 2018. Remember, this was to discuss a policy that was due March 31, 2019. The entire committee only met three or four times in the 2018-2019 school year, with one of these meetings falling after the deadline.

I left each of these meetings feeling hopeless and seething with anger over the lack of progress and communication. Often, it felt like excuses were being made as to why any possible suggestion for change wouldn't work at Acadia. Time was wasted on debates over the usage of a single word, and there was an endless argument about whether we should focus on developing the policy or new procedures (spoiler alert: one cannot develop without the other). This argument resulted in splitting the committee in half, one group to focus on each of these elements. I was on both committees, and all of the subsequent meetings continued to be unproductive. So little was achieved over the course of these months that I find it hard to recall any significant changes. God bless every single friend who would listen to me rant and rave about those tedious meetings, because if there is anything worse than seeing your friend upset, it's seeing a friend who is upset and complaining about university policy.

Finally, at a meeting between representatives of both groups, the committee shrank back down to a workable size. Those who could dedicate consistent time would continue to meet, and a few other interested faculty members and incoming University officials would be joining. The committee was renamed "The Sexual Health Policy and Procedure group," SHPP, which we pronounced "ship." This group had twelve to fifteen regular members, which changed as titles were passed down and contracted positions expired. We began to officially meet under this title bi-weekly in August 2019.

When SHPP was formed, I finally started to feel like progress was happening. Much of this is due to another passionate student and a few driven faculty and staff members who joined the committee and spoke up in major ways, particularly another student—Steven Wilton— as well as Dr. Erin Crandall and the new co-chair of the committee, Dr. Kelly Dye. Now, the committee still had discussions over details like effective language, but we were also finally addressing the matter of making policy changes versus developing procedure. Up until this point, we'd been trying to find a way to make the existing systems and offices work in a new way. Each of these potential solutions ended up going nowhere. In a moment of extreme frustration, I told the committee that *we were never going to find a solution within our existing structure because the university structure was built to perpetuate sexualized violence and protect the people who commit it.* Between this and similar conversations, we realized that we needed to put forward something completely new.

As we started to brainstorm what this might look like, we also began to do some groundwork with students. I became the coordinator and lead organizer of the "Now What" campaign. The name came from the idea that we know that sexualized violence on campus is a problem—so, now what? Where do we go from here? I spent weeks coordinating events, setting up a bystander training opportunity, and making posters. It rolled out in October 2019. The stand-out event was a closed kickboxing class called "ReClaim" where survivors of sexualized violence could learn some badass kickboxing self-defence from a trauma-informed counsellor. I didn't attend the class out of respect for the privacy of the survivors, but the counsellor told me it was fully attended and impactful. The group continued to meet a few more times.

Surprisingly, the longest-lasting impact the "Now What" campaign had wasn't an event, but the posters and stickers I created, which went up all over campus. The posters asked specific questions about sexualized violence that students may face from day to day. They were put up alongside supports for survivors of sexualized violence. We received a great response about these, and many of the posters continue to be printed and put up each year. The entire SHPP committee was hugely supportive and helpful in making the "Now What" campaign a campus-wide reality, and the continued impact it still has is well worth the weeks of sleep I lost to make it happen.

That week, my team and I also hosted a Q and A session on what the Sexualized Violence Policy looked like at the time. The goal of this session was to inform students of where we were at, but it ended up giving us an important perspective on issues unique to international students. Thanks to the brave students who spoke to us that day, we were able to edit our policy to help address these concerns. Being able to take those concerns back to the committee and see an immediate effort to address them within our policy highlights a crucial difference between the original and the current draft; not only were students the primary concern, but we were leading the charge. If another student or I brought up a problem with the policy or explained how we felt certain elements wouldn't benefit students, it was immediately revisited and reworked. We were encouraged to discuss our work on the policy with people who might bring in relevant insights or new ideas. We were never made to feel ashamed if we felt out of our depth or had trouble understanding more complicated policy elements. Instead of leaving meetings feeling angry, I left feeling encouraged and empowered. I was seeing the true power students had to push for change on campus.

While hundreds of students engaged with the "Now What" campaign, every single Acadia student, current and future, could rely on having a safe and effective Sexualized Violence Policy. While the campaign was happening, our radical solution for new procedures was taking shape. Our committee was preparing to suggest to the university that a new permanent office should be dedicated to response, investigation, and education on the topic of sexualized violence. This office would not only facilitate investigations in cases of alleged sexualized violence but provide support to anyone who reached out. The office would also offer regular training and education to campus groups on what sexualized violence is and how we can create a safer community. We wrote our entire policy around this office and reiterated to the university that protecting students in this way should be a priority. Thankfully, it was approved. The other committee members and I were beyond thrilled! It was a major win after what felt like an endless series of doors slammed in our face. I began to plan a second week of "Now What" events and had a new series of posters created. Unfortunately, all this great progress was happening in January and February of 2020. In March, our world stopped turning, and we were all sent home as COVID-19 hit Nova Scotia. Although round two of the "Now What" campaign was cancelled, SHPP continued to meet virtually and iron out the final details of the policy. The hiring of the coordinator for the new office, a position that was now known as the "Sexualized Violence Education and Response Coordinator" (SVREC), was halted along with all university hiring.

When we returned to campus in September, we were told funding for the SVREC was cancelled due to COVID. The pandemic—a traumatic yet temporary situation—was being used as an excuse to save money at the cost of student safety. I was livid. Our committee was outraged. Every student I spoke to reacted with utter disbelief at how little the university and those in charge seemed to care for our well-being. Thankfully, an ally among the university higher-ups spoke to one of our student union executives and suggested a plan of attack for us to change the rest of their minds.

Some of the students involved wrote a letter telling the uiniversity president and provosts that if this position was not permanently funded and hired as soon as possible, we would be contacting the media to show everyone that Acadia was prioritizing their pockets over the safety of their students. This was happening at the same time that multiple Atlantic universities were being criticized for their lack of support for survivors of sexualized violence. Had we gone forward, it would have fanned the flames towards Acadia next. The letter was signed by every major student leader on campus, including club presidents, Internal Organization Coordinators, Senior Residence Assistants, and our Students' Union executives. On October 28, 2020, I got word that our letter had worked. Acadia University had committed to having the SVREC hired full-time by January 2021, with a higher salary than the dismal amount initially promised. When I read that email, I started to openly weep in the meal hall. I was excited, happy, and exhausted after two years of fighting. We'd done it. Everything the other members of SHPP and myself had tried so hard to make happen for our students was finally going to be a reality.

From here, our policy spent the next few weeks going through final edits to make sure everything was smooth and consistent, as well as coherent with other university policies, particularly the Harassment and Discrimination policy, which I'd also helped to draft over the summer of 2020. With this complete, the policy was ready to be released. On December 16, 2020, the policy was announced in a campus-wide email alongside a quote from me: *"I am proud to be a part of the committee, which has worked incredibly hard to create a policy that is truly and finally to the benefit of students," says Cameron Smith, an Acadia student and Coordinator of the Acadia Mental Health Initiative. "This policy is a major step for us to be able to keep students educated, aware, and safe. Sexualized violence is a systemic problem, but I believe this policy marks real progress towards us creating a new and better system for everyone at Acadia."* Who would have known that one of my proudest achievements would be summed up by a few lines in an email I'm sure no one bothered to read?

The following semester, some of the committee members and I hosted an event to introduce the policy and the newly hired SVREC to all students, staff, and faculty. On March 18, 2021, our event was attended by over thirty people, numbers which were pretty impressive for an in-person event during COVID. At the time of writing, the live stream has been viewed by over seven-hundred people. You can watch it yourself on Instagram, @acadiastudents. The reaction was overwhelmingly positive, and people were excited to meet and learn about the SVREC and see the full development of our policy.

Some elements in the new policy are worth being excited over, and I want to highlight them to show the kinds of developments we can and should be pushing for. First, the policy is not only targeted towards survivors and perpetrators but also provides support for witnesses, by-standers, support people for the survivor and perpetrator, and anyone else who feels affected by the weight of sexualized violence on campus. It is built on survivor-centric and trauma-informed approaches, both of which are explicitly defined in the document. The new policy officially extends to any off-campus events the university has a vested interest in. This means almost any off-campus event in which a student reports under this policy can be dealt with through the university, instead of having criminal reporting as the only option. Transparency about the nature of this policy is also a core component, which means no more hidden numbers and secret matters of sexualized violence.

Acadia's Sexualized Violence Policy also includes a non-investigative approach in addition to the typical investigation methods. If chosen, a survivor can work with the SVREC and their alleged perpetrator to make the perpetrator aware of the problems with their behaviour and provide opportunities for education and understanding. With this approach, people now have the option of going through a process of growth and progress instead of only being able to seek out repercussions. I believe this approach will be extremely helpful when it comes to attacking the ignorance that helps sexualized violence thrive on campuses. Perpetrators won't merely be slapped with an investigation; they will have to sit down and learn about the harm of their actions. This path could also offer healing to survivors, as they may get to see that their perpetrator has learned from the incident and is far less likely to do harm going forward. Alleged perpetrators must show willing engagement in order for this option to be practised. The survivor can also pull out of the process at any time. The survivor and SVREC retain the right to move to an investigative approach if non-investigative measures are deemed insufficient. An approach like this takes time and care, and I believe its inclusion in the policy helps to show the attitude change I've witnessed while doing this work. Even though it took a long time, we kept pushing to create the best system possible. It took some heavy convincing, but student-focused solutions to sexualized violence have finally been recognized as a priority both as a campus issue and as a financial matter.

I was hired as an intern for the summer of 2021 to work on making the jargon-heavy policy into several plain language documents. No one in crisis should have to sit down with a dictionary of legal terms when they're seeking support and justice. In order for the policy to be effective for the community it serves, everyone must be able to understand it. I'm excited for the opportunity to start doing the work and to take whatever steps I can to make it accessible for all members of our campus community. The fact that this intern position exists at all is yet another sign of the progress campus advocates have made at Acadia.

When I graduated in May 2021, I was given an award recognizing my service to the university. It felt odd to be recognized for working on a subject so many students before me have been silenced over. When the previous AMHI coordinator left, they were angry and disappointed in what they had seen. They had no desire to continue relationships with the Students' Union or the university. And having seen what they went through trying to make change? They were right to feel that way. But after two more years of doing this work, not only did I graduate having finished what we set out to do, but I'm returning to Acadia for my second degree. Though I've left my official position, I'm continuing my work with the Sexualized Violence Policy and the Harassment and Discrimination policy as a student representative. I have positive connections and faith in our Students' Union to keep doing good work in this area. Though I dealt with significant resistance over the last few years, what I ultimately saw was the majority of people pushing for what was right, changes in attitude when it was most needed, a campus full of students hungry for change, and a new structure that was built with student well-being at its core.

Last I heard, the man who groped me was still on the football team. However, four years later, I have a lot more hope that reporting similar actions today wouldn't feel so pointless. Now, there are options for students to report solely to receive support, where the perpetrator and incident never have to be named. Now, we have education and training in the works to make sure everyone understands what consent and sexualized violence are and that there are consequences in place for those who ignore these concepts. Now, our system is built on support, prevention, and education, not just on reporting and managing after an incident has happened. To build something like this, you need a lot of people dedicated to doing the work, which will undoubtedly be incredibly difficult at times. Sexualized violence is a tough subject to handle, and it's an uphill battle, but it's a fight that's worth it every time to protect and support survivors.

I wrote the prior pages in late May of 2021, and revisiting them over two years later in August of 2023, I feel a wealth of emotions. Since writing this chapter, I have started and finished an education degree, graduating in May 2023. I have had the opportunity to pivot my skills and learning from behind-the-scenes policy work to more public-facing anti-violence and anti-oppression efforts. I have also witnessed incredible work by a dedicated group of folks at Acadia University. With all of this in mind, I would be remiss if I didn't report back on the policy and other works in action.

One piece of the Sexualized Violence Policy acknowledges that ongoing training on the subject will be a regular part of campus life. Since I began working, I have trained several hundred people, both on campus and in our surrounding community, in Bystander Intervention, 2SLGBTQIA+ history and allyship, and respecting gender diversity. The team of trainers at large has trained upwards of a thousand people in those and other related trainings. Notably, our football team now receives annual training on fighting toxic masculinity and being emotionally healthier men. Though I was not a part of this training, the fantastic team who remains at Acadia has blown me away with the new work they're pushing for, even when meeting resistance.

A key member of that team is the aforementioned Sexualized Violence and Response Coordinator, an astonishing human named Allison Smith. Having spent the last two and a half years with the honour of working with her, I am consistently shocked and grateful we ended up with someone so perfect for this role. I could list Allison's stunning resume of degrees and experiences, but I think it is more important to mention what makes her the person students adore and trust when they are experiencing the deep trauma of sexualized violence. Allison radiates a kindness and gentleness that comforts and removes pressure from the students who see her. She consistently goes above and beyond to create and assist with campus events and initiatives. I have never before seen a university department or representative have the high regard of the students in the way Allison does. Personally, she has been a supportive and encouraging presence in my life like I have never had before. So much of the work I have done over the last two years has been with Allison's constant advice and guidance. I owe much of my ongoing hope in a rather dark time for our society to Allison, and knowing there are more people like her making the world a better place. I write this not to sing

Allison's praises and show my gratitude for her, but in hopes that future Acadia students may see this, and know exactly the kind of person who is going to be fighting for them.

In fall of 2021, *Maclean's* revealed its annual university rankings. For the first time ever, sexual violence prevention was included in the criteria. Acadia was ranked number one nationally. I was overwhelmed, thrilled, and humbled. It was not national recognition that made me emotional, it was that all of the rankings are selected from student feedback. Acadia students took the time to report that they felt safer, more protected, and cared for than ever before. All I cared about when I joined the policy committee was people being safer and building a more supportive community. This was a clear answer from students, we had done that. There are certainly still issues and things that need to change in our system, but it had changed for the better in a big way.

Within a few hours of the Macleans rankings dropping, I had received numerous texts and calls from friends and campus members thanking me for my work. I had talked to Allison and we got to share in the joy that what we had been doing had resonated with students. I couldn't believe it, because I still don't think my work was anything extraordinary. To me, I was just using the skills I had to do what I feel is right, as I have always done. That is how we progress, not by sitting around, voting for pople we're pretty sure will make the right call and then tuning out. It takes the groundwork at the personal, institutional, local, provincial, and federal level. I did what I could in my little campus community. It doesn't mean that much overall I suppose, but it means a lot to me to know I did my part to make a space I love a better place to be. Our campuses are changing, but there's more work to be done. I, for one, am going to keep up the fight to make it happen.

Engaging Men in Sexual Violence Prevention: Challenges, Barriers, and Ways Forward

Maddie Brockbank

I have vivid memories of the things I heard around the halls of my high school. While attending a Catholic secondary school in an affluent neighbourhood in Southern Ontario, I was at the mercy of a deeply engrained rape culture without any tools, language, or knowledge about how to manage, identify, or address it. During my walks up and down the hallways in between classes, so-called "rape jokes" flew over my head, and my flinches were punctuated by boisterous laughter. In grade nine, a boy in the twelfth grade taunted me for weeks on end with lewd comments whenever he saw me with a male friend; he constantly asked whether I was "giving it up" to him. In grade ten, a male friend made continuous comments about my body and my appearance, telling me once that I was a "six" in the looks department and then calling me "shallow" when I didn't want to date him. He then told people that we hooked up, which led to weird looks, whispers, and titters as I walked by classmates who heard about it. In the eleventh and twelfth grades, boys in my classes started pursuing incoming grade nine students, dubbing it the "LG Hunt," which represented the sexual pursuits of "little girls." In the weeks leading up to prom, my graduating class nominated and cast their votes for a host of prom superlatives, framed as "awards," ranging from "most likely to die a virgin" to "best body," without the consent of anyone nominated. Throughout the entire four years I spent in high school, I heard countless stories about outrageous parties and the hook-ups that happened there, and I watched many young women come to school on Monday with their heads bowed and their cheeks flushed, as the alleged details of their weekend activities were spread like wildfire.

Upon entering university, I knew that these things were still happening; however, as a commuter student who kept to herself, I didn't have the same immersive experience of it. The things I'd witnessed and experienced while growing up always sat uncomfortably with me, bubbling just underneath the surface of my skin, but I struggled to name it. My attempts to do so during high school were quickly and harshly shot down by my administration, and I didn't think it would be much different at university. Burned by memories of rape jokes and body shaming, I kept my head low and moved quietly through my first year of university without incident.

However, things changed rather drastically when I set foot in my second-year feminist social work class. I distinctly remember sitting at the front of the class and being completely engrossed in the content every single week. After fourteen years of Catholic elementary and secondary school education, this course marked the first time I had heard certain terms—like consent and patriarchy—and the first time I felt I had the ability and the words to name the things I experienced and witnessed. Our course covered so many topics, experiences, and concerns—ranging from the criminalization of HIV non-disclosure, to child-rearing, to gender-based and sexualized violence, to arts-based interventions and research—that I felt continuously empowered, challenged, surprised, and affirmed in every class. In retrospect, it was truly a quintessential coming-of-age moment for me, a clear turning point marked by a shift in my thinking that paved the way for the next several years of my life.

However, I remember being troubled. While I was inspired, reaffirmed, and touched by the stories shared by many women guest speakers, foundational feminist writers, and my own peers in the course, I felt that something was missing. Overwhelmingly, I got the sense that survivors of violence, women, and gender diverse people were burdened with the responsibility of redressing cisheteropatriarchal harms in all their various forms. Every story I heard and read detailed the steep and treacherous processes of resisting interpersonal, state, institutional, and ideological violence, where feminists were continuously thwarted, dismissed, and attacked for their work. Often, it seemed that the perpetrators of this violence were invisible or mere shadows, hovering namelessly and facelessly somewhere in the background. Put simply, I felt frustrated that men appeared to be completely absent from this conversation despite the stark realities of their overrepresentation as perpetrators of gender-based and sexualized violence and as leaders of institutions resisting feminist work. My own experiences solidified my frustrations about how men were not necessarily reflecting on the spectrum of sexual harm that they perpetrated when they shouted obscene comments at women walking by or spread intimate details about women they had hooked up with.

Armed by my questions and constantly evolving ideas, I stayed behind one day after class to tentatively approach my professor, who had rapidly become my feminist idol.

"So," I remember beginning, feeling awkward, uncertain, and nervous.

Her answering smile was reassuring and pushed me to continue.

"I kind of have an idea. I want to talk to men about sexual violence."

From that initial statement, my professor became my supervisor. We began to have extensive discussions about men's roles in gender-based and sexualized violence perpetration, intervention, and prevention. She supported me in actualizing my whirlpool of questions and reflections to make them a research proposal, which sought to explore male university students' perspectives of sexual violence on Ontario university campuses. In the Summer of 2017, I was thrilled to be funded to conduct my project, where I had hour-long conversations with seven male university students about sex, consent, sexual violence, masculinity, and prevention. The interviews revealed some things I inherently knew, things that shocked me, and slivers of hope that excited me. While some men demonstrated concerning (mis)understandings of consent and violence that had me hiding visible cringes as they talked, all of them spoke earnestly and honestly about wanting to be involved in conversations about and movements against sexual violence. However, they often felt like there was little opportunity to do so, or they didn't know where to begin.

———

On the day of my poster presentation for the project, held in a large hall at McMaster in late October, I remember feeling like this work wasn't finished. While my research evoked some great conversations and insights, the absence of actionable steps or opportunities for men to engage more readily in this work was troubling. It felt like I was merely contributing to a growing body of work and not offering any kind of solution to a well-known issue, one that feminists have continued to name for centuries. After another brief chat with my supervisor, I set out to pitch a project at an advocacy and active citizenship funding competition at the university. First prize was $3,000. The night before the event, I pieced together a quick slideshow for my pitch, titling it "Fostering Men's Allyship in Violence Prevention."

I was so nervous when I arrived at the event on a sunny day in March 2018; there were about twelve other competitors who all were dressed nicely, had polished posters, and oozed confidence in their ideas. The smudged screen of my laptop and my simple slideshow seemed deeply inadequate. When the judging began, I tried to watch the judges' interactions with the other presenters subtly and carefully. They spent a good twenty minutes with each person, seemingly peppering them with questions and writing vigorous notes. I prepared myself silently for a barrage of questions that were all too common when you announce that you do anti-violence work with men: are you suggesting men are to blame for all sexual violence? What about the good guys? Why are you attacking men? It was a rhetoric that I became familiar with after presenting my research informally and formally over the six months prior to this competition.

However, I was a bit stunned each time a different judge approached my table. I gave my pitch, citing statistics about men's violence, naming the processes that forced women and gender-diverse people to historically bear the brunt of this work, talking about my previous research, and requesting funds to support an event specifically geared towards men's roles in violence prevention. Once I finished, I steeled myself for questions that simply never came. Each judge smiled at me, thanked me, scribbled a few notes, and moved on. I stood there, wondering absently if this was a test, and immediately jumped to the conclusion that things weren't going well.

My nerves livened even further when the donor for the event, a sleek business alum from McMaster, approached me to receive my pitch. I went through my script again, watching his reactions warily. His brow was furrowed, fingers pinching his chin as he listened. Once again, I braced myself for the worst. Here I was, talking to a white businessman about how men need to play a role in violence prevention due to their proximity to cisheteropatriarchal privilege and power. I fully expected to be criticized, scoffed at, or waved off.

Pinching the hem of my shirt, I waited for his reaction when I finished speaking. He peered at me through his square glasses for a brief moment, then said, "This is really, really interesting." I was floored. I thanked him as he nodded at me and walked away.

When it was time to announce the winners, my dad—who took time off work to attend—was absolutely certain that I would be announced in first place. My palms were slick and my heart hammered as I tried to ignore the bit of hope bubbling in my throat. I listened distantly to the donor's remarks about the strength of the projects being presented and all that they would offer the university. I watched in a daze as the second and third place winners were announced. My heart was thundering in my ears as the dean picked up the first-place certificate. Just before they announced the winner, my dad whispered, "It's you." When my name was called, I jumped to my feet, beaming at the applause, and wobbled up to the front of the room. After cursory pictures and handshakes, I lingered to talk with the donor, the dean, and the judges.

The donor looked at me again, this time with a wide smile. "You convinced me that this was needed," he said. "You took a well-known story and flipped it on its head. It was excellent."

On the car ride home, I was bursting from exhilaration, lingering adrenaline (that still trembled my fingers), and hope. Perhaps this work was becoming more accepted. If a room full of prestigious representatives from the university could believe in this work, then maybe it would all come together, fitting together perfectly like pieces of a puzzle. With $3,000 to put this together, I felt invincible.

———

Four months later, my hope had dissipated.

I was bone tired, deeply frustrated, and rapidly approaching a kind of debilitating hopelessness that concerned my family and friends. After the successful pitch and obtaining the funding, I began to organize meetings with people on and off campus who were invested in this work. I met with people from the Equity and Inclusion Office, the Student Wellness Centre, student-led peer support organizations, and community services that addressed men's violence. What started out as a chipper, excited, and hopeful endeavour quickly devolved; I left every meeting with a McMaster employee, a student peer support representative, or a community worker with several more things to jot on my to-do list. I felt alone and isolated as I ran from meeting to meeting, leaving with more things to do and feeling defeated by the lack of partnership and collaboration that I envisioned. Many people that I met with were overburdened with their own work expectations and schedules. While many supported the event, many gave me ideas to improve it without any ideas for how to make it happen. Administrators who held power didn't answer my emails at all.

I also appeared to unknowingly wade into rocky politics that I hadn't anticipated. Namely, I observed some key agencies in the greater Hamilton community, who are involved in gender-based violence intervention and prevention, appear almost possessive or territorial over men's engagement in anti-violence work. In other words, some key community shareholders were not pleased with the idea of myself or McMaster facilitating an event on male allyship when they felt it was their domain. It became more complicated by my efforts to make this event charitable to benefit the important work of Hamilton's local sexual assault centre. I was really uncomfortable when I discovered, mere weeks before the event, that some other agencies were unhappy, particularly because they did not feel that they would benefit materially or because their work felt unrecognized. I felt frustrated and embarrassed. I felt like I was failing. What began as something I was so hopeful about had turned into something I could barely stand the thought of without feeling nauseated. Everything felt doomed.

———

The breaking point came unexpectedly. All summer, I had been in talks with McMaster's Athletic Department about supporting the event, along with other male-dominated departments, like STEM, and general campus organizations (e.g. Residences). I'd heard countless stories about instances of sexual harm within these spaces. One story stood out: during a consent seminar, one male athlete air dropped sexually explicit photos and rape jokes to unsuspecting attendees, many of whom were women. When people expressed these concerns to administration, nothing really happened, which is an all-too-common story for survivors of sexual violence on university campuses.

I felt that Athletics could play a major role in this event; despite their previous disengagement from anti-violence efforts (including dodging commitments to an allyship campaign for months), I thought that engaging male athletes in this discussion would perhaps inspire other men on campus to take part and would facilitate a sense of accountability for men in Athletics to challenge rape culture within their own organization and the institution at large. After several voicemails and emails, I finally scheduled a meeting with the athletic director at the time and one of his assistants in the summer of 2018.

The athletic director did not show up. I met with his assistant who assured me that this was an initiative Athletics would stand behind. She promised me that athletes and coaches from various teams would attend and that they would support advertising the event. While she indicated that they could not support financially, she assured me that she would put it in Athletic calendars and assist me in coordinating their attendance.

I was elated. Not only did I have the support of the Hamilton Tiger-Cats and Hamilton Bulldogs organizations, but I was also now going to have McMaster Athletics' support. It felt like such a significant step in the right direction to de-stigmatizing sexual violence prevention efforts with men.

They even gave me a booth at Homecoming in September. I donned McMaster gear and stood proudly behind a sexual violence prevention table at the entrance to the stadium, with a colourful homemade sign taped haphazardly to its edges. We had flyers for the event, brochures for local organizations and on-campus services, a donation bucket, and a crisis number on the sign. My sister, one of my constants throughout the whole process, and I stood there for four hours. Of the hundreds of students that passed by us, no one took a flyer from my outstretched hand. No one approached us. No one made eye contact. They passed by us quickly to play games at the booth next to us. It seemed like our booth was a damper on what was meant to be a fun, wild, and carefree day. The realities of sexual violence—especially the stark fact that it is more likely to happen within the first eight weeks of school—were steadfastly ignored as if they were too uncomfortable and taboo to even think about. In retrospect, it felt like an omen.

Over the next few weeks after Homecoming, things fell apart. The athletic director and his assistant stopped answering my emails. Eventually, the assistant told me that she couldn't guarantee that any athletes would show up. I was panicked. It felt like such a covert form of institutional resistance: promise support, but don't come through with anything material. Something they claimed was important to them was suddenly not worth any time or energy. Promises were empty. I wondered if anything had been real or taken seriously at all.

The night I received that email, I sent over twenty-five emails to coaches and administration in the department and department administrators from various faculties. I asked for their teams, students, clubs, classes, whomever, to attend the event. I wrote about how important it was for men to be an active part of this conversation, how significant it would be for people to see men in their communities stepping up, and how much it would mean to the Sexual Assault Centre of Hamilton (SACHA) to see support for their organization. After writing emails, I remember lying on the floor of my living room, glaring at the ceiling. *Community work sucks*, I thought bitterly.

My phone lit up a few minutes later with an email from the coach of McMaster Football, the largest team in the entire department. The email was simple, but made me yell out, "Thank God!" which startled my dog who laid beside me on the floor.

His email read: "Hi, Maddie. Football will attend."

The event venue set, the speaker arranged, the peer-support spaces planned, the Hamilton Ti-Cats, McMaster Athletics, Mohawk Athletics representatives ready to attend, and with the MC—a popular host on a local news station—hired, I was on cloud nine. Things were finally coming together. I'd struck a balance with McMaster employees supporting the event after I'd implemented their suggestions, I'd settled some tensions with local organizations who were now readily attending the event with their own booths and supplies, and I budgeted to adequately compensate everyone who was playing a role in the event. It was now one week before the event, and I fully anticipated to have the 130-seat venue full.

I'd sent casual emails to many people reminding them about the event for the weeks leading up to it. I'd given up hope in emailing the athletic director. Most coaches and administrators didn't reply or acknowledge me at all. Some coaches sent regrets for flimsy reasons, but I was alright with it. As long as the football team attended, I was okay. Perhaps they were the gateway to greater entry into the department. However, I began to notice that the football coach was not responding to my reminders. An unsettled feeling began to brew.

The breaking point came when I saw the news story. The football coach had been suspended for using offensive and harmful language toward an official. A small piece of me ached to mutter, the irony is not lost, but I continued scrolling through various news articles covering the incident. I was stunned. It had happened a week or two before the event. He hadn't been replying in that time; some of my emails he likely ignored, but some he probably didn't even see.

I quickly looked up the phone numbers and emails of assistant coaches, many of whom I'd reached out to previously with no reply. On a whim, I called an assistant coach. He answered at 6 p.m. on a Sunday night. I nervously went over everything that happened: the head coach committed that the team would attend. I hadn't heard from him. I didn't know he was suspended. I'm begging you to uphold this commitment. The team needs this conversation now more than ever.

He assured me that football would still attend. I was relieved. Then, Monday morning, I got an email from another assistant from the team, which informed me that no one from football was coming. Shaking, I dialed the number he'd pasted placatingly at the end of the email. When he answered, he was instantly sheepish. Sorry, but not going to happen. I said something curt and snide, bade him goodbye, hung up the phone, then instantly broke down. It was three days before the event. I pictured an empty hall, an empty donation bin. I was so upset, frustrated, and defeated. I thought about all the experiences I'd had, the things I'd witnessed, the feelings that I had every time I bumped up against rape culture. I thought about my sixteen-year-old self who was always wondering if anything would ever change, if I could ever walk down hallways without fear. I thought about how many men would be missing out on conversations and events like these, how many dismissed them as something that simply didn't apply to them when, in reality, they were all implicated in the impacts of sexual violence. It felt like it was over.

I allowed myself thirty minutes to cry, to be angry, to write down unpleasant things in my journal. Then, I was back in motion. I emailed and texted practically every person I knew. Even though I'd done so much reaching out over the last six months, even though I'd paid for and submitted advertisements for local papers, websites, and radio stations, I pushed myself harder. I couldn't let this event fail. I couldn't fail SACHA. I couldn't let this resistance break me. I knew that there were countless activists, feminists, student organizers who had experienced the same things I was, who felt the way I was feeling right now. In the face of adversity, institutional resistance, and a general unwillingness to acknowledge the significance of this conversation, we push forward. And we are surrounded by a community of care who holds us up.

The event was a smashing success with over one hundred attendees. I don't remember much because I was running around like a chicken with my head cut off, but I remember the joy, the relief, the gratitude I felt when I saw people trickling into the event, some faces familiar and others not. My community came through for me in ways that I will never be able to adequately describe. The donation bin was overflowing, the volunteers were greeting people with friendly smiles, the organizations that attended were mingling easily.

The speaker, a wonderful public educator from a men's violence prevention program in Calgary, delivered a beautiful, interactive presentation. I watched, touched, when I saw male athletes from Mohawk College chatting happily with my social work friends in the row in front of them during a consent-based activity. I marveled at the fulsome dialogue emerging from the gender boxes activity, which revealed the constraints and harms of traditional gender roles and cisheteropatriarchal masculinity. I grinned at text updates from Safer Space volunteers who waited in another room in case anyone in the event needed support and who commended the event. I couldn't stop looking around at the attendees, seeing two Ti-Cats talking to mildly starstruck McMaster students, male ally volunteers from an organization nodding along to the discussion and taking notes, and student volunteers working diligently to make sure the event was being live streamed.

Though some things are a bit hazy from all the adrenaline—the crescendo and release of six months of stress—I will never forget the hearty applause when I announced that we had raised $3,000 for SACHA. And I will always keep the emails I got after the event tucked away in a folder in my email to remind me that all of this is always worth it.

In the few years since the event, which I cheekily named "Commit(men)t & Allyship," I have continued to pursue sexual violence prevention with men in various forms. I continue to traverse the rocky terrains of institutional resistance, backlash, tension, and the insidious presence of rape culture that underpins every setting that I do this work in, now as a PhD Student. I continue to feel uplifted by incredible student organizers, feminists, and grassroots organizations who work tirelessly to address sexual violence on their campuses and in their communities. I feel immense solidarity with them; I don't really feel so alone anymore. Things at McMaster continue to bloom in hopeful ways, even though there still is a long road ahead.

It feels a bit daunting to think about what I learned from this process and what I can pass along to students who feel compelled to mobilize and organize against sexual violence. There is so much merit in the frontline resistance, the posters and strikes and protests and campaigns led by survivors that call out their perpetrators, their institutions,  and the state. I admire the work of Students for Consent Culture Canada, the Women and Gender Equity Network at McMaster, and the tireless work of survivors on campuses across Canada. These organizers likely have much more profound and meaningful things to say and suggestions to follow when engaging in sexual violence prevention. My work feels a bit like a tributary, a smaller branch within the broader flow of a river. It is one part of a whole. I think that engaging men in sexual violence prevention is a key piece to this puzzle; when men hold the power to make a difference in positions of authority, when they're overrepresented as perpetrators, when our society is structured by white cisheteropatriarchy, they must be an active part and supporter of this work.

This story is part of a greater narrative of resistance. While we meet resistance in various ways when we do this work, ranging from tangible institutional rejection to ideological invalidation, we also resist and persist. We refuse to be silenced, dismissed, and ignored. We do this work even when it's hard. We come together and lift each other up even when we're being pushed down. We build communities in the ruins.

How We Survived

Building practices of self care and community care

Baggage

Kylee Graham

Heavy as a billion suns
as one / ocean on the inside of my eyelids
blisters on her feet
do not tell me
these things all weigh the same
when we are built with different strengths
different frames
if you put me in the lightweight category
I may uppercut your smile
onto my face / all by mistake
don't try to convince us
a pound of bricks is the same as a pound of feathers
only one will weigh you down
underwater
only one
still makes that noise in your head
a fork stuck in the bottom of the dishwasher
the feeling of ribs running over knuckles
un -com -fort -able

in public

call me Atlas
my back is worn
arms have grown

[I carried it for way too long]

call me Romeo
but they are the ones who left too soon
and I'm to blame

call me any woman's name
there ever was
because we all have something that makes our pants sag
we just can't shake off
forget

some have only just picked theirs up, muscles fresh
toned
they think they have it under control
I wish you luck and love
maybe all that milk you drank when you were young
will keep your bones in place
joints square
nerves ready
if you feel fatigued
know this is normal from long hours of lifting—
things you didn't want to

and when your back gives out
legs go weak
ground yourself, adjust your positioning
according to the morphology
your mother gave you

if you train enough
at some point it'll all just be muscle memory
and things will feel a little lighter
eventually
the strength will come
you'll learn to bear loads outside your comfort zone
hypertrophy takes time, and power even longer

but in the meantime
all I really want you to know is

the weight feels heavier
if you carry it alone

How to Heal Your Heart at Home

Anonymous

Content Warning: Moderate description of eating disorders, mild description of sexual assault
To skip to the next story, turn to page 282.

This story follows "They Watched Me Burn," from section one.

Part 1, Solitude

I started my mornings with familiar, comforting rituals: wake up, recollect the scattered remnants of dreams, decide whether to keep them, then drowsily, lazily, allow the warm shadow of sleep to ebb away. I would lie in bed for half an hour or more, losing myself in meditation or fantasy. Shafts of sunlight streamed between the blinds while morning marched on beyond my window.

I would lift sheets from bare skin and be reminded of many things. There was a gap between my thighs, a brushstroke of stretch marks where feather-soft fat used to be. When I grazed my chest with dulled fingertips, I could feel the embossment of my sternum, the unguarded curvature of my ribs. For the first time in my life, I could see the shape of my emerging skeleton without holding my breath. I wondered if thinness might make me pretty; after self-correction, I concluded that even anorexia couldn't make me *less ugly*. My arms were thinner, my wrists more sharply angled—at the ulnar head, if my anatomy lessons weren't mistaken—and in them, I saw my mother's wrists as her hands glided gracefully across piano keys. The triangular webs across my skin had deepened too. In my skin cells, I saw tracings of my matrilineal heritage, mapping paths where wrinkles would form with the passing of years. My struggles had prematurely aged me, and, for weeks, I was startled when I looked down at my forearms and failed to recognize myself in an increasingly skeletal body.

——

Hi Professor X, I just wanted to give you an update on my studies and health. I've been quite sick for some time now, but I'm doing my best to keep up with the material. I've spent too much money on doctor's notes this term and I can't afford to ask for more. I've attached an image of my recent prescription and the weight loss I've had over the past month. I won't make it to today's class, but I'll definitely be at the final. Regards, Y.

The email was from my final year at the university. I eventually lost twenty pounds, about fourteen percent of my body mass, over a thirty-day period. If the bioimpedance on my scale was to be believed, there was a substantive drop in muscle—not just fat—which partially explained the weakness creeping into my limbs. In spite of the lethargy, the fatigue, the dizziness, and the unending heart palpitations, I just couldn't bring myself to eat anymore. Nothing tasted good. My favourite foods were gummy, wasteful ash—expensive, nutritionally deficient, and prone to inducing wave after wave of nausea. Instead, I developed new habits. In the mornings, I drank a flask of black tea with a teaspoon of milk, plus a large tablespoon of peanut butter to help swallow my pills. In the evenings, when I'd return from The University, a single bowl of food. My one weekly food expense was a two-kilogram bag of frozen veggies purchased for four dollars—impeccable fare for the inconsolable diner. Sometimes, I was too depressed to even put the bowl in the microwave, so my dinners were always unseasoned and often unthawed, with frost desolately gripping the corners of carrots or parabolas of peas. It was the only food I could eat.

———

After shedding my bedsheets, I would pause in front of my closet, peer thoughtfully at the sunny world behind my blinds, and plan my outfit for the day. There were breezy sundresses and loose shorts that beckoned in the hot May weather. For a few brief moments, I would frown to myself and wonder, *Are you going outside today? If so, where are you going? What are the chances that you'll run into someone from school? What if they see you and take a picture? Are you covering enough skin to avoid harassment?* Then I would pause again, grimace, and think, *No. I'm going to wear whatever I want, and the "feminists" can't stop me anymore.*

When I explained to people that I'd experienced sexualized violence, the "feminists" responded with a cavalier, "Yeah, but what were you wearing?" One instance happened at a nightclub. I was sober, and he'd been drinking. He boisterously wrapped his arm around my neck and plastered a kiss on my cheek. I privately thought that he was using drunkenness as an excuse to test the waters, to see if it was alright to push my boundaries further and determine whether I would reciprocate the gesture. A polite inquiry would have been preferable. It was fairly minor in the grand scheme of my experiences, but I still felt awful and cried for the rest of the night. It was the straw that broke the camel's back, if you will. My camel definitely needed spinal reconstruction surgery.

"It's just that you tend to wear pretty revealing outfits sometimes," said the "feminists."

I protested, of course. I knew one or two feminist talking points: "Clothing is not consent," and all that. It didn't seem to matter, however, and I stopped speaking to women about my problems. The men in my life said that they were sorry to hear about my experiences. They tried to make me feel better. None of them understood, though, and I would quickly receive well-meaning recommendations to "brush it off." At least the men in my life, of all people, did not imply that my clothing invited violence.

Fully dressed, I would then begin making my bed. I was unknowingly going through the motions of behavioural activation[1]. Every morning, my routine included the arranging of pillows and the smoothing of sheets. Then, I'd tuck in one of my stuffed animals, neatly folding ears and arraying arms in a comfortable position. I would beam at that stuffed animal, offer thanks, and exclaim my love. Consequently, every morning began with tidying, gratitude, and a genuine sense of happiness. I'd pick up a stuffed animal, see the sprightly animation of its limbs, and hear its words of affirmation, "You're doing a great job! You're working real hard! You can do it! I love you!" It took me many years to realize that my stuffed animals reflected my inner dialogue; after all, to show kindness

---

1. Behavioural activation is a type of therapy used to treat depression. It is essentially about increasing positive reinforcement and decreasing negative reinforcement to improve mood. The routine of making your bed every day, for example, is one of the most common behavioural activation patterns.

and love to them was to show kindness and love to myself. After that realization, my self-talk became gentler.

After dressing and tidying, it was time for tea. I lived in a crowded two-bedroom basement suite with two roommates. I managed to get up before them on most days and would enjoy a few quiet moments to myself. I'd boil the kettle, pop in a tea bag, splash in some milk, and sip calmly while gazing out the kitchen window. I was still wounded and weak, but it was much easier to lick those wounds in isolation. Having hours to myself each day was deeply restorative after so many years of scheduling my time around romantic partners.

"I think you're right. It's time."

I was sitting next to Isabelle on a tiny couch when we decided. The mood oscillated between nervous apprehension and growing certainty. We had been together for six years. She had taken well to gender-affirming treatment, and her dysphoria had improved. She had also discovered that she preferred the company of men. I supported that. There were other underlying issues in our relationship—all long-term relationships have a few—but I felt that many of them could be traced to a core cause: she simply wasn't attracted to me anymore. She loved me, but platonically. We both wanted freedom. I fiddled absently with my engagement ring.

I told Isabelle that I loved her but I knew there was a man that she was deeply interested in. From the very beginning of our relationship, I had always reaffirmed my belief in the idea that if you love someone, you'll let them go. I wanted her to be happy. She cried when I said that.

I thought about the sacrifices I'd made throughout our relationship, how I'd schedule my weeks around her, eking out hours to make time for games and appointments and meals; how I'd wordlessly, meticulously clean the house to decrease her burden. My entire life was planned around hers. I couldn't end things without affirmation of my own. I asked her if she'd been happy. She said yes. I asked if I'd treated her well. She said yes. Tears tumbled over my smile. We cried together and said farewell to our love of six years. I had finally pushed us forward into an unknown but promising future.

I enjoyed my sunlit sips in the kitchen. Occasionally, my tea rituals would wake up my roommates. A door would creak open, and out would emerge a half-lucid Isabelle, rubbing tiredly at her eyes. We'd smile at each other before she attended to her own morning. Then, a little later, Russell would stagger out, and we'd have our own amiable exchange. I'd make them both a cup of coffee, savouring the everyday bliss of living among friends, then return once more to solitude.

Part 2, Love

After tea, it was time for productivity and planning. I would slip into my room, shut the door behind me, and start by skimming my emails. I always avoided the stressful ones in the morning. Then, I'd peruse my calendar. *Let's see, what's on the docket today,* I'd muse as I scrolled through lists of tasks and colourful blocks of time. Delight spread across my face and heart when I read the words "date with Jason."

For two years, I poured everything I had into the Students' Union. I sacrificed health, grades, relationships, desires, and dignity. Nothing escaped my asceticism. Fortunately, however, I was prescient enough to plan for the inevitable burnout and correspondingly built in a failsafe. Through Isabelle, I kept tabs on a cohort of students. Over those two years, I would periodically check-in with her: *any student issues I should know about?* I would have loved to solicit feedback directly from *all* students, thus dodging even nascent claims of nepotism; alas, limited resources and low student buy-in made such efforts nigh impossible. Car accidents, delayed buses, personal struggles—if it was within my power to help, actions were taken and assistance was offered. I made a few meaningful changes based on their experiences. In the end, I decided that my reward for two years of service would be the simple pleasure of introducing myself to that cohort and observing their successes from a distance. That plan quickly changed for the better.

Before I knew it, I was hanging out in their laboratory, chatting about music while other students browsed car listings or played flash games. I learned their names, their hopes, their goals. As they learned about me, in turn, they dubbed me "Lab Mom" for my comparatively maternal presence. I found it equally funny and flattering; they actually seemed to like me. In the midst of that uncomfortable and foreign elation, one student in particular captured my interest.

As you might have guessed, his name was Jason. His vibe could be described as "small town eclectic." He wore grey sweatpants splattered with automotive grease and paired them with a chakra bracelet. When class was over, he'd fish out his keys, sling a rainbow canvas backpack over one shoulder, and climb into a beat-up car with dicks carved into the paint and a bolt lock haphazardly welded onto the door. I was immediately invested in the premise.

I'd met him for the first time at an annual general meeting. Isabelle had convinced that cohort of students to attend. Before they could all leave, I strode over and thanked each of them for their attendance, evenly distributing eye contact and firm handshakes among the bunch. They didn't know me, but thanks to Isabelle, I knew them. I had asked Isabelle to prime me with identifying information beforehand to smooth over the introductions. That's how I recognized him. He smiled as he shook my hand. I saw blue eyes and crow's feet, clean-shaven cheeks raised high with affability, and immediately forgot everything that came after.

Jason was an unusual partner. We spent a summer together where sleep was just a suggestion and passing out at 4 AM became the norm. The days were for video games and hijinks; the nights, anime and conversation. Laughter flowed freely from two hearts lighter than they were before. My memories of this time always stream past in vivid montage—daylight like diamonds, glittering on a lake; stargazing on the roof of his car; rain pouring outside my window while we remained, cozy and quiet, in the warm glow of my bedroom. He was dearer to me than my own blood. These fond moments would patinate over the years and become the bittersweet prelude to a very acrimonious ending. Still, at the time, that joy nourished my starving soul. I needed that. I found the time to heal in solitude, but I found the means to heal in love.

Part 3, Community

It is now the summer of 2021, and the sun is rising. My day begins. Jason—at this time, a close friend—snores erratically in his room. When he wakes up, he'll find a chilled carafe of coffee waiting for him in the fridge along with a hastily-drawn sketch of our two plush dogs. Isabelle and Russell live farther from me now, so I can't easily sauce them up with a morning brew, but on a rare occasion, I'll call Isabelle and let her know how all of our stuffed animals are doing. Those lighthearted exchanges are probably better than the acrid instant coffees I used to prepare, anyway. My interactions with all parties involved are sturdy and stable, or strained and strange, depending on the day. I keep trying, even still.

I also recently joined a national nonprofit called Students For Consent Culture Canada (whose story you'll also read about in this book), hoping to correct the still-unchanged SVP at The University. As a result, today's agenda is a blur of emails and readings. I didn't think I would fit in as an activist or advocate—but, somehow, among an intelligent, hypercompetent, and compassionate group of people, I've found some shred of belonging. I'm cagey and skittish when working with women. I tried to explain by pouring my heart out and telling my stories. For once, I was met with understanding. For once, my pain was validated. I bore my grief and wasn't admonished or shamed.

It was the first time that women had treated me with kindness since the abuse started. I finished Zoom calls and Jitsi meetings, collapsed on my bed, and didn't hold in the tears of relief that followed. *So that's what it's like,* I thought. *That's what it's like to have someone understand and care.* I never knew. It was like the last puzzle piece slid into place. Suddenly, I was whole again.

I need to be cautious against overpromising and underdelivering. I need to keep the promises I make to myself. I need to be compassionate and remember the sage words I heard among this benevolent circle of women: "Progress is not linear." They were right. As my circuit completes and my circle connects, I see that this journey is always going to be a cycle. Dark days will come again. But I've survived many winters, and I think I can weather even more. It is summertime in my life now. I'll step into the wide world with grace and poise. I'm going to dance in the sun and marvel at the rain. I found the time to heal in solitude. I found the means to heal in love. I found a place to heal in this community.

Valkyries and Memories

Anonymous

The person who came before me was metal.

They spoke with an alkaline, bitter-sharp tang. To hear them was to taste blood.

Their heart, ribcaged in iron, steeled each beat against endless siege.

I wanted to understand them. I hoped they would heal.

The person who came before me was more than metal.

The woman who came before me was chaos.

She averted her eyes, always. Her gaze was true sight, unseen, focused on focus, unfocused.

Her spirit hid harm beneath an iridescence of bruises, hallowed in her shadowed halls.

I wanted the best for her. I hoped she would heal.

The woman who came before me was more than chaos.

I was the woman who brash-bravely bore arms.

I remembered The Ironheart and The Rainbowspirit.

I was bruised and bloodied, flayed and felled. My broken bones could parry no longer.

I wanted to survive. I hoped I would heal.
The woman who brash-bravely bore arms became lesser.

I was the woman who could not mend.
I quit the field—a pyrrhic victory. I did not escape
I'd lived with demons at the gate. They slowly learned to exist among the people.
I wanted to live again. I believed I could heal.
The woman who could not mend began to breathe once more.

I am the woman who stands defiant.
I am shrouded, armored, ferrous, prismatic. Demons serve in the legions I command.
My banner is kindness; my warpaint is tears.
I can live again. I know I can heal.
The woman who stands defiant will honour the memories.

Strategic Policy Reform and Celebrating the Delayed Wins

Caitlin Salvino

Undoubtedly, the year following the publishing of *Our Turn: A National Action Plan to End Campus Sexual Violence* was a whirlwind. Over the course of that year, I didn't spend more than a week in the same city. I travelled (in many cases multiple times) to Toronto, Montreal, Quebec City, Halifax, Charlottetown, St. John's, and Vancouver. Other members of our team were visiting even more campuses across the country to provide as much behind-the-scenes support as possible to student survivors on the ground. These trips were focused on meeting with student survivors, student leaders, media, and government officials, advocating for intersectional survivor-centric reforms. The majority of our efforts were directed at supporting students who were advocating for change at the grassroots level. We would share pre-existing resources to adapt and work with them to conduct research to strengthen the reforms they were advocating for.

When I reflect on this time in my life, I must admit it was a period of immense exhaustion and crushing disappointment. The only way I can describe it is akin to the first part of this story, where I wrote about the disappointment we felt when we had our efforts shut down by Carleton University administrators. Our group at Carleton had worked so hard to mobilize individuals and groups representing thousands of students across our campus, and it didn't matter. The administration decided they weren't going to reform anything, regardless of the harm it would cause survivors. It wasn't right, and it wasn't fair, but there was nothing we could do.

Working with student groups and survivors across Canada for the OurTurn Action Plan, I felt as though we were experiencing this unfair rejection over and over again. In many cases, regardless of the number of students who mobilized, the extent of the media coverage, or the depth of our accompanying research, administrators would not concede to any reforms. This was hard enough for us to experience once, let alone on repeat with student survivors across the country.

To cope with these feelings of disappointment, I want to share two ways I was able to survive. First, the kindness of students involved in this movement made our efforts possible. There are countless experiences I could share to illustrate how important it was to be able to meet and support fierce student survivors and leaders who were fighting for change across this country. It was deeply inspiring and provided us with the strength to continue this work despite facing so much rejection and dismissal.

I can recount one exceptional example of kindness at the inception of OurTurn, when the report drafting was in the initial stages. The project had hit a wall and was at risk of not being able to continue moving forward. From an airport hangar, I called a fellow student leader who I had met just a few weeks earlier and explained the situation. At that moment, this person who I had only met once before, saved the OurTurn Action Plan. They listened, provided comfort, and unilaterally engineered the transferring of the action plan to the McGill student's society, who offered in-kind services to help get the action plan published. Beyond orchestrating formal support for the OurTurn action plan, they also provided an immeasurable amount of personal support. They offered me a room in their apartment in Montreal, at no cost, and an office space to work from. This support came at a time when I had been working full-time on the OurTurn project without any compensation or a space to operate from. This altruistic act of kindness from a stranger, who later became one of my closest friends, meant more to me than I can ever express.

However, this kindness was not an isolated incident. On multiple occasions after difficult meetings with administrators, students would provide me with space to decompress and sometimes shed a few tears in frustration. Whether it was in a student-run service centre, a student-run sexual-assault support centre, or a student union office, I greatly appreciated the space to recover and the moments of solidarity I shared with the students in those moments. With our early budget of approximately $0, I slept on more couches across this country than I can count. These fellow students sharing their homes were central to our survival during this precarious time, both for us as individuals and the organization as a whole. I also appreciated the kindness that stemmed from students being comfortable to share their stories with us and remain grateful for the friendships that emerged. The students I met in the year of writing and publishing the OurTurn Action Plan are among the best humans I have ever met. To this day, I have friends across the country. I appreciated all the coffeeshop introductions, the impromptu meetings, and the invitations to non-work-related things (like getting "screeched-in" while in Newfoundland and Labrador), every time I was alone in a new city. Through these acts of kindness, every moment I got to spend with other students was re-energizing and helped me have the strength to keep fighting.

In addition to the kindness of students, the other way I survived was through maintaining the unrelenting belief that we were building a better future. Regardless of whether the changes we were advocating for were made immediately (spoiler: they were not), I survived by knowing that eventually, our reforms would become best practices and transform responses to campus sexual violence. For example, when we were initially doing advocacy at Carleton University, a central issue was the acknowledgement of the term "rape culture."[1] Advocates who pre-dated our efforts with the open letters were working to have officials at the University recognise the pervasiveness of sexual violence on campus. The same week that the OurTurn action plan was released, the sexual assault experiences of women against Harvey Weinstein were shared publicly[2] and the #MeToo movement, led by Tarana Burke,[3] went viral on social

---

1. Per the OurTurn Action Plan, the Ontario government defined rape culture as: "A culture in which dominant ideas, social practices, media images and societal institutions implicitly or explicitly condone sexual assault by normalizing or trivializing male sexual violence and by blaming survivors for their own abuse." See Government of Ontario, Office of the Premier, It's Never Okay: An Action Plan to Stop Sexual Violence and Harassment (March 2015), online: at 9. We note in the action plan the criticisms raised as it relates to the use of the term "rape culture", including the possible implication of hierarchizing certain forms of sexual violence. See Salvino, Caitlin, Kelsey Gilchrist, and Jade Cooligan Pang. "OurTurn: A National Action Plan to End Campus Sexual Violence." Montreal, QC: Student's Society of McGill University, October 2017, 8.

2. Ronan Farrow, "From Aggressive Overtures to Sexual Assault: Harvey Weinstein's Accusers Tell Their Stories," The New Yorker, October 10, 2017.

3. Tarana Burke first coined the term "Me Too" in 2006 when she first used the phrase to bring awareness to the prevalence of sexual violence. Following the publication of the Harvey Weinstein sexual assault disclosures, the term #MeToo went viral on social media. It is recognised with starting national and global movements to raise attention to the high prevalence of sexual violence. See Salvino, Caitlin, and Connor Spencer. "OurTurn: One Year Later Report." Montreal, QC: Concordia Student's Union, April 2019, 37.

media. Since the #MeToo movement, there has been a societal shift in the recognition of sexual violence in our communities, including campus communities. Post-#MeToo, we no longer have to convince governments and institutions of the existence of sexual violence on campus. Rather, we have been able to move on and focus our advocacy on other important campus-related gender-based violence issues. As a group of student activists who have operated both pre- and post-#MeToo, we have seen firsthand that change is possible, but often takes time paired with unrelenting advocacy.

We have also seen the slow progress of change in campus sexual violence policy reform. Compared to when we first began this advocacy work, there are so many standards for sexual violence policies that are now widely recognised. It is important to reflect on the victories, on where our efforts have achieved significant policy reform on campus, albeit after many of us have moved on. For me, one of the survivor tools I have relied on has been reflecting on where my journey began at Carleton. For example, I periodically check-in on Carleton University's Sexual Violence Policy. Although all our suggested reforms in the second open letter were completely shut down by the campus administration in 2016, this rejection was only in the short term.[4] In the five years since I have moved on from Carleton, there have been significant reforms to the Carleton Sexual Violence Policy to better align with the needs raised by student groups. This includes an extensive and comprehensive consultation process that sought out the voices of students, with an added

---

4. Salvino, Caitlin and Jade Cooligan Pang, edited by Jody Miles, Sally Johnson, and Omran, Fa'Ttima, "Open Letter to Reform Carleton's Sexual Violence Policy." Carleton Human Rights Society, February 10, 2017.

focus on the needs of students with marginalised identities.[5] Following the student consultation process, numerous reforms were made in 2019 to the Carleton University Sexual Violence Policy, including:

- Adding timelines to the complaint procedures (section 8.6);

- Adding a conflict of interest clause (section 8.8);

- Adding an immunity clause, referred to as "no prosecution of minor drug and alcohol offences" (section 8.9);

- Expanding and clarifying the interim measures available to a survivor (section 8.12);

- Clarifying the application of the policy to visitors on campus and including information on other options available to a sur-

---

5. "Sexual Violence Policy Consultation - Sexual Assault Support Services," Carleton University. <https://carleton.ca/sexual-violence-support/sexual-violence-policy-consultation />. In A 2017 report provided to the Carleton University Board of Governors, there was recognition of the numerous reforms sought to the Carleton University Sexual Violence Policy. This included the need to redress the perceived barriers of: (1) the perceived requirement within the Policy for the Complainant and Respondent to face each other in a formal hearing; (2) adding an immunity clause or statement which protects Complainants or those seeking help from punishment for minor violations relating to alcohol or drug use; (3) reconciling the perceptions of cross-institutional applications of FIPPA as it relates to sharing information about disciplinary actions or consequences against the Respondent, and; (4) articulating the types of statements which are prohibited within the confidentiality section in the Policy. The report also acknowledged additional reforms being sought to the Carleton University Sexual Violence Policy, including: (1) clarify timelines throughout the Policy; (2) include visitors and alumni into the scope of the Policy under the definition of "University Community"; (3) clarify the accommodation process, and; (4) specify how the Policy is applied to incidents which occur off campus. See Carleton University, *2017 Annual Report on Sexual Violence, Presented to the Board of Governors*, 8 February, 2019. <https://carleton.ca/equity/wp-content/uploads/Carleton-2017-Annual-Report-on-Sexual-Violence.pdf>.

vivor in this situation (section 9.1);

- Adding information on alternative accommodations for survivors in the complaint process (i.e. face to face protections) (section 9.6);

- Adding a requirement that all those on the complaint review committee and appeal committee will receive "sexual violence and procedural fairness training" (section 10.2).[6]

Reflecting and celebrating the "delayed wins" we have achieved collectively has been central to my personal survival in this work. Although serious challenges remain with the Carleton Sexual Violence Policy, as well as with every campus sexual violence policy across Canada, we must still take moments to reflect on the progress we have made. To have our recommendations of standards, such as timelines and immunity clauses, added to the Carleton Sexual Violence Policy is meaningful. Less than a few years ago, we were ignored, dismissed, and gaslit by officials who told us that our asks were impossible, and now some of these suggestions have been implemented. Being mindful of our history and all that we have achieved serves as an important reminder that ultimately, we will win. As we continue to advocate for reforms that are labelled as impossible, such as comprehensive mechanisms to address sexual violence by professors, provincially mandated minimum standards for campus sexual violence policies, and oversight bodies to ensure meaningful implementation of policy text, these past successes are an important reminder. For me, they help me to remain hopeful and inspired as the next generation of students pushes the movement forward.

---

6. Carleton University Sexual Violence Policy, revised April 25, 2021.

ghost girls

Olivia Landry

We left the café as it closed, rushing to pack our bags. It was cold, late November, dark and dreary. Somehow you needed glitter for a school project, and I wasn't ready to say goodbye so I walked with you to the Jean Coutu. On the way home, you pointed to a piece of sidewalk not covered by snow. *Isn't that the Venus symbol?* Despite living in this tiny town for a year and walking down this street nearly every day, I'd never seen this symbol carved into the cement. *I knew this meant something.* Sackville was the same, but somehow you made things brighter. Neither of us felt like we belonged here, like we were ghosts in the street. Being a ghost is an awfully lonely thing. There are no school clubs for ghosts, no support groups for ghosts. But that was exactly it; we were ghosts of girls who had more hope and we stopped wanting to be real girls. We were bitter ghosts with nothing to lose, and maybe we were better off that way. We made our own club, with crisscrossed baseball bats as our calling card. What we did wasn't decided yet—maybe we would save each other, create new worlds together, teach each other tenderness. Maybe we'd just get coffee, cold, late at night, while a café was trying to close, and walk each other home.

Where Do We Go From Here? Building a Container for Care, Solidarity, and Empowerment

Connor Spencer, Chantelle Spicer, and Tia Wong

Chantelle, Connor, and Tia are two generations of Chairs and Co-Chairs of the organization Students for Consent Culture Canada (SFCC). They are bound together not only through the organization, but through a long-lasting dedication to anti-colonial work and stewarding institutional memory, care, grassroots leadership, and solidarity between groups of survivors, students, leaders, and activists.

"I have always thought that what is needed is the development of people who are interested not in being leaders as much as in developing leadership in others."

—Ella Baker

"Our hands live and work in the present, while pushing in the past. It is impossible for us not to do both. Our hands make a future."

—Beth Brant, "A Gathering of Spirit"

A protein bar handed to you after a rally by a sympathetic professor who sensed you had not eaten all day. An administrator telling you it was nice to see you can be reasonable sometimes. Another telling you your work is anti-survivor because it makes students distrust the policy. Meeting a comrade doing similar work on their campus across the country in person for the first time and being shocked by how much taller or shorter they are than you thought. Feeling overwhelmed and exhausted and bawling (read: mourning) in a quiet spot on campus. Getting a call from a dear friend weeping on the streets of Montreal because we were just given our first real piece of funding after years of unpaid, anti-sexualized violence work. Taking calls and leaving class at a moment's notice to offer someone support. Years later, still feeling all of this incredibly present in your body.

Few of us would have imagined when we started our post-secondary careers that what we would learn most would be institutional procedures and strategies for silencing students facing systemic violence on campus. Instead of spending time writing papers or figuring out our academic interests, many of us found ourselves doing anti-sexualized violence work—where we were constantly gaslit by our institutions, made to feel like we were alone, and constantly told that our own personal experiences navigating the culture, policies, and procedures that existed on our campuses did not count as expertise.

It is within this context that Students for Consent Culture Canada (SFCC) emerged.[1] The creation of this national network of student anti-violence movers and shakers started from a place of much-needed validation, especially when we were being told by our institutions that our work—especially in 2016 (pre-#MeToo)—was not real or necessary or that anti-violence work wasn't something that institutions should be

---

1. For more on the organization, see sfcccanada.org.

concerned about. One of the great things about SFCC was that for the first time, we were able to connect with folks from other campuses who were doing and experiencing the same things. It started from a place of validation and care, and—let's be honest—deep anger and exhaustion.

In October 2017, many of us were working on the publication of the OurTurn National Action Plan.[2] It was the first document outlining best practices for sexualized violence policies on post-secondary campuses from a student survivor perspective. It was also the first project that linked many of us to each other across the country. We knew this document—and the months and months of unpaid labour that went into it—were incredibly important, but at the time we didn't know just how big of an impact it was going to have.

A week after the National Action Plan was published, #MeToo and the Harvey Weinstein story broke, and all of a sudden, a lot of the conversations that had been happening on campuses really changed. We saw politicians and schools wanting to figure out how to even begin to be accountable for some of the revelations that were coming out. However, many of us knew this desire for accountability didn't come from a place of wanting to end sexualized and gender-based violence, but rather from a place of wishing to get ahead of any possible activism. It was a push for containment. Damage control. Institutions were in desperate need of skills and expertise and all of a sudden there was this National Action Plan which, at its core, is a document outlining student survivor expertise. It was the first time there was any sense of what a 'good' anti-sexualized violence policy on campus looked like. This became a

---

2. Salvino, Caitlin, Kelsey Gilchrist, and Jade Cooligan Pang, "OurTurn: A National Action Plan to End Campus Sexual Violence," Montreal, QC: Student's Society of McGill University, October 2017.

way for us to humbly contribute—by sharing best practices, supporting students to grade their policies, or assisting in other initiatives.

Born of spontaneous mutual support among and between survivors across the country during the creation of the National Action Plan, our network was formalized into a non-profit structure to gain a sense of 'legitimacy' and (in a perfect world) funding. It was definitely not an easy process, not one that we felt we had a lot of choice over, and many of us were quite hesitant. We knew we needed to be incredibly intentional with the way that we set ourselves up, rooting our work in our values rather than mimicking and perpetuating a deeply problematic idea of what a "credible" organization looks like. We took our time.

SFCC emerged as an organization in October 2019. It is a product of our love, rage, labour, solidarity, and commitment to change and to each other. Because of the prominence of the OurTurn Action Plan and the work we were doing on campuses across the country, in no time at all a very new SFCC found itself connected with students across the country who were seeking support for their anti-sexualized violence work, swapping best practices, scheming strategy to deal with horrible administrators, and, most importantly, helping to develop leadership, capacity, and support on each of these campuses where we could. We also found ourselves invited into spaces that had formerly been closed to us—government consultations, campus committees, and administration—and we do our best to bring those who still have doors closed to them into these rooms with us.

Much of our experience with on-campus organizing in October 2017 and the creation of SFCC in 2019 is described in the OurTurn: One Year Later report, including a snapshot of statistics on the impact of the

OurTurn National Action Plan in the year after its publishing.[3] Those statistics include:

- 115 media articles written about OurTurn,

- Being involved in five provincial governments' consultations/lobbying,

- Participating in eight federal consultations,

- Four mentions in the house of commons, and

- Over four-thousand signatures on various OurTurn open letters across the country.

What these statistics don't give you is a sense of what was actually, for many of us, the most meaningful part of this work: a sense of community, shared values, validation, and mutual aid as we pushed forward. It was a sense that we could interrupt power dynamics on campus by uplifting students and survivor expertise. We have also been able to interrupt toxic organizing practices by honouring slowness, relationship building, capacity, and boundaries. We have worked to strengthen relationships with survivors, and wherever possible, our fellow student groups. It is these kinds of relationships that create the trust and sustainability required to make change.

This kind of work feels immense, especially as we intentionally carry out our anti-sexualized violence work in a way that sees sexualized violence as a symptom of the larger capitalist, colonial system that "Canada" is built on and continues to maintain. We cannot affect change in

---

3. Salvino, Caitlin and Connor Spencer, "OurTurn: One Year Later Report," Montreal, QC: Concordia Student's Union, April 2019.

a culture where sexualized violence is an everyday occurrence without addressing other forms of violence in our approach. But we no longer feel alone. It is challenging to find the words to express the sense of relief many of us felt in finding each other initially, and the continued relief we feel being in a community with each other and figuring this out together. Our journey has been incredibly hard, but it has also been incredibly healing.

SFCC as an organization is not perfect, and we have and will continue to make mistakes and learn more about ways to work that best reflect our values as a community, and our commitments to care for ourselves and each other. We are navigating the non-profit industrial complex, rooting ourselves always more and more firmly in our focus of giving students the tools they need to help do their work, and trying to resist perpetuating the power structures that exist on our campuses. What we are doing is also not new, but a continuance of generations of survivors and activists who have demanded and worked for better worlds. We could not do this work without the generations of people—particularly Black, Indigenous, disabled, trans, queer, and Brown peoples—who have carried and shared the pain, labour, and radical imagining of anti-violence work on campuses and beyond.

So, here we are in 2023. Policy experts who don't believe in policy. People who are healing in our own non-linear ways and at our own pace, individually and collectively. Within an organization that maybe—just maybe—can begin to look and work like the world we want to create.

my love will not be institutionalized

CHANTELLE SPICER

my love is not for you
to consume.[1]
you are hungry
and i am tired of crafting your forgiveness

when i do not have the space to forgive myself.

my love is for me
this time
i will turn this world inside out[2]

for me, for sisters, for land
for empty-abandoned-industrialized places
for hearts held together out of necessity *but barely*

because they are me too.

my love will be for you
when you are ready to hold it

in a sacred way.
when it won't wash over you
as an absolution.

this love might be a bridge for us
if only you could be trusted to cross it.

do your own work.

---

1. Flowers, Rachel. "Refusal to Forgive: Indigenous Women's Love and Rage," *Decolonization: Indigeneity, Education & Society,* 4, no. 2 (2015): 32-49.

2. Nora Samaran, *Turn This World Inside Out: The Emergence of Nurturance Culture,* AK Press, 2018.

Beautiful and Expansive Love

ANONYMOUS

I wrote this poem,
Because I'm in my first relationship.
And someone close to me told me
That I deserve beautiful and expansive love,
Without fear.
She said that we all do.

But still,
I am sorry.
I am sorry because I vowed that I would love myself
Before giving my love to somebody else,
But everything happened so quickly
And I'm still not there.
I am sorry that there are moments
When I am more of a victim
Than a survivor,
And I am sorry he will have to see them.
I am sorry because I wanted to be complete
Before I committed myself

To another human being
And there are still so many parts of me
That are broken.
I am sorry, that I am hurting,
And I am sorry that there are things
He cannot make better,
And I'm sorry, if he ever feels at fault,
For the things that I feel.

I wrote this poem,
Because I'm in my first relationship,
And I want him to know that sometimes I hurt,
And that is not his fault.
It is not his fault that when he tells me to relax
I will tense entirely.
It is not his fault that I still flinch
When his hands grab onto mine,
It was not his hands
That caused the bruises
But it is his hands
That feel them now,
And it is not his fault
That the places his fingertips graze
Still
Ache.
It is not his fault
That when he said he loved me
I could say nothing
In return

And it is not because
I didn't love him
But because the words were ripped
Out of my throat
By the same hands
That held it so tightly
And that is not
His fault.
It is not his fault that the feelings of fingers
On my neck
Won't just give me chills
But will freeze me
To my core,
And it is not his fault
I freeze.

I wrote this poem,
Because I'm in my first relationship
And I'm beginning to learn
That the hurt that I feel
Is not my fault either—
But somewhere along the way
I learned that my voice
Is not loud enough.
I learned that my body
Belongs to more
Than just me.
I learned that falling in love
Makes you crazy

That caring at all
Makes you weird
That if you don't leave first
You will be left empty
So you should just never care
At all.
I learned that love
Is something
That can only
Be taken, so please,
Be patient,
While I unlearn all that I know
So I can give back
Willingly.
It is not my fault
That some are raised
Without boundaries
And it is not my fault
That they've erased mine.
It is not my fault
That building myself back up again
Is going to take time,
But I am sorry
That it must take his.
He deserves someone who can love him entirely
Without being afraid
And I love him entirely,
But I am afraid,
And that is not his fault.

I wrote this poem
Because I'm in my first relationship.
And my friend recently told me
That I deserve beautiful and expansive love
Without fear.
She said that we all do.
We deserve to be with someone who sees our hurt
And then accepts it.
They accept that there are things in our past
That they cannot change.
They accept that scars are something
They cannot kiss better
But then kiss them anyway.
They accept that there are some types of hurt
That will never feel better,
But they promise
To never add to your pain.
They will see you through days
Where you're just barely surviving
And they'll see you through days
When you aren't at all,
And you may seem to be more of a victim
Than a survivor,
But you will always
Be enough.

I wrote this poem
Because I'm in my first relationship.

And I'm learning
That I deserve beautiful and expansive love,
Without fear.

We all do.

Surviving Ten Seconds

Kate Mullin

Content Warning: Mention of suicide, mild descriptions of sexualized violence and victim blaming
To skip to the next story, turn to page 312.

To skip to the next story, turn to page 312.

If you can make it through ten seconds, you can make it through anything. This philosophy has saved me a number of times—even when I could only count to four.

At an early age, mental health struggles made a major impact on my life. The loss of both my grandparents to suicide was a hidden topic that deeply affected my childhood. It became evident in my adult life that I was raised in the aftermath of grief. It was the tension and separation that came with grief that led to the further loss of family members. Family members who didn't die of suicide were pushed out or disowned, a consequence that came from not understanding consent and boundaries—preventing the healing that would have come with understanding and support.

It wasn't until later in my life that I saw the direct impacts of those struggles, when I dealt with my own suicidal tendencies. Those tensions I grew up with provided an unhealthy example that encouraged me to act on these thoughts. It was those moments of hardship that ultimately led me to my passion for leadership and advocacy.

When I started university—a time meant to be full of learning, growth, and self discovery—a long line of intergenerational trauma stemming from sexualized violence began to reveal itself. While some people may feel the effects of family trauma without direct experience, that wasn't my story.

I knew of family members who had experienced sexualized violence throughout my childhood, but I only truly understood the impacts of what they went through after my own experience. It took three years, an abusive relationship, and a traumatic party for me to realize that the issue of sexualized violence isn't something that can be ignored.

Both of my cases were full of peer and self-doubt. Like the majority of those who experience sexualized violence, I was never the "perfect victim." Rarely is sexual assault what the media portrays. Rarely is the perpetrator a stranger in a dark alley. It's someone you know, someone you trust, love, or deeply care for, and whether you're unconscious due to alcohol, or coerced into submission, these are experiences of sexual assault.

Growing up and seeing the impacts of mental illness and later having sexualized violence affect my own mental health, I saw a need to learn and fight against the stigma of both. Not only was I not aware of these topics before they affected me personally, but it was evident that others around me weren't either.

"Weren't you drinking?"

"But you're dating them."

"You can't say things like that."

These victim blaming comments tried to silence my story but succeeded in doing the opposite. They pushed me to fight for awareness even more.

It's become normalized in society to tell young women to cover up, to provide safety tips rather than change how we view women and marginalized groups. This is evident in the prevalence of behaviours that perpetuate a culture of sexualized violence. A staring eye, a rude comment, or sexualized gestures are common, and while those in power refuse to support survivors in sentencing this behaviour as a criminal act, women and marginalized groups have learned to adapt. It is a cycle that causes harm to survivors and their idea of their place in the world. Constantly hearing comments about one's appearance creates a false idea about one's own self-worth, and places sexual attraction and sexuality over comfort and health. It's this oversexualization that harms individuals and creates contradictions; when women and marginalized groups embrace their sexualities and take control of their own bodies, the comments still don't go away and people continue to take issue with their autonomy.

Having been personally affected by this cycle of violence, I learned to heal through my advocacy efforts, and by envisioning a better world.

Looking back, my activist work started more broadly as a child through my elementary school's student council, where I learned what leadership meant to me. Leadership allowed me to have the courage to express my voice and effectively support others, something that became immensely valuable as a survivor. It gave me the skills to connect with the people around me while completing our collective goals, and created opportunities to encourage growth. I learned that leadership isn't about being in power, but about understanding yourself, your passion, and having the determination to act on it. Leadership is about valuing the people around you and the opportunities you're given, as it provides a place surrounded by different minds   to further your knowledge. Leadership builds skills that can shape your everyday life, as it did mine.

It wasn't until later, in high school, when I spent another two years in various positions on a new students' council, that I learned to develop my leadership further. At the time, I saw my return to these positions as a coincidence. I viewed it as an opportunity for me to make an impact on the schools that played an important role in shaping me and was the setting that introduced society's beliefs. I now realize that my return to student council was me rediscovering my passion for this type of work. In this period of my life, I learned the foundation of who I am in activism and how much value it holds to me. It was through leadership that I built my strength to fight against the different traumas I've encountered. It wasn't until university that my drive in leadership narrowed into the sexualized violence prevention movement, and learning those fundamental leadership skills at a young age helped me to do that.

Now, attending university, I continue to use my activist efforts to impact this new community of students around me. The University of Alberta has a variety of different volunteer resources people can access to learn about a range of topics and have their work be supported in a variety of ways. From specific hobby interests to mental health aid, these student volunteer groups help   build meaningful peer connections. It's through these student groups that I've helped provide students a way to improve their mental health and generate funds to support different nonprofits and charities. Through the teamwork involved in running events, we were able to bring awareness, encourage self-care practices, and host fundraisers to help provide both financial and material support. It was through these activities that we were able to make a difference. These opportunities helped me realize the vast ways people can use leadership to create different types of change and encouraged me to discover my passion for sexualized violence prevention work in education and my personal writing and art.

While sexualized violence affects most people, directly or indirectly, there is still a heavy stigma against discussing it. Promoting education and awareness about the issue increases the possibility for gender equality and safety. When facing these heavy issues, I've learned to embrace my identity as a survivor. I do this through my volunteer work, where I show my support to organizations that encourage change. This includes the most empowering team I've been a part of; Students For Consent Culture Canada (SFCC) is where I've been the Education Lead and consent educator for fellow students and activists. Here, I've been able to create space to discuss the different nuances of boundaries, sexual and not, that societies do not often bring to people's attention or comfortability to discuss. Not only does it relate to romantic relationships but also family, friends and our workplace and activist settings. Ultimately, having more platforms fighting sexualized violence, we encourage more leaders to talk about it and lead our peers to challenge the culture of sexualized violence, reducing its acceptance in social circles.

I have also developed my own understanding of the broad topic of sexualized violence through my work. This growth has helped me recognize my own emotions, better categorize them, and recognize how they're affected by trauma. Being more aware of the effects of sexualized violence, I'm better able to make these distinctions. I'm also now prepared to start conversations and accommodate those who have had similar experiences. I am able to see how violence can affect many aspects of someone's life, including their mental health, and through activism I can help ensure people are gentle with themselves throughout their healing process, directly as a peer supporter but also through encouraging a society of acceptance.

SFCC and the other projects I've engaged with have connected me with like-minded individuals who are also working tirelessly to address the social injustice that is sexualized violence. Seeing these individuals and witnessing our collective passion has provided me with hope and healing. Knowing that there are steps being taken, conversations being held, and voices that want change makes advocacy my key tool for healing.

It is through advocacy that I'm trying to end my family's line of intergenerational trauma.

Each generation has their own specific issues for activists to tackle. While general themes such as gender or racial discrimination have been intergenerational, they've transformed from voting rights to ending sexualized violence. People today are using the momentum generated by past activists to fuel the fight against our current issues. Sometimes the world seems like a negative place that allows for issues such as sexualized violence to persist, but there is hope. It is because of past activists and seeing how the world is always developing and changing that I recognize the power we hold to create change for future generations, and to ensure that those who come after us feel safe, as they deserve.

I know that through this work, we will make an impact on society, so that one day people won't need activism to heal or to count to ten to survive.

E

ADDY STRICKLAND

i'm flying home,
you say,
and i want to tell you
not to fly too far
but i don't know how
so instead i say

okay

and the moon is low and red
and it's the second day of spring
and i thought
that spring was supposed to be okay

but this isn't okay

and i can't get the water hot enough
to forget what i'm feeling
so instead i hold my breath
and wait

for fire to take root in my lungs

and i think about fire,
what it would feel like to burn

i feel like i'm watching you burn.

Shoulder to Shoulder

ADDY STRICKLAND

"If you are marching, fighting in the streets for social justice—tell us. We will be there, marching with you, shoulder to shoulder."

This is the promise a Mexica elder named Balty made to the group of twenty-some young people I was travelling with in Arizona. We had spent the last hour learning traditional Mexica dance and were sitting on the sun-warmed concrete listening to a history of the land we were staying on. He spoke about how the Mexican-American border interrupted the migration path of his people, and about the erasure of their history from the American curriculum. Living with that history, they weren't concerned with studying social justice, but rather with living it, and he encouraged us to do the same—promising to stand with us along the way. He may very well have made the same promise to every group of eager young activists he had the opportunity to work with, but there is no doubt in my mind that he meant every word.

At the time, while I was appreciative of this statement, I'm not sure I really understood the weight of a promise like that, but over the past four years I've found myself coming back to those words time and time again. I was that kid in high school who wanted to change the world, and I enrolled at St. Francis Xavier University so I could study social justice, but I didn't know what that meant until I was thrown into it headfirst.

Sure, I'd organized fundraisers before, or taken part in food drives, but actively protesting and fighting for change that directly impacted my life and the lives of my friends was a different experience entirely.

Having read the earlier stories in this anthology, you'll be familiar with a number of movements that happened at StFX. Within these movements, we put so much of ourselves into the work that we did. We spent hours in organizing meetings, painstakingly safety-pinned hundreds of teal ribbons, sat in on more open forums and information sessions than I can count, recounted our stories to reporters and news outlets like broken records, listened to our friends narrate their traumas over and over again, were repeatedly gaslit by the institution we were fighting to change ... It wasn't easy work by any means, and throughout all of this, we were still students. By November of my second year, almost everyone I know was utterly burned out and exhausted.

In our fourth year, we were pushed into action once again, and the emotions and stress I thought I'd moved past came back in full force—further exacerbated by the collective trauma of a global pandemic. Someone once told me that social justice never comes tied with a bow; on post-secondary campuses, it comes in fragments—slivers of victory painstakingly chipped from foundations of violence and deceit. Celebrating those victories, no matter how small, was one thing that kept me going, and that has allowed me to continue doing the work to this day. Another, perhaps even more significant motivation, was the networks of support and the communities of solidarity that we built along the way.

Every protest, every open letter, every news article or interview—there was no one person behind any of them. Rather, there was a community of survivors and supporters pouring their time, energy, and love into imagining a better future—offering resources on Facebook groups or in-person; swapping poetry via text message; debriefing after protests on auditorium floors; sharing quiet eye-rolls and knowing glances in meetings with admin; sitting side-by-side in silence or ranting and yelling at the top of our lungs. None of us could have achieved the change we did on our own. Activist work is hard, and messy, and heartbreaking—but we survived. Marching together, shoulder to shoulder.

———

There's a tradition at StFX where students in their final year of study purchase a class ring, the "X-Ring," which is supposedly the third most-recognized ring in the world. For many, it's a symbol of pride, and a lasting, wearable reminder of "the StFX experience." I know people who chose not to buy or not to wear their rings because of what happened during their four years on campus. To wear a ring symbolizing institutional pride seems ironic, looking back at it all.

Getting my own ring, I wanted to commemorate the four years of activism, policy work, and protest that were central to my so-called "StFX experience," and I wanted to honour the communities of support and solidarity we built along the way. And so, on the inside of my ring, engraved in tiny, almost illegible script, are the words "*shoulder to shoulder.*" I finally understand the weight of Balty's promise, so instead of wearing my ring as a symbol of institutional pride, I wear it to extend my own: if you are marching, fighting in the streets for social justice—tell me. I will be there, marching with you, shoulder to shoulder.

The Power of Art and Activism to Heal and Transform the Self and the Collective Body

Sasha Askarian

My time as a former collective member for the Simon Fraser University Women's Centre in British Columbia challenged my ideas around rape and sexual assault. In particular, individual stories often spoke to the societal structures that continuously support and sustain rape culture. The stories we would learn about often ran across familiar patterns of pain and relative powerlessness in historically traumatized communities in Canada. That is, traumas conditioned by media images around gendered and sexual norms, inequitable policing practices, precarious immigration status, and the ongoing histories of colonialism, racism, and patriarchy. I wrote "Yes" to touch upon the intuitions of victims living with these realities, emanating from society and invading both the individual body and the communal body alike. Sexual assault and the subsequent mental crises it creates needs to be understood within this nexus of power linking the dynamics of class, citizenship, race, and gender.

This is especially the case for vulnerable people within Indigenous communities, international students, and racialized peoples on campus seeking support in the women's centre. Campus culture often fails to provide safe spaces for women and adequate resources to mitigate the impacts of unsafety, in particular, resources addressing food insecurity and mental health. During my undergraduate years, the women's centre was one of the few designated safe spaces established after years of feminist activism. However, the cozy lounge and carefully selected library was not necessarily just a space for victims, or a place to grapple with issues of gender inequality head on. It was, during my time there, also a space for women to rest, resist, and simply be.

When it came time to address rampant oppression on campus, the collective's team utilized both creative and classic forms of social activism. Namely, we participated in women's marches, body positivity campaigns, workshops relating to gender-based violence, and peaceful protests advocating for women's bodily autonomy. In dealing with these complex social conditions, one particular medium of resistance and strength was channelled through the power of creativity. We actively learned to centre the body as a means to tap into the heavy social impacts of violence and oppression, subsequently opening a portal into healing. This was most memorably exercised during a special visit from activist, artist, and writer Carmen Aguirre. She introduced our team of volunteers to the power of theatrics with its ability to unlock the pain sitting within our bodies and spirits. In fact, her exercise in portraying stories through decisive movements of our limbs unearthed pains rooted in my own body. Meaning woven into each movement expressed the hardened hurt viscerally pushing out through my belly and welling in my eyes. This critical and artistic approach allowed participants to exercise novel and creative outlets for their fears, passions, and knowledge.

After several years of reflection, I understand this innovative and therapeutic method to be an act of rebellion communicating our collective pain and intergenerational traumas. It cultivates new spaces for transformative healing. To continue this practice of rebellion, I wrote "Yes" to invite readers to rethink structural violence that impacts our being and the collective body in its entirety.

Yes.

Rape is the act of brute force that projects not only unto the body of the victim but thrusts from a world which the rapist constructs, a world that drags a shallow "yes" from her mouth. This is a world imbricated with assumptions and interlocking ideologies and Lorde knows, it is a power structure wrestling down the erotic into surfaced desires—positioning the receiver as ever receivable. It is a particular universality, for the "yes" in this world is a hollow one indeed.

- S. A.

Letter to a Classmate

ANONYMOUS

Content Warning: Moderate description of sexual assault
To skip to the next story, turn to page 330.

[REDACTED],

I am writing to you, in order to outline for you, a wrong that you have committed against me. This isn't going to make sense to you right away. You will need to read carefully and, after that, re-read what I have written again and again. Please take the time to do this.

This letter is something that is difficult for me to write. It took me several months to get this down. It took me two years before I decided to send it. I wasn't sure that I could actually do it. Facing this, for me, is facing a monster ...

I wonder if you ever thought this day would come? Did you live in fear, anticipating my anger? Was it a small worry that dogged you occasionally as you tried to drift to sleep? Did you make excuses to appease yourself, to heap the blame on me or factors outside of your and my control, like the alcohol, the music, the night? Or did it never even cross your mind that you had done something wrong, something criminal, something like rape?

Had you forgotten that night? Is this letter a shock, something "out of the blue?" Do you, too, experience small "triggers" that can root you back there to that moment? Did you even experience a fraction of the panic, dread, fear, and overwhelming shame that I felt and still feel? Do you remember that I forgot all the details of that night? I forgot everything. All I remember is the panic, fear, dread, and overwhelming sense of shame.

Have you ever told anyone what happened? I never have. Not a single soul. I tried to erase it from my memory completely. I tried to will it out of existence. I told myself, "This kind of thing happens to everyone," "You will look back and find it funny," "It happens on TV all the time!" Such a childish approach, don't you think? For the record, I find it ugly and humiliating, but never funny. For the record, I never want to have to form the words in my mouth that say what happened. I never want to tell a single soul. I can only write it down. And only to you. I need to get the ugliness and shame out of my system. You will be my dump site. You owe me at least that.

I know what you think happened. You told me the next day, remember? I couldn't remember anything, not a thing. I have to trust your version. I don't know if I trust your version. I know that I don't trust your analysis. I don't trust you, either. But I did. Isn't that funny? Me, the feminist in the department, the one who hates men; I trusted you! A nice guy. One of the few in the department, I thought. Are you smiling as you read this? Do you feel pride? Nostalgia? Or are you ashamed of yourself? I honestly don't know what to expect.

Maybe you want to hear what I think happened ... I don't know that I am ready to write this. I've thought about it for a long time, but I have been too scared. I wonder what is the bravest thing you have ever done in your life? Have you ever been brave? I've been brave. I have to be brave.

I wonder if you know that feeling of bravery, where your entire body trembles, you are sweating, your entire nervous system is telling you to turn around, not to do what you are trying to do, but your courage, your integrity, are telling you that you must continue.

We took political philosophy together. Remember when we read Kant? The only real virtue, as Kant would say, is doing your duty when every part of you does not want to do it, when there is no real reward. Will I be rewarded for writing to you? It feels somewhat liberating to get it all down, but I know that if I send it, I will live in fear of the worst-case reprisal you can bestow. I won't be able to sleep at night out of worry. I will have to go to therapy, which I already do, but you will be a fresh, new topic to bring up. I wonder if writing this is virtuous. I wonder if virtue means the same thing to you as it does to me.

Listen, I've done some research that I want to share. A free lesson! Peer-to-peer. After all, aren't we equal members of an egalitarian society?

1. Consent. Everyone says consent is a tricky concept, but it's not. Have you ever gone through the ethics process for your research? It's a lot like that. Consent must be verbal, not under threats or duress, informed, voluntary, and able to be revoked at any time. So far so good?

   a) Let's think this through. I've thought about it a lot. An ethics committee would likely not accept the consent of a person who is intoxicated. That would be unethical. But personal life is different, right?

   b) For consent to be valid, for a "yes" to mean "yes," the person must have the option of saying no. This is why consent under duress is not acceptable. Which brings me to my next point:

2. How alcohol affects the brain. Alcohol inhibits the higher-order functioning of the brain, including decision making. Alco-

hol also increases the body's instinctive functions. Sexual response/arousal is instinctive—it is not controlled by higher-order logical thinking and decision making. This is why a person who is incapacitated can still experience sexual arousal. An intoxicated "yes" then, can be understood as the result of this instinctive functioning and not lowered inhibitions as people frequently think. Interesting research, I know.

3. Consent and Alcohol. For some reason, when these two very logical and scientific areas of understanding become mixed, all logical thinking goes out the window! Things are changing though. Let's carefully consider the following guidelines developed by sexual violence prevention programs that teach consent: It's not consent if:

a) "Your acquaintance/friend/date/partner is passed out, asleep, incoherent, staggering or not aware of his/her environment."

b) "You don't think the person would agree to sex if they were sober."

c) "You and your acquaintance/friend/date/partner have never talked about having sex together before you became intoxicated, and you don't know what that person would want."

d) "Someone has stated what he/she is comfortable with, but when they are intoxicated to the point they are unable to articulate permission, you go farther than agreed upon."[1]

Please, for my sake, take a second look. Read through each of those points carefully. Re-read them again. I know this is hard to take in, understand, and especially to apply to one's

---

1. "Student Safety in Nova Scotia: A Review of Student Union Policies and Practice to Prevent Sexual Violence," Martell Consulting Services Ltd., January 13, 2014.

own behaviour, so take your time. I can wait. Think it over. Thinking it over might have been a good decision in the first place.

4. Consent and the law. Guess what isn't acceptable as a legal defence in criminal court? You're right, being drunk! If you are drunk, you are still responsible for your heinous behaviour. A less drunk person taking advantage of a very, very intoxicated person is a crime. Especially if that less drunk person recognized the signs that the other person was indeed very, very intoxicated. If a reasonable person could recognize those signs, a less drunk person is also supposed to recognize them.

Now, I know, bringing up the law is shitty behaviour of me. Maybe you feel panicked. Maybe you are freaking out just a little right now. Relax. Don't call your attorney. I already told you I don't ever want to speak these words out loud. Not to anyone. I only want to impart upon you the seriousness of what you have done. I only want you to feel a fraction of the fear, and only for a moment, of what I felt that morning. Besides, our legal system almost always favours rapists. Also, I have had very bad experiences with the police in the past, and I do not wish to put myself through that again.

I want to believe that after your panic or fear subsides you will take the time to think carefully about what I have written. I want to believe that although it is difficult, you will engage in self-reflection, even if it's just a little self-reflection. Does it make up for everything? Does this make you a good guy? No. But it's better than nothing.

---

1. "Student Safety in Nova Scotia: A Review of Student Union Policies and Practice to Prevent Sexual Violence," Martell Consulting Services Ltd., January 13, 2014.

Here are some key points that will not stop circulating through my head. I had cuts on my body. You said that I fell when we were up on the roof. You said that I spilled my drink. Someone who cannot stand, who is spilling things, surely this person is too drunk to consent ... I was also acting in ways that I had never acted before around you when sober. That must have given you some pause ... did you pause? Did you think about what you were doing? Or was it all my fault?

There are ways to tell someone that they are too drunk, that they need to drink water or eat some food, that they can sleep in your bed while you take the sofa, that you will call them a cab, that they are acting out of character ... Did you try any of this? Should I believe you?

Here is another moment that keeps flashing in my head: waking up that morning, alone and undressed. I had no idea where I was. Think about that! Imagine that! Try! Imagine waking up with no idea where you are! I didn't recognize anything around me. I felt too ill and too weak to get up and look around. I lay there in fear. In terror, actually. Think about that ... I had no idea where I was, if I was safe, why I was undressed, who was around ... Have you ever woken up like that, not knowing where you are? Vulnerable? Unclothed? I doubt it. And even if you have, it's not the same when you are a man. It's terrifying. It wasn't until you came back into the room later that I realized where I was and then again, more terror, but also shame and humiliation.

I was not relieved to see you. I was not happy to ask you what happened. I felt deep revulsion as you recounted the events of the night before. And you seemed sober, maybe slightly hungover. There was a wide gulf of experience between us that morning. I think there still is. I wonder if it is even possible for you to see things from my perspective—to cross that gulf.

When I remember that morning, I still tremble with fear. I attended a Take Back the Night march this year. At the marches, women talk about their experiences with sexual violence. I told, without naming you, the story of that morning. As I spoke out loud, words that I never wanted to speak, my hands shook so hard that the paper I held fluttered to the ground. My legs shook and I could barely stand. My voice wavered and stuttered. I couldn't even look up at the crowd of strangers in front of me. That is bravery. It's not pretty. That is how I feel about what happened. Terrified but finally able to face it.

This isn't a simple regret. Regret is one thing. Shame and vulnerability and the humiliation of having put yourself in a bad situation, of having done something you never ever wanted to do, of being literally stripped of your dignity, this is what I felt. Try to imagine that. Please, it is easy to dismiss me and blame me, but try, for one moment, to imagine what I felt, the breadth of it, the depth. I felt as though I lost my dignity. Try to cross over that gulf and to feel what I feel.

Look, here in bold type I will say it:

1) **What happened was wrong.**

2) **You are responsible for committing that wrong action.**

3) **You could have and should have acted differently.**

Look, I don't want much from you. I really just needed to get this out of my system, to let it stop poisoning me slowly from the inside. I will not tell anyone what happened. I can't face it. I won't make any major demands of you. It's entirely up to you to take accountability for this, if you want to take accountability. If you don't, I can't do anything to force you.

Should you choose to respond please consider the following cycle of emotions first:

1. You might be in shock. You might not be able to believe that

this is happening. You might think that something is wrong with me, causing me to see the situation from an angle that feels bizarre and irrational. You might think that I sent this letter to the wrong person by mistake. That I have mixed up my memories. This is a normal response.

a) I haven't. This letter is for you, [REDACTED].

2. You might be numb. You might feel a total lack of emotion and empathy. You might want to tear up this letter, throw it in the trash, and never think about it again. Also a normal response.

a) Please don't do that. I assure you that it is not so easy to forget a disruption like this letter by simply not thinking about it.

3. You might be angry. You might think that I am a bitch. That I am vindictive. That I am a whore that cannot deal with my own whorishness. Maybe I am.

a) That rage will subside.

4. You might be terrified of what this means and what I will do.

a) I assure you, I want nothing from you and I will tell no one. All I want is for you to read this and think about it. That's all.

5. You might start rationalizing the situation. That would be the easiest thing to do. You will think back to that night and come up with all sorts of reasons why your behaviour was acceptable, why it was rational, and why it should not and could not be considered hurtful. This is the most likely response.

a) In many ways you are right to think this way. We all do this when faced with the accusation that we hurt someone, especially someone that we like. *But* please, although it is difficult, try to see things from my perspective ... You don't have to agree with me, but at least try to empathize with me ... to feel my hurt, my terror ... Empathizing with someone we hurt is a difficult task for anyone. I don't expect you to be any better than me at that, I struggle with it too. But please try.

6. You might get depressed. You might think you are a terrible person.

a) Allow yourself to feel what you feel. Allow it to guide your reflection. But understand that you are the only one who gets to decide how you feel. How you feel about yourself is not my responsibility and not my fault.

Here are the responses that I will accept from you should you choose to respond: An apology. An acknowledgement of the harm you caused. Total silence (AKA a non-response).

Here are the responses that I will *not* accept from you under any circumstances: Excuses. Your "side" of the story. Self-deprecating bullshit. (If you are tempted to respond with any of these, by all means write them down, get them out of your system, and then, *burn them*. I don't want them).

I will not contact you again, with one exception: If I am ever made aware of any other accusations against you by any other women or children, no matter how much time has passed, my silence will be broken no matter what awful damage it does to my reputation. You have my word on that.

You are not the only person to have done what you did to me. The others were more blatantly violent. I write to you and not to them because I have hope (maybe foolish) that you can learn and reflect on what you have done. If I am wrong, if there are others suffering in silence as I suffered, I will bear the guilt.

Anonymous

[REDACTED] responded. He responded within two minutes of the email being sent. It took me years to write this and more years to build up the courage to send it. He responded in two minutes. I find that fact so illustrative of the differences in our experience.

He apologized. I don't care about that. It means nothing to me. I don't trust his apology or him. But he also wrote, "Everything you wrote is true." That line has stuck with me. It affected me so much more than I ever thought I would. To me, that line feels like an admission of guilt. That line tells me, "You are right." That line tells me, "You are not crazy." That line tells me, "You can trust yourself again."

I printed out his email and my email. I put them in an envelope labeled [REDACTED]. I put the envelope in the same folder where I keep all my important documents: my birth certificate, my SIN number, my student loan documents, my university transcripts, my checkbook, old passports, and this letter. Having that letter in a safe place, that letter with that line, makes me feel powerful. I feel like I could pull that letter out at any time: release it to the media, to his employer, to his family. I doubt it is enough to hold up in court, but it is enough to make me feel powerful.

When I wrote this letter initially, I had no plans to send it, but I am glad that I eventually worked up the courage to do so. I like to think of the power I got in response as a gift. Since I never want to feel even an ounce of gratitude to him, I choose instead to thank myself for the courage it took to write and send that letter.

Arrival

Anonymous

To which destination is this place?
Does it exist?
An imagination?
Yet, it does exist
in my realization of worthiness,
a paradise materialized.
Completion,
morning walks,
sensual meals,
talking to my body.
Feet, where will we go
Where will you take me?
I speak to my heart.
I know you hurt,
my love for you transcends the imaginations of love offered in this world.
I will never betray you;
lean on me.
Feel my touch as I travel from your crown
to your ankles,
to the tips of your

toenails.
Leaving no area untouched.
I am soft; I am kind; I am gentle.
I do not inflict harm.
I linger in your
tenderest areas leaving only after
its release,
releasing you of aches,
releasing you of shame,
Releasing you of regrets and creating new
memories.
Kind ones.
Great ones.
And, each day is better than
the last because— I —
have learned
you.
I know you.
More profoundly
than anyone else because I am in you.
I am you.
We are one.

Advice from the Front Lines

Though we aren't convinced that there's such a thing as an "expert" activist, the combined knowledge and experience of our contributors is something we wish we'd had access to when we started out. Here, we've asked each of our contributors to share a piece of advice from what they've learned engaging in campus activism against sexualized violence.

———

Sasha Askarian—The years I spent active in social justice projects taught me to keep an open and investigative mind. What we understand to be justice will reshape itself as we are challenged by different lived experiences. Practicing an empathetic approach to social causes is necessary in freeing us from dogmatic and insubstantial claims to freedom and justice and works to centre communities most systemically vulnerable. This has been evident in my ever-evolving ideas around gender and justice, all of which have changed dramatically in learning from Indigenous, Black and many other critical feminist thinkers. Embrace the discomfort that comes from unlearning dominant worldviews—only then our work will build upon an inclusive future against a divisive-inducing system of violence.

Johannah May Black—Never back away from the work of imagining a better future. Do not give in to sanctimonious or patronizing proclamations that your ideas of justice are unrealistic, utopian, or impossible. Remember that the world has not always been this way. There have been massive changes to social and political systems in the past and there will be again in the future. There have been societies without patriarchy. There have been societies without structural violence. There have been nurturing and communal societies. We have been given boundless imaginations for a reason. The future is something that we have the collective right to create for ourselves. We must nurture our utopian ideals and use them to guide us to a more just world.

Maddie Brockbank—This work often feels unforgiving, but we continue to push boundaries to imagine a world free from violence. While it feels almost impossible to gather insights and ideas for emerging activists from the rubble of my own experiences, I've pulled together a list of my major takeaways as a final note of hope and encouragement for anyone who wants to do this work. They are not exhaustive, but they are lessons and reflections that I hold close to my heart.

1. Connect with organizations, people, and stakeholders who are invested in this work. Ask them what they need or what role you can play in their larger efforts. Invite them into spaces and forge partnerships and collaborations thoughtfully, proactively, and intentionally. Become a part of a coalition. There is strength in numbers

2. Apply for every funding opportunity you see. This work is important, so don't let your institution deter you from pursuing it. You

deserve to be compensated. The organizations you work with and care about deserve funding.

3. Always be sure to check your tank. Feeling burned out, distressed, and angry is common in this work. Some of it can be motivating, inspiring, and moving, but it can also take a lot out of you. Practise self-care and community care in whatever ways you can.

4. Engage with feminist texts and videos that fill you up. I attended Tarana Burke's public talk one week after the Commit(men)t & Allyship event I ran, and it healed the part of me that had been beat down by six months of organizing

5. It sounds trite, but listen to your gut. If conversations with administrators don't feel right, push on, but don't put all your eggs in one basket. Know that this resistance is built into the very fabric of the institutions we're working within. It's designed to get you down. Never stop holding them accountable, but also be sure to take care of yourself, intentionally direct your energies, and trust your instincts

6. Remind yourself why you do this work. Hold your own stories and the experiences of others close. When I feel hopeless, I always think about my sixteen-year-old self, my mom, my friends, anyone who has been scarred by sexual violence. I think about the communities of care that we've built, and it pushes me forward. We're still here. We will win.

Julie Glaser—
1. Utilize creativity to engage with the actions: it lifts the spirit, helps others connect to the message, and can create new pathways of seeing and doing.
2. Always be humble and thankful for the strides we make: the path has been a long one to get here, with many who will never be named or honoured having paved the way, and of course there is still a very long

way to go.

3. Surround yourself with beautiful souls, connect with nature, and never stop dancing.

Penelope Hutchison—We are strongest when we work together, support each other and lift each other up. Respect diversity of opinion and experience, but do not let our small politics take away from our larger purpose—to put an end to the patriarchy.

Micah Kalisch—When we are building movements, coalitions, events, resources, and communities it is important to remember whose voices are being heard and whose aren't. Remember that survivors are not a monolithic group and there is no one-size-fits-all approach. Everyone you work with is going to be at a different stage of their healing. For survivors doing this work, particularly feminized and/or racialized survivors, many people may tell you that you are not cut out for this work, that you are not strong enough for it, especially faculty members. They are wrong, and they are afraid of seeing you make meaning and empowerment out of your situation, producing change, and exposing the systemic failures and salient rape culture on campus. Reflect on why and for whom you are doing this work. How can you make space for other survivors? Remember to take breaks. Burnout is real, and this is not easy work. Taking a break is one of the most powerful and important things you can role model for others. You deserve safety, rest, love, and care. Often this work reminds us how corrupt and dilapidated the system is. As survivors and allies, we can get lost in this and attempt to fix everything at once. Eradicating gender-based violence will not occur overnight. However, every time you offer peer support to a survivor, shut down a rape joke, share a resource, and create art and space for survivors, you make an impact. Don't dismiss and downplay the significance of that. Don't dismiss yourself, your feelings, and your work.

Emma Kuzmyk—When you're told you're being "too idealistic," remind yourself there's no such thing, and then keep going.

Sufia Langevin—Include voices from as many different places as possible. When working in activism, it's easy to see issues through your lens alone or think that yours is the most important. By surrounding yourself with other brave souls who may see things differently, the work is enhanced and the results are so much more rewarding. Activism, advocacy, and all this hard work also require a great amount of trust. Remember to respect and appreciate everyone who has given you their trust and pick who you give yours to wisely. The road may look long but sharing the journey with others will ease the burden for all of you.

Anonymous—We all walked a different path to get here. I look at the most competent of my activist peers and think, "Wow. They're amazing. They were successful because they organized people (and went to therapy)." Some of you will be alone and many of you will have few resources. You've been walking your path isolated from the people who could help you most. Know that there are others. Know that their compassion and courageous strength can be a beacon of hope in dark times. (Know that you *might want to go to therapy* if you're so much as picking up this book.) For me, doing this work has been therapeutic in and of itself. Speaking with other people who lived through the same pain created a sort of healing resonance in me. When I spoke with peers at SFCC, for the first time since the violence started ... I felt truly understood. The tears—of catharsis, grief, loss, and belonging—started me on the path to becoming a whole person again. Always walk your path with others, if you can.

Vicki Mackintosh—Never stop advocating for yourself and for others, take a break when you need to, but never stop. Surround yourself with like-minded people—they ease some of the exhaustion. Never be afraid to ask for help, other people may not offer, but will be there when asked. Celebrate small victories, and try to look at the big picture and what you've accomplished overall; fighting for change takes time, don't get discouraged and don't give up. Always be inclusive of all, the more diversity your movement has, the more voices will be heard and the better it will be.

Rebecca Mesay—When I first started this type of work, I sometimes found it difficult to conceptualize a world other than the one I was living in. It felt like things and people were so set in their ways that no amount of conversation or advocacy could change them. At that time, I quickly realized that envisioning the "changed world" I wanted to bring about was so important because that is what would act as my motivation for the hardest of days. I would think about specific goals, like comprehensive consent education starting in elementary school or increasing access to sexual and reproductive healthcare services for women in rural areas. I would combine all of these objectives and start building a world that was equitable and feminist in my mind, then I would go out and advocate for that world to become a reality.

Shelby Miller—If you have an idea about making something better for others, roll with it, because like-minded people will come together if given the opportunity.

Kate Mullin—I am proud of you for picking up this book and hearing the stories of activists. Often our work is hidden, we are told our stories are wrong or pointless, but, really, it's the opposite. We are powerful. Each one of us holds a perspective fueled by our passion for change. Change that will prioritize consent and desexualize marginalized groups. It is this passion that provides us momentum. It's important to understand what empowers you to do this periodically taxing work.

We are in the midst of change and every voice is valuable in amplifying our demands for equality. Comments and events can be triggering but know for the amount of people supporting these harmful acts there are more actively fighting against it. You are not alone, people are here to support you in your own personal fight for justice. Find like-minded individuals that encourage your work and always keep learning from the people around you.

Michelle Roy—Stop thinking you have to change the world to be successful in your activism. Impacting the life of one person means you have made a difference, and that is powerful. Focus on the ones around you, and build a better and stronger community

Caitlin Salvino—Transforming systems takes time. Change is often not linear, but it is possible. Always ask for compensation for your labour. Be skeptical of the "experts." Take the time to ensure your movement is fully accessible. Among the hardship and challenges, seek out even the smallest moments of joy. It is okay and often necessary to lean on your friends and loved ones for support. Never forget that this movement has been and always will be student-led.

Cameron Smith—When you're working to raise awareness, make sure there is also a plan and the right people in place to do the hands-on work. It's easy to be loud, it's hard to make permanent changes to powerful structures. Fight to be in the room where decisions are made, that's where activism becomes progress. Make sure all along the way that your priority is taking care of yourself—you're a person before you're an activist.

Connor Spencer—Cherish and actively nourish your friendships with the people you do this work with. You are humans who love each other doing this work together first—your relationships and commitments to each other will be what gets you through the tough times <3. And especially for my fellow white cis women who the media and administrators like to incorrectly look to as the experts/leaders of this work—have you done the work to be able to hear from your comrades when you have perpetuated harm? And are you ready to change the way you do things? This is some of the most crucial (and ongoing) work we can do—get better at hearing when we have messed up and changing our behaviour accordingly. Often receiving constructive feedback is immensely triggering for survivors, and part of our work is navigating those triggers in a way that is both honest and rooted in a deep love and commitment to your relationship with the person you have received the feedback from.

Chantelle Spicer—Don't let anyone tell you what justice and healing look like for you. It is and will be a multitude of things during the course of your life. At the moments when justice feels like fighting, fight. When justice is resting, rest (rest, by the way, is also resisting <3). Take the time and discover practices for listening to your heart, body, and spirit and let them guide you. Otherwise, you could end up getting pulled in directions and undertows that are not actually healing for you any longer.

Addy Strickland—Since the start of my activist journey, I've learned a number of ways to make activism, which is heavy work, a bit lighter. The best piece of advice I can give is to celebrate the little victories, no matter how small they may seem in comparison to the end goal. Allow yourself to be revitalized and re-energized by every win along the way. The losses and the goals unachieved will always feel more significant, will always set in motion spirals of "what went wrong?" or "what could we have done differently?" but most of the time, some good is better than none at all. This work is hard, and overwhelming, and so rarely celebrated—so let yourself be joyful when things go right, even if only for a moment. Those moments sustain movements.

Riley Wolfe—I often become overwhelmed reading the news and seeing all the ways oppressive systems continue to function, and it seems impossible that the work I do will make any difference. I cope with these feelings by thinking about my sphere of influence and if I am making a meaningful contribution to that sphere. It also helps to remember I'm not working alone, even if the others doing such important work are not always visible. Looking forward, it can be disheartening to see how much further we have to go, but looking back can show us how far we have actually come in creating change, as much of that change is incremental. Both these perspectives are important as we put in emotional and physical labour.

Conclusion

Addy Strickland and Emma Kuzmyk

Dear reader,

Thank you. Thank you for making time to read these stories and for holding space for our contributors' voices. We know that this book isn't easy to read—that the stories weigh heavy and may feel all too familiar—so we thank you for sticking with it. It means a lot to us that these stories have a home here, and that their words—which have, until now, existed precariously in news clippings, or been passed on through whisper networks—are permanently inked on these pages. Campus activism is cyclical by nature and thus is often missing the collective memory that is necessary for sustaining movements. This anthology has allowed us to bring together stories that span more than three decades, and that start to draw lines of connection between those of us who are doing this work. No more reinventing the wheel of anti-sexualized violence activism—we do this together.

We (anti-sexualized violence activists in general) have so much in common. While putting this book together, it was difficult not to notice the similarities between our stories. These similarities tell us that we are not alone—not even close—and that while the trauma of our collective experiences may be immense, our work, and our response, is immense too.

We have seen major institutional failures, the prevalence of rape culture, the difficulty in fighting within a system that's stacked against you at every level, and yet, when we read these stories, the feelings that we come away with are ones of gratitude, inspiration, and hope. Gratitude because there are so many amazing people who are doing this work, who are creating real, lasting change, and who refuse to be silenced. Inspiration because we know that we are not alone, that should we choose to stand, we know others will rise up too. Hope because we understand that sexualized violence is so ingrained in our society that this fight can't be individual, or campus-specific, and, in reading these stories, we know that it is not. We know that we are all fighting.

Sexualized violence transcends our campuses, and so the work we do must do the same. We know that we need a holistic approach in order to revolutionize the system. We know that our work must be connected, that we must build off each other's momentum and learn from each other's mistakes, and that we must also pause and celebrate along the way. That is the mission of this book, and we are so glad it's found its way into your hands.

Calls to Action:

1. Connect with your community.

Perhaps the most important thing we learned in our years of activism, which has been reemphasized in creating this book, is that no one should have to do this work alone, that no one *should* do this work alone. Activism is far too heavy for any one person to carry on their own, and so, we ask you to call on your community—whatever that looks like for you. Draw energy from being with each other and learn from the experiences of those around you. There are people in various iterations of community who have been doing this work, or versions of it, for ages—there's no need to start from scratch when so much knowledge (that is not limited to academic spaces) already exists in the world, and our communities can help us find and make sense of it.

When you're thinking about what community is for you, and who might be part of that, we also urge you not to worry if the answer isn't clear right away. As we first get into this work, we often don't recognize the communities we're a part of; rather, they reveal themselves along the way as we discover who among our ranks is a natural organizer, who loves to hold the megaphone, who has connections higher up, or who designs the best protest signs. As we move forward, we connect with those on our own campuses who are committed to driving change, but we also connect with those across the country who are doing similar work, through projects like this one, that aim to bring us together.

There are always people—you just have to find each other. Do the work, show up consistently, and fight for the things you believe in. Community will reveal itself.

2. Apply what you've learned.

When you reach the last page of this book, when it finds a home on your bookshelf or in the stack on your nightstand, please don't let what you've learned remain between these pages. The stories in this book are raw and heavy, and above all, they are real—about real people in real places dealing with the unfortunate reality that our campuses refuse to take adequate action against sexualized violence. What you do next is just as important as what lives on these pages, and we hope that when the time comes to close this book, you'll take action.

What we hope you've learned from this anthology, as well, is that action doesn't look like any one thing. Protests, walkouts, and sit-ins are all actions—but so are poems, policy change, and self-care. Challenge loved ones when they say something problematic, call out rape jokes, support your friends, and continue to educate yourself with the hundreds of resources that activists have fought to create and make public. Act. No matter what action looks like for you.

3. Take time to rest and heal.

It's easy to tell others to prioritize their well-being—to focus on their mental health and do what they need to do to feel okay—but it's much harder to tell ourselves. It's also easy to underestimate the importance of our own recovery, to push it off as something we'll do later—when we have the time, the resources, the support, or whatever else we may need. But the truth, which can be hard to accept, is that healing is not a perfect process. We can't afford to wait for the perfect moment or the perfect plan to start our healing journey; rather, healing must be intrinsic to everything we do.

Often, when we think about healing, we think about time. About taking time away, time off, time alone—but sometimes it might not be time that we need to take. Sometimes we need space. Space away from the environments where we were harmed, where our voices were silenced, where we suffered. Here, I think about plants who outgrow their pots, or who were comfortable in their spot during the winter but now the leaves on the trees are blocking the light, and they can't grow there anymore. Leaving a space behind when it means you'll have more space to grow is an act of self-love.

Sometimes, space is not enough. Sometimes, we might need to walk away—even though we are passionate, even though we are courageous, even though we want to keep fighting—even though doing so might be the hardest decision we make. And with that being said, please take comfort in the fact that there will always be good people fighting the good fight, and they will always be willing to welcome you back among their ranks when you are ready. This work is not going anywhere.

4. Believe survivors.

Always and without hesitation.

Contributors

Sasha Askarian (she/her) is a PhD candidate at York University's political science department, active in the pursuit of social justice and a creative writer. Sasha conducts innovative arts-based research at UBC's Centre for Gender & Sexual Health Equity in Indigenous Health and continues to advocate for health equity as a senior policy analyst at FNHA. She is passionate about bridging research with community and has done so by curating gallery exhibitions that amplify Indigenous voices through art. Sasha is also a poet who delights in cultural and creative expressions. Her work conveys the power of art to reflect and shape our social and political realities. This fusion of creativity, research and activism is exemplified in her co-authored publication in *New Sociology: Journal of Critical Praxis Becoming (Un)Productive: Grieving Death, Reclaiming Life*, volume 1.

Johannah May Black (she/her) is an activist, writer, and educator. After volunteering for the Survivor Support Phone Line at York University during her PhD studies, she realized that her unpaid volunteer work was more meaningful to her than her research and academic studies. Since then, she has worked in sexual violence prevention and response work in various settings. Johannah is currently located in Ki?lawna? (Kelowna, BC), the traditional, ancestral, and unceded territory of the Sylix Okanagan nation.

Maddie Brockbank (she/her) is a PhD Candidate and Vanier Scholar in the School of Social Work at McMaster University in Hamilton, Ontario, which sits and meets on the traditional lands of the Haudenosaunee Nation and is protected by the Dish With One Spoon

Wampum Agreement. Maddie received her BSW (2019) and MSW (2020) at McMaster as well, where she has spent over five years researching, practising, and facilitating community engagement around anti-carceral gender-based violence intervention and prevention with men. Maddie has been published in *The British Journal of Social Work and Critical and Radical Social Work*, with additional articles and chapters forthcoming. Maddie is a lifelong learner and enjoys reading as much as possible, spending time with her family (and dog!), and Halloween.

Heather Chandler (she/her) was born in Nunavut and raised in Nova Scotia. Heather is a large animal veterinarian specializing in dairy and beef cows. A member of the Canadian Veterinary Medical Association's Animal Welfare Committee Auxiliary, she is passionate about farm animal welfare and the intersection of animal abuse and domestic violence. Happiest when outdoors, she spends her free time paddle boarding, swimming, camping and hiking with her rescue greyhound Rupert.

Julie Glaser is published in numerous anthologies including Fireweed, Tessera, Bent On Writing (ed. Elizabeth Ruth), Womanisms & Feminisms (ed. Althea Prince), and filling Station Magazine. Julie has worked in the film and cultural sectors, and as a consultant engaging communities in activism and social change on issues of homelessness, sexual and gender identity, diversity and inclusion, the environment, and accessibility. When not on horseback, she can be found in the garden, furiously trying to finish a novel.

Kylee Graham (she/they) is a queer feminist poet, advocate, wildlife veterinarian, and PhD student currently located in PEI, Canada. She is passionate about addressing gender-based violence, the effects of capitalism, interconnectedness, respectability politics and healing. Live music, her cat Olive, and the ocean, are what brings Kylee joy. Her work has been published in the literary journal Laurels and Bells, Beyond Words Literary Journal, Headline Poetry and Press, The Sanctuary Magazine, Tiny Spoon Magazine and Ariel Publishing. Check her out on instagram @k.gpoetry_ !

Penelope Hutchison (she/her) is a lifelong women's rights crusader. After graduating from Queen's (1990) she completed a Bachelor of Journalism (1991) and a Masters of Health Administration (2003). She has worked in and written about women's health for decades. She is currently a senior leader with BC Family Doctors. For more than twenty-five years, she has been privileged to work and swim in the ocean waters and lakes (her favourite pastime) of the unceded territories of the Coast Salish Peoples, including the traditional lands of the xʷməθkwəy̓əm (Musqueam), Skwxwú7mesh (Squamish), and Səl̓ílwətaɬ (Tsleil-Waututh) Nations.

Micah Kalish (she/they) is an activist, educator, student, author, poet, artist, and survivor. Micah lives and works on the unceded territory of the Mississaugas of the Credit, the Anishnabeg, the Chippewa, the Haudenosaunee and the Wendat peoples and under the Dish with One Spoon Treaty. She completed a specialist HBA in Women and Gender Studies from the University of Toronto and is currently doing her master's. Micah is the founder of The PEARS Project and has been honoured to work with survivors in post-secondary institutions across Turtle Island. Micah has worked with numerous anti-violence organizations and prioritizes using an intersectional feminist survivor-centric and holistic lens in her advocacy, peer support, policy work, and everyday life.

Olivia Landry (she/her) graduated with a Bachelor of Arts in Women's and Gender Studies from Mount Allison University (2018) and a Master of Arts in Gender Studies from Queen's University (2019). Since 2019, she has worked in community and post-secondary in the field of sexual and gender-based violence prevention, particularly in rural communities. She is from Kjipuktuk (Halifax, Nova Scotia), and is grateful to live so close to family, friends, and the ocean.

Sufia Langevin (she/her, they/them) graduated from Bishop's University with a Bachelor of Arts in Secondary Education and Social Studies in 2024. She spent her undergraduate years heavily involved in student advocacy, primarily focused on building equitable structures and diversifying decision-making tables, winning her a 3MNational Student Fellowship in 2022. Exploring life beyond graduation, she has expanded from student advocacy to youth advocacy, taking on leadership positions in nonprofits and starting her research career on rewiring the Canadian higher education system for equity and flourishing. She believes in the power of community and centering underrepresented voices; her leadership work has the goal of both equipping students/youth with the skills they need to succeed while dismantling structures that create barriers to that success. When she's not working and volunteering, she can be found reading, enjoying nature, and laughing.

Vicki Mackintosh (she/they) is located in Mi'kma'ki, the unceded territory of the Mi'kmaq. Vicki graduated with a Master of Science degree (2023) and spent much of their education advocating for underrepresented groups in the campus community. Vicki is a strong advocate for the 2SLGBTQIA+ and dis/ability community and strives to find a career which allows her to pursue this passion. During her graduate degree, Vicki held many roles, but mostly proudly President of the 2SLGBTQIA+ support group, Co-founder and president of SAGE (Sexual Assault Group Empowerment) and EDIA Employer Outreach and Development Assistant. Her passions include education, fighting for equity and inclusion, as well as advocating for those who feel they don't have a voice. In their spare time, Vicki enjoys traveling as well as hiking, beach glassing and camping with her two corgis or curling up with a cup of tea, a Rupi Kaur book and her two cats.

Rebecca Mesay (she/her) is a political science graduate of St. Francis Xavier University and Malmö University (Sweden) and completed her Juris Doctor at Lincoln Alexander School of Law. As a student, she was involved in advocacy groups focused on equity for underrepresented populations, increasing access to education, and the prevention of sexual violence at universities. She previously worked as a consent educator and for the Government of Canada. In law, her professional interests include examining sentencing for young offenders, the overincarceration of vulnerable populations, and racism in the justice system. Her writing typically explores intersections of blackness, womanhood, and resistance to colonial structures.

Shelby Miller (she/her) is a Clinical Therapist who works with a variety of clients as well as crisis counselling work. She obtained her undergraduate degree from Mount Saint Vincent University in psychology and religious studies and completed her Masters of Arts in Counselling Psychology from Yorkville. For fun, she likes to surf, run, read, and listen to her record player. She is passionate about surfing and providing the necessary help for individuals with mental illness, specifically PTSD, and sometimes combines the two with her clients. She got into activism due to the continued mishandling of sexual assault cases on university campuses. She hopes this book can help others take action against injustices in their own schools.

Kate Mullin (she/her) is a proud activist, consent educator with Students For Consent Culture Canada, undergraduate at the University of Alberta in Psychology and Gender Studies, and doula. She crafts creatively as a writer and artist but also as a mother who has birthed two of the next generation of change makers. As a fellow survivor with intrinsic knowledge, Kate also holds multiple certifications to support survivors in their process of healing through disclosures. She uses this knowledge in many non-profit spaces and advisory boards, including the Federal Ministerial Advisory Council on GBV. Her current advocacy work is within speaker, moderator and research roles by creating Student' Unions' sexual violence policies and providing consent trainings to students. Ultimately, her work has focused primarily on the connection of bodily autonomy and representation which provides inspiration for her work and motivation for promoting a world of solidarity.

Michelle Roy (she/her) is an education specialist born and raised in Fredericton, New Brunswick, where she currently lives with her baby and partner. Michelle has been a survivor of sexual violence since the age of seven. Beginning in her early teens, her activism focused on survivors of sexual violence and their rights. After many years of activism at Mount Allison University, she was fed up with the way her campus continued to treat survivors, and made a now viral Instagram post exposing the truth and realities of many survivors. After leading a protest of four-hundred students, Michelle has been part of her campuses Sexual Violence Prevention Working Group and the New Brunswick's Sexual Violence round tables. She is a strong believer in how our personal trauma and experiences create knowledge and theory in academia through self reflection.

Caitlin Salvino (she/her) is a law student at the University of Toronto and Junior Fellow at Massey College. After completing a B.A. in Human Rights at Carleton University, she completed an MPhil and DPhil in Law at the University of Oxford where she studied as a Rhodes Scholar. She co-wrote the 2017 OurTurn a National Action Plan to End Campus Sexual Violence. This bilingual action plan has been signed by more than forty student groups across Canada and has been used at various levels to transform approaches to campus sexual violence policy design. Reflecting her community advocacy on gender-based violence and disability rights, she received the Governor General Award in Commemoration of the Persons Case in 2022.

Cameron Smith (she/her) graduated from Acadia University with a Bachelor of Arts in English and Classics in 2021, and a Bachelor of Education in 2023. In her time as a student, Cameron filled many roles on campus: coordinator of the Acadia Mental Health Initiative, a Residence Assistant, and an intern and educator with the Acadia Sexualized Violence Response and Education Coordinator. Cameron is passionate about social justice and working to better her community, which made activism focused on sexualized violence a natural step. Cameron currently works in education, and engages in activism by providing training sessions to community organizations and writing pieces on social issues. She tries to bring an anti-violence, anti-oppression focus to all she does. Cameron hopes to continue working in the field of sexual violence education and prevention throughout her life. She also knows a dizzying amount of fun facts and can make any three-sentence story into a ten-minute experience. Her writing and the events discussed within took place in Mi'kma'ki, the ancestral and unceded territory of the Mi'kmaq People.

Connor Spencer (she/her) does her best to be a patient agitator. She lives, organizes, and works with groups such as Students for Consent Culture Canada, Briarpatch magazine, and the labour movement on unceded and unsurrendered Algonquin territory.

Chantelle Spicer (she/they) is dedicated to Indigenous sovereignty and futures, consent in all forms of solidarity, accountability, and care in and between our social movements. Chantelle has been involved in work with Students for Consent Culture Canada, West Coast LEAF, the Downtown Eastside Women's Centre, the Nanaimo Women's Centre, and the Teaching Support Staff Union. They are also a poet, an artist, a gardener, a weaver, a dreamer and those things have to be mentioned because they are important to change-making. The lands Chantelle works with should be under jurisdiction of xʷməθkʷəy̓əm, Səl̓ílwətaʔ, Skwxwú7mesh nations but due to structures of genocide that target Indigenous women and two-spirit people, are illegally claimed by Vancouver & Canada.

Riley Wolfe (they/them) is a queer history PhD who studied at York University. Their focus is on Mexican queer and trans activist history and transnational activist networks. They completed a BA in history from St Francis Xavier University and a MA in history from York University.

They were the president of the student 2SLGBTQ+ student society and a co-coordinator for the Peer Support Program at StFX during their undergrad. They continued to pursue their passion for 2SLGBTQ+ education and mental health support as a youth educator at their hometown high school. They live on the traditional and unceded territory of the Abenaki people and the Wabenaki Confederacy. They believe in the power of history to inspire future activism and solidarity through understanding where we've been and how we got here.

Tia Wong is an artist and community organizer based in Ottawa (unceded and unsurrendered territory of the Algonquin Nation). She graduated with a Bachelor's degree in Health & Community Services from the University of Victoria, having previously attended Carleton University for Global & International Studies. Tia now works as a designer for web-based climate science initiatives. She was formerly Co-Chair of Students for Consent Culture and is passionate about creating a culture of consent through peer-led education and strengthening the anti-violence movement across so-called Canada.

Acknowledgements

This book is the culmination of several years of work, and would never have been possible without an extensive community of support.

Thank you to Tina and Alex at Rising Action, for believing in this project and helping us bring it to the world.

Thank you to the organizers, editors, and publishers who provided the first homes–in print or on stage–for several of these stories. The space you've carved out to share these voices is so necessary.

Thank you to those in the university community—the badass staff, faculty, and student union leaders who have supported us along the way–showing compassion, granting extensions, or going to bat for us when our voices felt like they weren't loud enough. Thank you for continuing to show up, year after year, and demonstrate what it means to walk the walk and be "for the kids."

Thank you to our family, friends, and loved ones, who have shown us support, encouragement, community, and love, and offered moments of levity.

Thank you to the amazing contributors who made this book what it is. Your courage in sharing your stories and your trust in us to bring them forward means everything.

Finally, to all of the activists who came before us: none of this would have been possible without you. And to all activists current and to come: we're with you. We're proud of you. Thank you.

About the Curators

We (Addy and Emma) met in our first year as post secondary students when we both enroled at St. Francis Xavier University in the first year Social Justice Colloquium. Considering the program, it makes a lot of sense that we quickly became friends, and then partners in activism. For four years, we worked together to combat sexual violence on our campus. We co-authored open letters and news articles, attended marches and protests, co-founded and developed a peer-led mental health and sexualized violence support service, and generally caused a fair amount of disruption.

We knew that once we graduated, we wanted to keep the partnership alive. In our four years of activism at StFX, we learned so much and had so many stories to tell, it seemed a shame that they might leave campus with us, and we knew that our experiences likely weren't unique. We are both activists, artists, and writers who want to channel our creative energy into building a better world, so the idea to create an anthology made a lot of sense when we thought about next steps.

Addy Strickland (she/her) is a writer, artist, and facilitator based in Antigonish, Nova Scotia. She graduated from St. Francis Xavier University in 2021 with a degree in Development Studies and English, through which she concentrated her studies on art and storytelling as tools for community development. She also recently completed a certificate in publishing from Toronto Metropolitan University. While at StFX, Addy was deeply involved in protesting sexualized violence. She co-founded the StFX Peer Support Program, facilitated sexualized violence prevention training, and helped coordinate numerous protests and collective actions alongside fellow activists. Since graduating, she's remained involved in anti-sexualized violence activism by volunteering with Students for Consent Culture Canada—contributing to the organization's podcast and supporting other ongoing initiatives. Currently, Addy works in the fields of community development and youth engagement, and enjoys finding ways to bring art into her facilitation practice—continuing to merge art and activism in each new chapter of her life.

Emma Kuzmyk (she/her) is a writer and coffee-enthusiast based in Kjipuktuk (Halifax), the traditional and unceded territory of the Mi'kmaq people. She graduated from St. Francis Xavier University in 2021 with a degree in English. While at StFX, Emma was a student-athlete, students' union executive, and involved in various activities aimed at ending sexualized violence. She's proud to have played small roles in different sexualized-violence awareness campaigns on campus, at the Antigonish Women's Resource Centre, in the development and facilitation of Waves of

Change bystander training, and in the founding of the StFX Peer Support Program. Believing in the activist capabilities and responsibilities of art, in all its forms, Emma has attempted to blend the two by helping to illustrate prevention programs, sharing spoken word poetry at marches, rallies, and protests, and in telling stories grounded in creating images of the future to which we can aspire. Currently, Emma is pursuing her Masters of Fine Arts in Fiction, and plans to continue dreaming about and expanding on visions of utopia and the many ways we might work towards it.

Glossary

Rape Culture—Describes the social attitudes of a group of people which trivialize, normalize, and stigmatize sexualized violence. Rape culture often perpetuates myths about sexualized violence and creates an environment where survivors are less likely to come forward due to the group's response. On a post-secondary campus, rape culture might look like sexist or misogynistic chants being sung during welcome week, or like school administration not taking a survivor's report seriously.

Survivor vs. Victim—In the context of sexualized violence, the terms survivor and victim refer to people who have experienced it. Both terms are limited in their ability to describe people's experiences, and some people may not identify with either, but it's important to have language to talk about the collective of people who have experienced sexualized violence. Typically, we (activists) use the term "survivor" while recognizing its limitations. The legal system uses the term "victim."

Sexualized Violence—An umbrella term, used somewhat interchangeably with the term "sexual violence," which "covers a broad range of behaviours and scenarios that instrumentalize sex or sexuality in ways that cause harm to either individuals or groups."[1] Throughout the

---

1. Johannah Black, *Basic Bystander: A Facilitator's Guide*, Antigonish, NS: Antigonish Women's Resource Centre and Sexual Assault Services Association, 2018.

anthology we use the term "sexualized violence" rather than "sexual violence" to emphasize that it is violence that has been sexualized rather than an act which is sexual.

Sexual Assault—Refers to sexual contact inflicted on a person without their explicit consent.[2]

Rape—A specific type of sexual assault.

Rape Myth—Attitudes and beliefs within society that, though false, inform the way we think about sexual assault and sexualized violence.[3] Many of these myths justify victim blaming, offer excuses to perpetrators, and make reporting an even more difficult process.[4]

#MeToo—A social-media movement started by activist Tarana Burke in 2006 for survivors to share their experiences that exploded into an international reckoning of abusers when actress Alyssa Milano used the tag in 2017.[5]

Consent—A mutual agreement between two people that is freely given, clearly communicated, and void of power imbalance, coercion, deception, or force.[6]

Rape Kit—A set of tools used by medical professionals to gather and preserve evidence during a physical exam, after a sexual assault has taken place.

---

2. "Sexual Assault," RAINN, 2021.

3. K.A Lonsway & L. F. Fitzgerald, "Rape myths in review," *Psychology of Women Quarterly*, 18, (1994): 133-164.

4. Johannah Black, *Basic Bystander: A Facilitator's Guide*, Antigonish, NS: Antigonish Women's Resource Centre and Sexual Assault Services Association, 2018.

5. "Me too Movement," November 4, 2021.

6. "What Consent Looks Like," RAINN, 2021.

"The Red Zone"—A period of time at the beginning of the post-secondary school year, usually one to three months, where incidences of sexual assault and sexualized violence are statistically higher than the rest of the year.[7]

Trigger / Triggered—Being triggered is a psychological and physiological response to trauma. A trigger can be almost anything—a word, an event, an object—that reminds someone of a past traumatic experience, and causes them to feel as if they're experiencing parts of the traumatic experience all over again. Being triggered is a very real and valid response to trauma and can be difficult to deal with in the moment.[8]

Perpetrator—A term favoured by the legal system which is often used to refer to a person who perpetrated sexualized violence or assault.

Activism—The act, no matter how big or small, of fighting for what's right.

Victim Blaming—When a victim of sexualized violence is handed the blame for the actions of the person who caused them harm, usually as a result of perpetuated rape myths, pervasive rape culture, and patriarchy.

Intersectionality—Coined in 1989 by Kimberlé Crenshaw, intersectionality is "the complex, cumulative way in which the effects of multiple forms of discrimination (such as racism, sexism, and classism) combine, overlap, or intersect especially in the experiences of marginalized individuals or groups."[9]

---

7. "The Red Zone: Sexual Violence on College Campuses," PDF. May 2020. Metoomvt.org.

8. Emma Kuzmyk, "Self-Soothing When Triggered While Organizing as a Survivor" (2021) in *Courage Catalysts: Creating Consent Culture on Campus (A Toolkit for Students, by Students)*, eds Carina Gabriele, Anoodth Naushan & Farah Khan, Courage to Act, 2021.

9. Merriam-Webster, "Intersectionality," Merriam-Webster.com Dictionary, 2021.

Disclosing vs. Reporting—Disclosing refers to telling somebody about your experience. This can be in an official or non-official manner. A disclosure requires no further action, though the person you disclose to may be able to help you find resources or support. Reporting is a form of disclosure made to an official body (think administration or law enforcement) in which you are seeking a formal process, an investigation, or disciplinary actions. You can receive help and support without reporting, and reporting is ultimately your decision.

References

Ahmed, Sara. *Living a Feminist Life*. Durham: Duke University Press, 2017.

Bindel, J. "The Montreal Massacre: Canada's Feminists Remember." *The Guardian*, December 3, 2012.

Black, Johannah. *Basic Bystander: A Facilitator's Guide*. Antigonish, NS: Antigonish Women's Resource Centre and Sexual Assault Services Association, 2018.

Black, M.C., Basile, K.C., Breiding, M.J., Smith, S.G., Walters, M.L., Merrick, M.T., Chen, J., & Stevens, M.R. *The National Intimate Partner and Sexual Violence Survey (NISVS): 2010 Summary Report*. Atlanta, GA: National Center for Injury Prevention and Control, Centers for Disease Control and Prevention, 2011.

Brodsky, Alexandra. "'Rape-Adjacent': Imagining Legal Responses to Non-consensual Condom Removal." *Columbia Journal of Gender and Law*, 32, no. 2 (2017).

Burczycka, Marta. "Students' Experiences of Unwanted Sexualized Behaviours and Sexual Assault at Post-secondary Schools in the Canadian Provinces, 2019." Government of Canada, Statistics Canada, September 14, 2020. https://www150.statcan.gc.ca/n1/pub/85-002-x/20 20001/article/00005-eng.htm.

Canadian Women's Foundation. "The Facts About Sexual Assault and Harassment." Last modified June 1, 2022. Retrieved from https://canadianwomen.org/the-facts/sexual-assault-harassment/#:~:text=Is%20sexual%20assault%20really%20as,General%20Social%20Survey%20on%20Victimization.&text=Women%20were%2010%20times%20more,reported%20sexual%20assault%20in%202008

Carleton University, *2017 Annual Report on Sexual Violence, Presented to the Board of Governors,* 8 February, 2019. <https://carleton.ca/equity/wp-content/uploads/Carleton-2017-Annual-Report-on-Sexual-Violence.pdf>.

Carleton University, *Carleton University Draft Sexual Violence Policy,* (Vice-President Students and Enrolment, October 2016), online: <https://carleton.ca/studentsupport/wp-content/uploads/Draft-Sexual-Violence-Policy-October-6-2016.pdf>.

Carleton University. *Community Update: Sexual Violence Policy.* Vice-President Students and Enrolment, October 2016. http://carleton.ca/studentsupport/wp-content/uploads/Sexual-Violence-Policy-Draft-Feedback-Summary.pdf.

Carleton University Sexual Violence Policy, revised April 25, 2021. <https://carleton.ca/secretariat/wp-content/uploads/Sexual-Violence-Policy.pdf>.

Dickie, A. "The Art of Intimidation: Sexism and Destiny at Queen's." *This Magazine,* March 1990.

Editorial. "Send in the clowns..." *Queen's Journal,* November 7, 1989.

Farrow, Ronan. "From Aggressive Overtures to Sexual Assault: Harvey Weinstein's Accusers Tell Their Stories." *The New Yorker,* October 10, 2017. <https://www.newyorker.com/news/news-desk/from-aggressive-overtures-to-sexual-assault-harvey-weinsteins-accusers-tell-their-stories>.

Flowers, Rachel. "Refusal to Forgive: Indigenous Women's Love and Rage." *Decolonization: Indigeneity, Education & Society,* 4, no. 2 (2015): 32-49.

French, O. "Sex Wars Still Rage on Campus." *The Globe and Mail,* November 11, 1989.

Graduate Student Association, "Statement from GSA Board of Governors Representative re: Sexual Violence Policy," December 1, 2016. <http://gsacarleton.ca/2016/12/statement-from-gsa-board-of-g overnors-representative-re-sexual-violence-policy/ >.

Kuzmyk, Emma. "Self-Soothing When Triggered While Organizing as a Survivor" (2021) in *Courage Catalysts: Creating Consent Culture on Campus (A Toolkit for Students, by Students),* eds Carina Gabriele, Anoodth Naushan & Farah Khan. Courage to Act, 2021.

Landsberg, M. "Students Learn Sexist Lesson at Universities." *The Toronto Star,* November 11, 1989.

Lonsway, K.A., & Fitzgerald, L.F. "Rape myths in review." *Psychology of Women Quarterly,* 18, (1994): 133-164.

Lum, Zi-Ann. "Canadian Universities To Face Funding Cuts If They Fail To Address Campus Sexual Assaults." *Huffington Post,* February 28, 2018. <https://www.huffingtonpost.ca/2018 /02/27/canada-bud-get2018-universities-funding-cuts-sex-assault-campus_a_23372615/>.

MacDonald, N. (Writer), & Mansbridge, P. (Host). "Montreal Massacre murderer's suicide note released." *The National,* CBC, November 28, 1990.

Merriam-Webster. "Intersectionality." Merriam-Webster.com Dictionary, 2021. https://www.merriam-webster.com/dictionary/intersectionality

Miller, Chanel. *Know My Name: A Memoir.* New York: Viking, an Imprint of Penguin Random House, 2019.

Mount Allison University. "Policies and Procedures with Respect to Sexual Harassment." Policies and Procedures. Retrieved February 2013 from https://mta.ca/about/leadership-and-governance/policies-and-procedures.

RAINN. "Sexual Assault." 2021. Retrieved from https://www.rainn.org/articles/sexual-assault

RAINN. "What Consent Looks Like." 2021. Retrieved from https://www.rainn.org/articles/what-is-consent

Salvino, C., Miles, J., & Johnson, S. "Open Letter to the Carleton Community and Administration on the Draft Sexual Violence Policy." Carleton Human Rights Society, October 28, 2016. <https://docs.google.com/document/d/1KsqT5BJUPH7S3U4TcOC6QawUmNPkFNAi0QwxJTH4NJw/edit#heading=h.5bfjawtiz3uc>.

Salvino, Caitlin, and Connor Spencer. "OurTurn: One Year Later Report." Montreal, QC: Concordia Student's Union, April 2019, <https://static1.squarespace.com/static/5bc4e7bcf4755a6e42b00495/t/5ca4bd76652dea6fb0eec244/1554300288926/SFCC_report_en_final.pdf>.

Salvino, Caitlin, and Jade Cooligan Pang, edited by Jody Miles, Sally Johnson, and Omran, Fa'Ttima. "Open Letter to Reform Carleton's Sexual Violence Policy." Carleton Human Rights Society, February 10, 2017. <https://docs.google.com/document/d/1opKlxJqF59L983CZbXEkMSWEpAZnO17pBDxcqjm1Up8/edit>.

Salvino, Caitlin, Kelsey Gilchrist, and Jade Cooligan Pang. "OurTurn: A National Action Plan to End Campus Sexual Violence." Montreal, QC: Student's Society of McGill University, October 2017, <https://static1.squarespace.com/static/5bc4e7bcf4755a6e42b00495/t/5c2fa6921ae6cf5f6c71821b/1546627650779/OurTurn+Action+Plan.pdf> at 20.

Salvino, Caitlin. "Opinion: Students can't afford to ignore call for feedback." *The Charlatan*, October 19, 2016. <https://charlatan.ca/2016/10/opinion-students-cant-afford-to-ignore-call-for-feedback/>.

Samaran, Nora. *Turn This World Inside Out: The Emergence of Nurturance Culture.* AK Press, 2018.

Schwartz, Zane. "Canadian Universities Are Failing Students on Sexual Assault." Macleans., March 1, 2018. https://www.macleans.ca/education/university/canadian-universities-are-failing-students-on-sexual-assault/. /

Sexual Violence and Harassment Action Plan Act (Supporting Survivors and Challenging Sexual Violence and Harassment), RRO 1990, Reg 132.

Sexual Violence Prevention Working Terms of References. Mount Allison Sexual Violence Working Group. January 21, 2021.

Statistics Canada. "One in Ten Women Students Sexually Assaulted in a Post-secondary Setting." Last modified September 14, 2020. https://www150.statcan.gc.ca/n1/daily-quotidien/200914/dq200914a-eng.htm.

Torrens, J. and Zima, J. "Residents try to 'lighten up' campaign." *The Queen's Journal*, October 13, 1989.

Tyler, T. "Why Campus Pranks Turning Nasty." *The Sunday Star*, November 5, 1989.

Weiner & Simpson, 1971, as cited in Sara Ahmed, *Living a Feminist Life*. Durham: Duke University Press, 2017, 65.

World Health Organization. "Violence Against Women." Last modified March 9, 2021. https://www.who.int/news-room/fact-sheets/detail/violence-against-women#:~:text=Sexual%20violence%20is%20%22any%20sexual,the%20victim%2C%20in%20any%20setting.

Wynn, N. *Canceling*. ContraPoint, January 2, 2020.

"Facts and Figures," Mount Allison University, n.d. Retrieved in 2021 from https://www.mta.ca/Prospective/About/Facts_and_figures/Facts_and_figures/.

"Me too Movement." November 4, 2021. Retrieved from https://metoomvmt.org/

"Queen's students apologize for crude signs." *The Ottawa Citizen*, November 3, 1989.

"Sexual Violence Policy Consultation - Sexual Assault Support Services," Carleton University. <https://carleton.ca/sexual-violence-support/sexual-violence-policy-consultation/>.

"Student Safety in Nova Scotia: A Review of Student Union Policies and Practice to Prevent Sexual Violence." Martell Consulting Services Ltd., January 13, 2014.

"The Red Zone: Sexual Violence on College Campuses," PDF. May 2020. Metoomvt.org.